MW00807453

In Close Association

HARVARD EAST ASIAN MONOGRAPHS 453

In Close Association

Local Activist Networks in the Making
of Japanese Modernity, 1868–1920

Marnie S. Anderson

Published by the Harvard University Asia Center
Distributed by Harvard University Press
Cambridge (Massachusetts) and London 2022

© 2022 by The President and Fellows of Harvard College
Printed in the United States of America

The Harvard University Asia Center publishes a monograph series and, in coordination with the Fairbank Center for Chinese Studies, the Korea Institute, the Reischauer Institute of Japanese Studies, and other facilities and institutes, administers research projects designed to further scholarly understanding of China, Japan, Korea, Vietnam, and other Asian countries. The Center also sponsors projects addressing multidisciplinary, transnational, and regional issues in Asia.

Cataloging-in-Publication Data is on file at the Library of Congress.

ISBN 9780674278257 (cloth)

Index by Rachel Lyon

∞ Printed on acid-free paper

Last figure below indicates year of this printing
31 30 29 28 27 26 25 24 23 22

For Maren and Michael

Contents

Figures

Acknowledgments

This book has been in the works for a decade, and I am grateful to the many people and institutions who have assisted and inspired me along the way.

I thank the archivists who have made the research possible. They include Leslie Fields and Deborah Richards at Mt. Holyoke College Archives and Special Collections, Christine Jacobson of the Houghton Library, Yamashita-san at the Okayama Prefectural Archives and the staff at the National Diet Library and Okayama Prefectural Library. I am grateful to the United Church of Christ Wider Church Ministries for permission to use the American Board of Commissioners for Foreign Missions archives.

In Japan, I received unexpected kindness from Jeremy Brooks of San'yō Jogakuen Junior and Senior High School. I am grateful to Noriko Ishii for invaluable information on Sumiya Koume and to Kumi Yoshihara for correcting my errors about Nakagawa. I thank as well Erik Shicketanz, Miyazaki Fumiko, Takagi Hiroshi, Mieda Akiko, Sekiguchi Sumiko, Bettina Gramlich-Oka, and Helen Ballhatchet. Closer to home, I am grateful to Laura Nenzi, Daniel Botsman, Hitomi Tonomura, Leslie Pincus, Jonathan Lipman, Kristy Johnson, Laura Hein, Amy Stanley, Julia Bullock, Michael Abele, Matthew Hayes, Garrett Washington, Sabine Frühstück, Dana Mirsalis, Anne Walthall, and David Howell for feedback at various stages of the project. My writing group colleagues— Ellen Boucher, Vanessa Walker, Mary Hicks, and Alec Hickmott—also deserve thanks. Audiences at Northwestern, Ochanomizu University, Yale, the University of Michigan, Harvard, and the University of California at Santa Barbara asked terrific questions. Brian Platt has my gratitude for reading and commenting on the whole manuscript before I turned it in. All errors are my own.

At Smith College, I am particularly grateful to Sharon Domier, Maureen Callahan, Susan Levin, Nancy Bradbury, and Richard Lim. Ernest Benz, Jeff Ahlman, Lucie Schmidt, and Beth Myers came through for me when I needed advice. Former provost Katherine Rowe, now the president of the College of William and Mary, showed me the difference outstanding leadership makes.

I am grateful to the Northeast Asia Council of the Association for Asian Studies for funding as well as to the Smith College Committee on Faculty Compensation and Development. I thank Bob Graham and the Harvard University Asia Center as well as readers for the press. Akiko Yamagata was a superb copyeditor.

Portions of previously published material all appear here with permission. Portions of chapter 2 appeared in "From Concubine to Activist and 'Anonymous Founder': The Role of Networks in Sumiya Koume's Life," in *Women and Networks in Nineteenth-Century Japan*, edited by Bettina Gramlich-Oka, Anne Walthall, Miyazaki Fumiko, and Sugano Noriko, 201–20 (Ann Arbor: University of Michigan Press, 2020) as well as "Critiquing Concubinage: Sumiya Koume and Changing Gender Roles in Modern Japan," *Japanese Studies* 37, no. 3 (2017): 311–29, © Japanese Studies Association of Australia, reprinted by permission of Taylor & Francis Ltd., http://wwwtandfonline.com, on behalf of Japanese Studies Association of Australia. Portions of chapter 3 previously appeared in "Women and Political Life in Meiji Japan: The Case of the Okayama joshi konshinkai (Okayama Women's Friendship Society)," *U.S.-Japan Women's Journal*, no. 44 (2013): 43–66.

My family and friends—my networks—have supported and uplifted me. Thanks to my wonderful students, including the scholars of Posse 6, who always asked how the book was going. I thank especially Maren and Michael for more than I can ever express.

Abbreviations

American Board	American Board of Commissioners for Foreign Missions
JWCTU	Japan Woman's Christian Temperance Union
Nihon josei undō	*Nihon josei undō shiryō shūsei,* edited by Suzuki Yūko
OWFS	Okayama Women's Friendship Society (Okayama joshi konshinkai)
Tsuikairoku	*Sumiya Koume-shi tsuikairoku,* by Onoda Tetsuya
WCTU	Woman's Christian Temperance Union
YMCA	Young Men's Christian Association
YWCA	Young Women's Christian Association

Note on Editorial Conventions

Following East Asian practice, I refer to all individuals by their surname after introducing them by their full name (surname followed by given names) except when multiple members of the same family appear, in which case I use the given name.

In referring to married women activists, I have used the names by which they are best known in the historical literature: Kishida Toshiko and Fukuda Hideko. Kishida was the maiden name and Fukuda, the married name.

All translations are mine unless otherwise indicated.

INTRODUCTION

In 1875, Nakagawa Yokotarō (1836–1903) took an eighty-mile journey to the treaty port of Kobe. Nakagawa had been a samurai before Japan's modern revolution, known as the Meiji Restoration (1868), took away that status. Now, he was an eccentric bureaucrat from Okayama, the capital of the newly established Okayama Prefecture, and he had become intrigued by new ideas about Western medicine and Christianity.[1] While in Kobe, he invited a Western Protestant medical missionary, Dr. Wallace Taylor (1835–1923), to visit Okayama and serve as an advisor at the prefectural hospital. Taylor could not accept the appointment because the Meiji central government would not issue passports for his family, but that bureaucratic impediment did not deter Nakagawa. In 1878, Nakagawa and the Okayama governor formally invited a group of missionaries affiliated with the American Board of Commissioners for Foreign Missions (American Board), the missionary wing of the Congregational church, to set up a formal mission station in Okayama, only the second in the interior of Japan after Kyoto.[2]

This book tells the story of Nakagawa and the overlapping networks of local female and male activists around him who engaged in political

1. Throughout the book, when I refer to "Okayama," I mean the city rather than the domain or prefecture unless otherwise specified.

2. See Cary, *A History of Christianity in Japan*, 119–20. Several other Protestant denominations sent missions to Japan.

and social reform as they forged new roles and created a new modern world. The networks comprised individuals who were related by blood or marriage; they included married couples and single people. In their emerging roles, they built schools, joined a political movement, promoted new policies stressing "civilization and enlightenment" (*bunmei kaika*) and hygiene, and worked to help those less privileged than themselves by supporting an orphanage. They met at political meetings, at schools, and sometimes at church. Many had ties stretching back a decade or more. Working alongside them were the Western Protestant missionaries affiliated with the American Board, who not only spread their religion but also served as educators, introduced new architecture, debated Shakespeare's works with local people, and taught bread-making and knitting.[3]

The combination of Okayama's historical commitment to education, the personalities of individuals like Nakagawa who were dedicated to modernization, and the early arrival of Westerners in the prefecture generated an intriguing set of reform projects and offer scholars a rich view of how local people built modern Japan.[4] By analyzing their efforts, we see that Japan became modern not just by a top-down process initiated by the central government in Tokyo. Much of the energy came instead from the middle—from local people of some wealth and means—and spread outward. Louise Young, in her study of interwar urban culture *Beyond the Metropolis*, has pointed out that Japanese modernity did not originate in Tokyo and ripple out to the provinces. Rather, modernity in Japan "was co-constituted through the dynamic interaction of provincial cities with the capital, as well as through the circulation and exchange of people and ideas throughout the country."[5] Although Young focuses on the 1910s to 1930s, I find that her point holds true decades earlier as well.

Standard stories of modern Japan give priority to the new Meiji state—and the group of elite men who governed. To be sure, the state did engage in radical reforms, building a new political structure and industrializing rapidly, with the primary goal of maintaining Japanese sovereignty in the

---

3.   Tanaka Tomoko has analyzed the Western missionaries' stories in Japan, amply documented in the American Board archives. Tanaka, *Kindai Nihon kōtō kyōiku taisei*.

4.   By modernization, I specifically mean the kinds of modern discourses individuals engaged with as well as the organizations and movements they built.

5.   Young, *Beyond the Metropolis*, 11.

face of Western imperialism, which had already encroached on other parts of Asia including China and India. Yet the ways individuals and groups seized the initiative to effect change—sometimes working with the state and sometimes independently—have remained relatively unexplored. Brian Platt has made a similar argument about the efforts of local people in shaping the modern education system, and Christopher Craig has taken up the pivotal role of local elites in modernization efforts from 1890 to 1912.[6] Neil Waters, James Baxter, and Michael Lewis have also scrutinized the era from the perspective of local history.[7] The early Meiji state was a "not-so-strong state," especially compared to the more powerful, better-resourced state of later decades, and the efforts of local women and men were crucial in making Japan modern at a time when the future was open.[8] They were, after all, the "protagonists of modernity," to use Carol Gluck's phrase.[9]

My account of this group of activists begins in the 1870s and extends through the 1910s. This period—coinciding with the Japan's modern transformation—marked a time of major change in Okayama, although the city had long been a regional center in southwestern Japan. During the Tokugawa period (1600–1868), the city was a thriving castle town, one of the largest in the region with a population of over twenty thousand in the early nineteenth century. By the 1870s, at the beginning of the Meiji period (1868–1912), Okayama's population stood at thirty-five thousand people, a sizable number for a regional city.[10] After Japan began opening treaty ports to Western countries from the 1850s, Okayama elites began to engage in modernizing projects, but most local residents had never seen a Westerner even two decades later. Westerners were visible in treaty port cities like Kobe and Yokohama, but not in the interior in places like Okayama, where most people lived. Indeed, much of the country remained closed off until the end of the nineteenth century. The only foreigners in Okayama in the early 1870s were single men from China

6. Platt, *Burning and Building*; Craig, "The Middlemen of Modernity."

7. Waters, *Japan's Local Pragmatists*; Baxter, *The Meiji Unification*; Lewis, *Becoming Apart*.

8. Gluck, "End of Elsewhere," 683.

9. Gluck, "End of Elsewhere," 682.

10. Young calls Okayama and cities like it "second cities," a designation referring to prefectural capitals that served as "the economic, political, and cultural centers of their respective regions." Young, *Beyond the Metropolis*, 7.

and other parts of Asia.[11] The arrival of Western missionaries in the late 1870s, then, represented a momentous occasion. Many of them came as couples, and a number of single women arrived as well.

The men and women at the heart of Okayama's networks formed an emergent local elite. They were mostly former samurai (*shizoku*) and rural entrepreneurs or wealthy merchants. Their projects included the Freedom and People's Rights Movement (also referenced here as People's Rights Movement; Jiyū minken undō), the first movement for democratic representation outside of the Western world. Born out of opposition to the concentration of power in the new national government, the movement advocated popular representation through a parliamentary system. Many of the male and female activists formed political associations and forged a vibrant political culture. At the same time, they engaged, to varying degrees, with projects related to Protestant Christianity, social reform, and education—especially for girls.

The story I tell highlights the transnational flows of people and ideas, including political rights, social reform, and Christianity, but this study is inherently place-based and people-centered. These new networks of men and women included Nakagawa, his friend Nishi Kiichi (pen name Bizan; 1843–1904), a former teacher and leader in the People's Rights Movement; Abe Isoo (1865–1949), a young Protestant minister who would go on to become a famous socialist; Sumiya Koume (1850–1920), a former concubine turned activist who ran the Okayama Orphanage (Okayama kojiin); Ōnishi Kinu (1857–1933), a divorcée devoted to the cause of temperance; and Kajiro Yoshi (1871–1959), who studied abroad in the United States and graduated from Mt. Holyoke College before becoming principal of San'yō gakuen, a girls' school founded by Japanese Protestant Christians.[12] The Western Protestant missionaries affiliated with the American Board also figured among their ranks. Some of the individuals, such as Abe Isoo, went on to become well known at the national level. Fukuda (formerly Kageyama) Hideko (1865–1927) is the best-known woman activist of the era, in part because she was the only woman involved in the 1885 Osaka Incident, an abortive attempt to foment revolution in Korea. She was arrested and imprisoned, earning a national reputation as a Japanese Joan of Arc.

11. Hamada, *Kadota kaiwai*, 14–15.
12. Over time, the school has undergone several name changes and has expanded the grade levels it covers. For simplicity's sake, I refer to it here as San'yō gakuen school.

My work joins biographies of non-elite individuals in modern Japan, including three by Simon Partner (*Toshié*, *The Mayor of Aihara*, and *The Merchant's Tale*) as well as Gail Bernstein's study of the Matsuura family, *Isami's House*. We also have sketches of individuals in Anne Walthall's edited volume *The Human Tradition in Modern Japan* and Ronald Loftus's collection of women's autobiographies, *Telling Lives*.[13] My approach is distinct in that it focuses on a network of activists rather than an individual or family. Though some of the people were related by blood or kinship ties, many were not. I showcase the many ways people worked together and the importance of how groups can effect historical change. This book also takes a deep look at an understudied yet crucial moment in Japanese history, since most biographical studies are anchored in the Tokugawa period or the era surrounding World War II. At the same time, it adds to the small body of literature on Meiji-era women, which has previously examined prostitutes, textile workers, and activists associated with the Freedom and People's Rights Movement and the Japan Woman's Christian Temperance Union (JWCTU; Nihon kirisutokyō fujin kyōfūkai).[14]

Some of my material overlaps with Japanese historian Hamada Hideo's *The Roads of the Kadota Kaiwai Neighborhood* (*Kadota kaiwai no michi*), which also discusses Okayama's vibrant social networks. However, Hamada does not address politics and devotes most of the book to male foreign missionaries and two Japanese people who led institutions: Ishii Jūji (1865–1914) and Kajiro Yoshi.[15] In contrast, my primary focus is on Japanese networks of both women and men. Moreover, I address reform in multiple registers, demonstrating how people seized opportunities opened by the Meiji Restoration, leaving lasting institutional marks.

By looking at major events from fresh perspectives, my project attempts what historian of the United States Mary Beth Norton has called "history on the diagonal," which focuses on "the perspective of groups that traditionally have not dominated the telling of history."[16] By adopting this approach, I provide a new view on the process of how Japan

13.   Another book that takes up a network is Hein, *Post-Fascist Japan*.

14.   See Lublin, *Reforming Japan*; Sievers, *Flowers in Salt*; Tsurumi, *Factory Girls*.

15.   Hamada, *Kadota kaiwai*. Hamada discusses two women who led institutions: Kajiro Yoshi and, to a lesser extent, Alice Pettee Adams, but he does not adopt a gendered perspective. I address some of the reasons why in chapter 4. On Adams, see the epilogue.

16.   Norton, "History on the Diagonal," 1. On former samurai women, see Matsuzaki, "Meiji ishinki no jendā kenkyū."

became modern, one that highlights the efforts and achievements of people far from the newly renamed center of government, Tokyo, who seldom receive scholarly attention. An example of this type of work comes from Simon Partner's recent study of a Yokohama-based merchant in the 1850s and 1860s. Partner demonstrates through the life of Chūemon that even before the Meiji Restoration brought monumental changes, new types of commercial relations centered on the treaty ports profoundly reshaped peoples' lives across the Japanese archipelago and beyond.[17]

Intersecting networks of human beings lie at the heart of the book. By studying networks, I shed light on how people connected not only to each other but also to ideas and institutions, including sex-specific associations.[18] As I map out ties, I distinguish between formal and informal networks. I identify three formal networks, all of which overlapped. The first centered on foreign missionaries affiliated with the American Board. The second converged around the Okayama Church (Okayama kyōkai), which was established by Japanese converts in 1880. The Church, in turn, supported the Okayama Orphanage, and a number of converts helped to found the previously mentioned San'yō gakuen school, suggesting that the Church constituted a central node in local activist networks. The third network was the local manifestation of the Freedom and People's Rights Movement, which strove to broaden political life and demand a representative government. This last network involved nearly all of the Japanese people under discussion and none of the Westerners.

In contrast to formal networks, what I call "informal networks" centered on families and neighborhoods and by their nature prove harder to document. The contributions of individuals to informal networks—what some scholars call "kin work"—give insight into the complex tangle of local connections and the ways they overlapped with more formal institutions and networks.[19] Network visualization illuminates the many different ways people connected: through families, schools, neighborhoods, churches, and political organizations (fig. 1).

17. Partner, *The Merchant's Tale*, 222–23.

18. Visualizing Historical Networks, accessed 15 July 2016, http://www.fas.harvard.edu/~histecon/visualizing/index.html.

19. For an example of the literature on kin work, see Micaela di Leonardo, "The Female World."

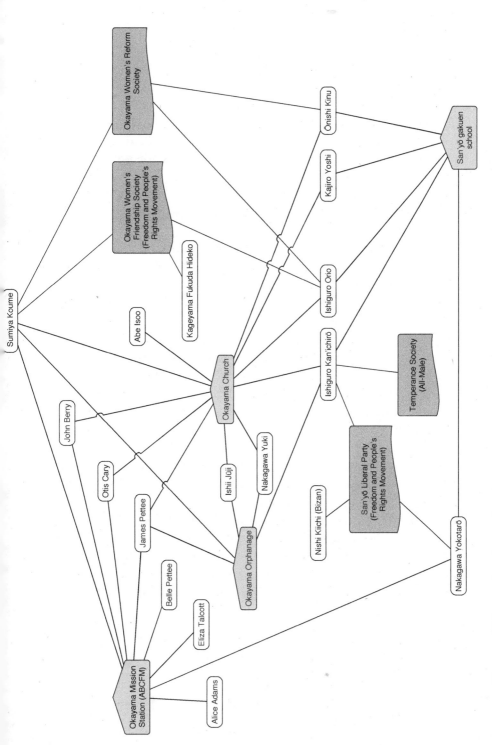

FIGURE 1. Diagram of Okayama-based networks.

On one level, this book is a local history. As scholar Moriya Tomoe has observed, Okayama Prefecture provides exceptional material for a social history of the Meiji period because of the high levels of activism. Moriya points to the significant percentage of Protestant Christians from all levels of society (everyone from former samurai to newly "liberated" outcastes, or *burakumin*), the number of social welfare pioneers like Okayama Orphanage founder Ishii Jūji, prison reformer Tomeoka Kōsuke (1864–1934), and Salvation Army leader Yamamuro Gunpei (1872–1940), and the deep connections between the churches and the local Freedom and People's Rights Movement.[20] Moriya also highlights the vibrant broader religious landscape in Okayama, where several "new religions" emerged, including Kurozumikyō and Konkōkyō.[21] I suggest that Okayama was distinctive rather than representative in part because of the area's longtime focus on education together with the early arrival of foreign Protestant missionaries relative to other places in Japan outside of the treaty ports. Yet the case of local people shaping Japan's modernity in Okayama illustrates historical dynamics that apply to other parts of the country, for example the People's Rights activists in Kōchi Prefecture and the Protestant movement in Kobe.[22]

On another level, this study highlights the transnational nature of late nineteenth-century Japanese life and sheds light on the history of global Christianity and social reform. Networks were transnational not only because they included foreign Protestant missionaries but also because a number of Okayama natives studied abroad in the United States and Europe; others went to China and Russia. Ties across the new nation were also strong as people frequently moved back and forth between Okayama, Kyoto, and Tokyo. To give but one example, take Konishi Masutarō (1862–1940), born in Okayama to a commoner family who resided near the castle. He served as a secretary to local magnate Nozaki Bukichirō (1848–1925), who headed a salt-making business. Konishi went to Russia to study theology in Kiev for seven years from 1886 to 1893 with

---

20. Moriya, "Auto sutēshon kara sutēshon e." Tomeoka hailed from Takahashi, about eighteen miles away from Okayama, and Yamamuro was born in the city of Niimi, some fifty miles from Okayama.

21. Moriya, "Auto sutēshon kara sutēshon e," 118.

22. Sotozaki, *Kōchi-ken fujin undōshi*; Tanaka, *Kindai Nihon kōtō kyōiku taisei*.

Nozaki's financial backing. While abroad, Konishi worked with Leo Tolstoy on a Russian translation of the Chinese Daoist classic the *Laozi* and translated some of Tolstoy's work into Japanese. Konishi returned to Japan in 1893 to take up a position at the Tokyo-based Orthodox Seminary and later taught Russian language and literature at Kyoto University. The rest of Konishi's career straddled academia and industry as he continued working for the salt business in colonial Taiwan and Hokkaido.[23] His story exemplifies the many intersecting ties one could maintain and cultivate at local, national, and transnational levels.

By putting my center of gravity in Okayama, I aim to "track histories that remain hidden in a more traditional framework centered on nations and capital cities."[24] A number of historians, including Jeremy Adelman and Lara Putnam, have called attention to the importance of the local in a globalizing era and the necessity of place-based research.[25] My analysis of the Okayama networks allows me to excavate new information about the ways local networks of people made Japan modern by building new institutions, cultivating novel ideas, and reshaping modern politics.

Okayama and Local History

Relative to some other areas of Japan, Okayama has received extensive scholarly attention in English. Part of the region's lure lies in its exceptional archives. Historians and anthropologists have been drawn to the area and have used it as a case study to understand the country more broadly. In particular, John Whitney Hall's *Government and Local Power in Japan, 500–1700* stands out, as does *Village Japan*, written jointly by Richard Beardsley, John W. Hall, and Robert Ward. Hall and other scholars conducted their research at the University of Michigan's Okayama Field Station, which operated in the prefecture during the early post–World War II years from 1950 to 1955.

23. San'yō shinbunsha, *Okayama-ken rekishi jinbutsu jiten*, 434–35.
24. Maza, *Thinking about History*, 71.
25. Adelman, "What Is Global History Now?"; Putnam, "The Transnational and the Text-Searchable," 397–98.

In the Tokugawa period, Okayama's regional culture, particularly the policies of the local Ikeda daimyo, facilitated the expansion of education, including education for male commoners and women. In 1670, the Ikeda lord set up an academy for male commoners and samurai, the Shizutani gakkō, nestled in a valley in what is now the city of Bizen.[26] After the Tokugawa government lifted the ban on importing Western books in the eighteenth century—so long as the books did not address Christianity—the Okayama area thrived as a center of Western learning.[27] Abe Isoo, who resided in Okayama for over a decade as a pastor, recalled that women also received excellent education under the Ikeda lords, though he did not mention specifics: "Before Okayama women got a modern education, they had received an education unique in our country."[28] One hint at the extent of women's education comes from statistics compiled by the Ministry of Education in 1880. They register that by the mid-nineteenth century, the Okayama domain had fourteen temple schools (*terakoya*) headed by women; only the shogunal capital of Edo (fifty-three) and Kumamoto (fifteen) had more.[29] Still, it remains difficult to piece together the overall picture—for instance, one school in Okayama did not compile attendance records since "teachers assumed girls would be embarrassed to have their names called in public."[30]

The leaders of Okayama domain, like those of most other Japanese domains, stood on the sidelines during the upheavals of the 1860s that led to the downfall of the Tokugawa military government.[31] But the area was far from immune to change. In the decades following the Meiji

26.   Shibata, *Kinsei gōnō no gakumon to shisō*.

27.   Nakamura, "Working the Siebold Network," 209.

28.   Murata Tomi, *Ōnishi Kinuko*, 49. See also Abe, *Shakai shugisha*, 142. Abe Isoo resided in Okayama off and on from 1887 to 1897. In 1841, nearby Tsuyama domain created a room to educate commoner women; it was the only domain to "take any interest in the education of women." Kornicki, "Women, Education, and Literacy," 9.

29.   Female-led schools drew higher percentages of female students. Sugano, "Terakoya to onnakyōshi," 144–46.

30.   Walthall, "The Life Cycle of Farm Women," 46.

31.   In the early 1860s, the Okayama domain adopted a neutral approach to the conflicts that pitted imperial loyalists against those whose allegiances lay with the Tokugawa government. But by the time of the Bōshin War (1868–1869), the Okayama domain was under the leadership of a new lord who fought on the side of the imperial army. On the complicated politics of the era, see Ravina, *To Stand with the Nations*, chap. 3.

Restoration, the prefecture became an important area for the textile industry, especially in the nearby city of Kurashiki.[32] Okayama's location facing the Inland Sea and its proximity to the industrial powerhouse of Osaka facilitated the area's economic development.

A study of Meiji-era Okayama drives home the importance of local initiatives. The 1870s marked a time when the Japanese government was working to attain parity with the Western powers by overturning the unequal treaties that put the country in an inferior economic and legal position—Japan lacked tariff autonomy and extraterritoriality in the treaty ports meant that foreigners were not subject to Japanese law. The era also saw all manner of social, political, and economic reform, under the slogan "civilization and enlightenment." As we shall see, the Okayama networks embraced the spirit of reform and carried it to various ends: members built schools and institutions for social reform. They embraced novel ideas about everything from modern hygiene to political rights. The American Board missionaries were able to establish a mission in the first place because of the work of the Okayama governor acting together with local notables like Nakagawa. Local officials continued to promote education, and the prefecture developed a national reputation for excellence.[33] In all these cases, Okayama's modernization was, above all, the product of local efforts.

On the Meiji Restoration and the Former Samurai

The networks I analyze center primarily on former samurai. During the previous Tokugawa regime, the samurai occupied a privileged hereditary status. Even those who populated the lower echelons of the samurai status and struggled with economic hardship received stipends and enjoyed certain privileges. The monumental changes following the Meiji Restoration forced the samurai into a new world in which the government

---

32. Tsurumi, *Factory Girls*.

33. Other standouts were Nagano and Yamaguchi. San'yō gakuen, *Ai to hōshi*, 22. For an early work on the transition to Meiji in Okayama, see Burks, "Administrative Transition from Han to Ken."

abolished their privileged status, took away their exclusive right to wear swords, and converted their stipends into bonds. Such experiences were wrenching, and naturally, some fared better than others. Government projects were instituted to assist the group economically and integrate them into the new society. These projects included land reclamation schemes and business ventures and yielded mixed results.[34] The goal was to help the former samurai find a new way of living that would sustain them and their families. Some served in the new government as bureaucrats. Others joined the police force or became lawyers.[35] Some were sent to Hokkaido as farmer-militia (*tondenhei*).[36] A great many converted to Christianity, for in the new religion they saw a "meaningful path to power."[37]

We know less about the fate of *shizoku* women, the wives, mothers, daughters, and sisters of modernity's usual male protagonists. In the 1940s, historian and socialist feminist Yamakawa Kikue noted that daughters of bannermen (*hatamoto*) often ended up as geisha or concubines after the Restoration because of their family's dire financial circumstances, but the subject has not received much attention.[38] More recently, in a review of the state of the field on gender history and the Restoration, Matsuzaki Rumi postulates that *shizoku* women "supported their households both from within and without" after the Restoration and calls for further research on this topic.[39]

This book excavates the stories of several *shizoku* women, including the orphaned concubine Sumiya Koume as well as married women like Ishiguro Orio (1864–1917), an activist and reformer. I also highlight the possibilities the Meiji period brought for lifelong single women including Sumiya, Kajiro Yoshi, and Ōnishi Kinu. Such women were able to have careers and exercise authority at institutions such as schools and orphanages and to move in spheres beyond the traditional household.[40]

---

34. Harootunian, "The Economic Rehabilitation." The projects were known in Japanese as *shizoku jusan*.

35. Glasnovich, "Return to the Sword"; Flaherty, *Public Law, Private Practice*.

36. Mason, *Dominant Narratives of Colonial Hokkaido and Imperial Japan*, chap. 1.

37. Scheiner, *Christian Converts*, 6.

38. Yamakawa, *Women of the Mito Domain*, 144; Dalby, *Geisha*, 195.

39. Matsuzaki, "Meiji ishinki no jendā kenkyū," 56.

40. On other former samurai women, see the discussion of divorced Sono Teru (known in English as Sono Tel) in Flaherty, *Public Law, Private Practice*, 109–20; Walthall, "Nishimiya Hide."

The experiences of Meiji single women have too often flown under the radar, limiting our understanding of gender roles in Meiji Japan.

The Work of the Networks

The three central causes of politics, education, and social reform are the lenses I use to explore the work of the networks. In practice, these pursuits often overlapped, but for analytical purposes, I separate them here.

POLITICS

The first cause, political involvement, occurred within the Freedom and People's Rights Movement, one of biggest challenges to the Meiji state in the 1870s and 1880s. It opposed the way leaders from two southwestern domains had concentrated power at the national level. Participants advocated the establishment of a parliamentary system as well as wider distribution of power in the new government. Inada Masahiro has noted that the People's Rights Movement also gave rise to a new conception of political culture, one whose impact was long lasting.[41] Male activists formed political associations and political parties. By 1882, women joined them and began creating their own associations, as I discuss in chapter 3. Some women enjoyed careers as political speakers alongside men, and newspapers recorded the presence of women at otherwise mostly male gatherings.[42] More broadly, Daniel Botsman highlights how the movement's ideas reshaped the parameters of what was possible and how "the language of nineteenth-century liberalism gradually came to take on concrete meaning in Meiji Japan, often becoming enmeshed in processes of social change that were already in motion."[43]

In 1881, the government partly met the movement's demands and announced that a constitution would be promulgated by the end of the decade. By 1890, the opposition movements had run out of steam, brought into line through a deft combination of heavy-handed suppression and

41. Inada, *Jiyū minken no bunkashi*; Bowen, *Rebellion and Democracy*.
42. Marnie Anderson, *A Place in Public*.
43. Botsman, "Freedom without Slavery," 1344. See also Kim, *The Age of Visions and Arguments*.

conciliatory measures. The government announced the Imperial Japanese Constitution (known as the Meiji Constitution) in 1889, and the following year brought the beginning of a national Diet and party politics.[44] At the very moment formal politics opened up for elite men, a series of laws blocked it for all women.[45]

EDUCATION

The second cause seized upon by activists was education. The Meiji oligarchs were acutely aware of the importance of universal education in forging a strong nation-state. The Ministry of Education enacted the Fundamental Code of Education (Gakusei) in 1872, which created a centralized system. Thereafter, primary education was to be universal for all Japanese subjects, though in practice, attendance lagged and the system did not become fully realized until after the turn of the twentieth century. The 1870s also saw the adoption of a Western-inspired curriculum that included geography, math, and science rather than one centered on the Confucian classics.

But the local reformers did not stand by passively. Several activists were interested in founding schools and promoting education for girls. Their enthusiasm for women's education deserves elaboration. Early Meiji advocates of "civilization and enlightenment" generally understood the education of women as necessary in order for Japan to be truly "civilized." They had fully accepted the nineteenth-century understanding of "civilization" as the final step on a universal ladder all societies necessarily climbed. Western countries justified the unequal treaties on the grounds that Japan was less advanced than the West, and Japanese leaders were eager to remedy the situation and attain parity on the international stage.

The focus on women's education should not be taken to mean that women were not educated in previous periods of Japanese history. Some were, and in elite circles in Tokugawa Japan, men assumed women's literacy.[46] However, the dramatic growth in late Tokugawa commoner education primarily took place in mixed-sex temple schools, and single-sex

---

44. Gluck, *Japan's Modern Myths*, 17.
45. Marnie Anderson, *A Place in Public*, chap. 4.
46. Gramlich-Oka and Walthall, "Introduction," 7.

schools for girls were rare.[47] Still, both worlds featured what Anne Walthall terms "gender-differentiated learning."[48] In the modern period, boys and girls were educated together in primary schools, though some aspects of the curriculum differed by sex and only girls learned sewing. Teachers taught penmanship separately to girls and boys as well. Middle and higher schools were sex-segregated, and women faced discrimination at the highest levels of education.[49] Nonetheless, prewar institutions did permit access beginning in the 1910s when three imperial universities admitted women. Tōhoku was the first in 1913, followed by Hokkaido and Kyushu. There were also colleges specifically for women, and women could attend some private colleges and universities. Many of these institutions were founded by Western missionaries, who saw the opening of schools for women as crucial to their work and more beneficial to their outreach than opening schools for men, a cause to which the Japanese government was already committed.[50]

Scholars typically associate the spirit of the 1870s with educator and journalist Fukuzawa Yukichi (1835–1901) and his famous tract *An Encouragement of Learning* (*Gakumon no susume*), serialized between 1871 and 1876. Fukuzawa championed education for all and seemed to embrace an egalitarian spirit. As Fukuzawa wrote in the text's opening line: "Heaven, it is said, does not create one person above or below another."[51] But Fukuzawa did not promote gender equality in the way the term is generally understood today. Rather, like the philosopher John Stuart Mill (1806–1873), he advocated for a more active role for women within the home.[52]

Fukuzawa was not the only figure advocating for a "modern" education. Many local elites were fully on board. A year before Fukuzawa began to serialize *An Encouragement of Learning*, Okayama bureaucrat Nishi Kiichi circulated the following set of precepts to the population announcing the fundamental direction of education in Okayama. One local source uses this document to claim that Nishi anticipated Fukuzawa as well as

47. Kornicki notes there were a few all-girls' schools in the Tokugawa period. Kornicki, "Women, Education, and Literacy," 15.

48. Walthall, "Women and Literacy from Edo to Meiji," 228.

49. Walthall, "Women and Literacy from Edo to Meiji," 226–27.

50. Noriko Ishii, *American Women Missionaries*, 12.

51. For an English translation by Dilworth, see Fukuzawa, *An Encouragement of Learning*, 3.

52. Marnie Anderson, *A Place in Public*, chap. 2.

the Fundamental Code of Education of 1872.[53] I reproduce the precepts here so we can understand how bureaucrats articulated local priorities in this particular moment, reflecting both new Western-inspired definitions of civilization and Tokugawa-period Confucian moralism:

1. As we revive and build schools, we should correct public morals. Theaters and the like cause harm and are without benefit.
2. The difference between barbarism and civilization can be found in the education provided by schools.
3. There are many countries in the world. The Western countries are civilized. Our country's previous statuses have now become one; we must urgently work to serve the country and build patriotism and compete with all foreign countries.
4. Civilized countries provide schools for children. We must build schools for girls and put in place teachers of writing, mathematics, and Western studies.[54]

Here Nishi embraces the language of civilization, the education of women and a broad curriculum in order to navigate the competitive nineteenth-century world. Like a good Confucian moralist, he enjoins his audience to practice morality and cautions against the damage caused by theater-going. He notes the dissolution of status categories—a process that unfolded gradually over the first half of 1870s—in an unusual manner. Instead of talking about abolition or dissolution, he explains that various groups have merged together.

SOCIAL REFORM

In addition to politics and education, the third cause advocated by the networks centered on social reform, the most broad and capacious of the categories. The impulse to reform society took off in the years surrounding the turn of the twentieth century.[55] Social reform in Okayama included advocating for modern hygiene, public health, and infrastructure, as Nakagawa did (chapter 1). A reforming spirit drove the founding of

53. San'yō gakuen, *Ai to hōshi*, 23.
54. San'yō gakuen, *Ai to hōshi*, 23.
55. For an analysis of juvenile delinquency, see Ambaras, *Bad Youth*.

the Okayama Orphanage by Ishii Jūji in 1887.[56] The Orphanage received extensive support from the people and institutions I discuss here, notably Nakagawa's former concubine Sumiya Koume, missionary James H. Pettee (1851–1920), and the Okayama Church. By the turn of the twentieth century, the Okayama Orphanage enjoyed renown throughout Japan as a model for social reform: it had even earned the support of Meiji officialdom and the imperial household.[57]

The cause of social reform in the Okayama networks was often—though not always—Christian-inflected. We see it in the work of women's groups to promote monogamy and abolish prostitution and in the sex-specific groups devoted to the cause of temperance.

The Missions and the Missionaries

Once the Meiji government lifted the ban on Christianity in 1873, foreign missionaries began arriving in large numbers.[58] During the Tokugawa period, the government had banned the foreign faith because of its perceived potential to disrupt the social order. The Protestant missionaries who set foot in Japan in the 1870s and 1880s were propelled by the Social Gospel, a movement that was just getting off the ground in the United States, where it had originated. Proponents of the Social Gospel were not only concerned with saving souls but also aimed to ameliorate the societal problems arising from rapid industrialization, including poverty and inequality. The men and women of the New England-based American Board, one of the largest—and certainly the oldest—of the nineteenth-century American mission organizations, had this mindset. By the 1870s, the American Board was composed entirely of Congregationalists, known in Japan as the Kumiai. Its initial efforts were focused on western Japan, especially Kyoto, Osaka, and Kobe, since the American Board was a

---

56. Maus, "Ishii Jūji." Ishii was inspired by Prussian-born British reformer George Müller (1805–1898).

57. Maus, "Ishii Jūji," 225.

58. Cary, *A History of Christianity in Japan*, 104; James Pettee, *The Japan Mission*, especially 14. Before 1873, the missionaries in Japan ministered to the foreign community.

latecomer among Protestant denominational boards to the country. Previous boards had already established a presence in eastern Japan, including Tokyo.[59]

In 1878, three members of the American Board based in Kobe made a prospective visit to Okayama, at Nakagawa's invitation, to consider the possibility of establishing a mission station. They were John C. Berry (1847–1936), Otis Cary (1851–1932), and James H. Pettee. Berry had a medical degree; this expertise was highly attractive to local Japanese elites and had been the primary impetus for inviting missionary Dr. Taylor in 1875. The three men accepted an invitation from the Okayama governor to establish a station the following year, and they were joined by their wives and a Miss Julia Wilson, who worked as a nurse (fig. 2).[60]

Setting up a mission station outside a treaty port was a challenge because it required permission from the national and local governments. Governor Takasaki Itsumu (1836–1896) and other local notables welcomed the missionaries, and the governor offered them rent-free lodging.[61] Far from partial to the Protestants, Takasaki also invited members of the Roman Catholic and Eastern Orthodox communities. Yet his expansive welcome did not dampen the enthusiasm of the American Board missionaries. Pettee, in a letter to the American Board headquarters titled "A New Call from Japan: Shall We Occupy Okayama?" could barely contain his excitement about the possibilities Okayama presented:

> To be earnestly invited to his city by a governor, to be told that a place should be made for us, if none now existed . . . to be offered by said official a portion of a public park for a building site, it being the most desirable one in the city, to be most courteously treated and at last to receive a present from this same dignitary—can I be a missionary and pass through such experiences?[62]

59.   Noriko Ishii, *American Women Missionaries*, 8.
60.   The wives were Ellen Emerson Cary, Isabella (Belle) Wilson Pettee, and Maria Gove Berry. Hamada, *Kadota kaiwai*, chap. 1–2; Nihon kirutokyōdan Okayama kyōkai, *Okayama kyōkai hyakunenshi*, 15.
61.   Hamada, *Kadota kaiwai*, 16–17; Cary, *A History of Christianity in Japan*, 146.
62.   James Pettee, "A New Call from Japan: Shall We Occupy Okayama?" 2 January 1879 (Kobe), American Board of Commissioners for Foreign Missions archives, ABC 77.1 (47:15). By permission of the Houghton Library, Harvard University.

FIGURE 2. The Okayama Station Missionaries around 1879–1880. Top row left to right: Belle Pettee, John Berry, Otis Cary. Middle row left to right: James Pettee, Maria Berry, Ellen Cary. Bottom row: Julia Wilson. Courtesy of Houghton Library, Harvard University and United Church Ministries.

The new Okayama Station was ready by 1879, and the missionaries again received a warm reception from the community. Local men took turns renting a "foreign suit of clothes" from an enterprising photographer, who purchased it for "commercial purposes." They then showed up at the missionaries' home to pay their respects.[63] The missionaries were aided by a general enthusiasm in the early Meiji period for all things modern and Western, which local people generally associated with the foreign religion. In a different context, China and India, religious studies scholar Peter van der Veer points to parallels between the process of conversion to modernity and conversion to a new religion, and that point applies to Japan as well.[64] Christian membership in Japan grew rapidly in the mid-1880s.[65] The Okayama missionaries worked with local converts; a group of whom would establish the Okayama Church in 1880. The missionaries developed ties to several Japanese pastors, including the first two pastors of the Okayama Church: Kanamori Michitomo (1857–1927) and Abe Isoo. The missionaries fundraised and arranged to send students abroad to institutions of higher learning in the West, notably to schools in New England. Berry and Wilson supported themselves through their work at the hospital, while Cary and Pettee taught at a local private school. The school, Gensen gakkai (Origin society), was founded by the Ikeda family, the former lords of the Okayama domain.[66]

The local enthusiasm for Western ideas and practices faded, however, by the 1890s, an era that saw a reaction against Westernizing trends, especially Christianity, and an embrace of "tradition."[67] The shifting reception accorded to the missionaries can be glimpsed in an overview of their various dwellings. When the American Board missionaries first arrived in Okayama, they stayed in a Japanese-style house on the top of a hill, offered by the governor until Western accommodations more suited to their tastes could be built. After the Western-style houses were completed,

63. Berry, *A Pioneer Doctor*, 96.

64. Van der Veer, *The Modern Spirit of Asia*, chap. 4.

65. Lublin, *Reforming Japan*, 44. In 1881, there were 3,811 registered Christians. Ion, *American Missionaries, Christian Oyatoi, and Japan*, 300.

66. Nihon kirutokyōdan Okayama kyōkai, *Okayama kyōkai hyakunenshi*, 15; Cary, *A History of Christianity in Japan*, 146.

67. Pyle, "Meiji Conservatism"; Fujimoto, "Women, Missionaries, and Medical Professions," 195.

the missionaries resided in them until the mid-1890s, when the buildings were torn down amid a wave of anti-Western sentiment among local people. One local chronicler recalled that a group of outraged locals thought the buildings' proximity to a Shinto shrine was problematic. At that juncture, the missionaries relocated to the heart of the city.[68]

A few years after their arrival in Okayama, many of the missionaries had moved on. Nurse Julia Wilson left Japan in 1880. The Berry family moved to Kyoto. The Carys followed them in 1892. The Pettees, however, stayed in Okayama for over three decades. Owing to their longtime residence, the Pettees left a deep impression on the local community. One chronicler remembered that James Pettee had a wonderful library and that he lent his volumes of gorgeously-bound works by Shakespeare and Milton to local people. Pettee's contributions were, this same author maintained, not merely in the realm of religion but also more broadly the modernization of Okayama. Pettee was particularly helpful to Orphanage founder Ishii Jūji, and Ishii mentions Pettee regularly in his diary.[69]

Although most accounts of the missions highlight the work of the men, married and single women also play a role in this story. Single women like Eliza Talcott (1836–1911), who taught and mentored Nakagawa's concubine Sumiya Koume, belonged to a wave of single American female missionaries who arrived in Japan beginning in the last decades of the nineteenth century. Increasingly, they were graduates of the women's colleges that had newly opened in the United States, including Mt. Holyoke Seminary (which became Mt. Holyoke College in 1893) and Smith College. A diverse lot, these women wielded more autonomy and influence abroad than they did at home, though they faced gendered constraints.[70] Married women such as James Pettee's wife, Belle Pettee (1853–1937), also appear in these pages, interacting with locals and writing about Japan-related topics for a Western audience that supported the missions. Initially, the missions welcomed only married women, but this

---

68. Tamaki Sugiyama, "Untitled Speech for the Japan-America Cultural Exchange Society, Miyoshino Hall, 15 March 1965," American Board of Commissioners for Foreign Missions archives, ABC 77.1 (47:15). By permission of the Houghton Library, Harvard University.

69. Tamaki Sugiyama, "Untitled Speech."

70. Yasutake, *Transnational Women's Activism*, 11–13; Noriko Ishii, *American Women Missionaries*, 5.

changed because wives were generally already stretched thin by household duties and had little time to work for the missions. The significant growth in the number of single women was such that by the turn of the twentieth century, the number of women missionaries exceeded men in missions around the world and the women's missionary movement had been professionalized.[71]

How to evaluate the legacy of women missionaries has been a subject of contemporary scholarly debate. Previous literature tended to understand these women "as simple pawns or agents of Western cultural imperialism," but recent scholarship calls this view into question and demands a reevaluation of missionaries' role.[72] The main contribution of this new body of work, Mona Siegel concludes, lies in understanding how female missionaries made "evangelical ideals about women's moral authority into a powerful claim for women's participation in the lively public debates regarding the meaning of national progress and citizenship sweeping Eurasia in an era of waning imperial influence."[73] This evaluation goes hand in hand with a new understanding of missionary outposts as "vibrant cross-cultural frontiers."[74]

A point to be made more generally is that the impact of the missions far exceeded the number of people the missionaries actually converted to Christianity. The education and health care projects that missionaries undertook exerted a profound influence on the trajectory of modernization in these societies.[75] Many of the schools they built exist today. And, at the same time, the missionaries themselves were changed by their experiences.[76] Some studied local religions, Japanese medical practices including

71. Siegel, "Transcending Cross-Cultural Frontiers," 192, 195; Noriko Ishii, *American Women Missionaries*, 5.

72. Siegel, "Transcending Cross-Cultural Frontiers," 189.

73. Siegel, "Transcending Cross-Cultural Frontiers," 196.

74. Siegel, "Transcending Cross-Cultural Frontiers," 196. For other work on foreign women missionaries in Japan, see Seat, *Providence Has Freed Our Hands*; Kohiyama, "No Nation Can Rise Higher Than Its Women."

75. See Van der Veer, *The Modern Spirit of Asia*.

76. As David Hollinger succinctly begins his recent study of United States missionaries abroad, "The Protestant foreign missionary project expected to make the world look more like the United States. Instead, it made the United States look more like the world." Hollinger, *Protestants Abroad*, 1. On doctrinal struggles among the American Board missionaries, see Campbell, "To Make the World One in Christ Jesus."

moxibustion, and the tea ceremony. They struggled to learn Japanese. On one occasion, a foreign pastor baptized a congregation by accident, believing himself to be giving a benediction.[77] Pettee himself confessed in a report sent back home: "My constant cry is, Show me the shortest road to a knowledge of this difficult Japanese language."[78]

The tensions generated by the cross-cultural encounter were many and ranged from mild—even humorous—to serious. The foreigners observed with apparent amusement that the Eucharist was usually celebrated with sponge cake instead of bread.[79] Some issues were more perplexing. Missionaries had to answer the question of whether silkworms could be attended to on the Sabbath (the answer was yes). Some problems had no simple solution: converts were at times compelled to pay Buddhist priests to stop praying for a deceased relative so they could be "properly interred as a Christian."[80] Other issues were more weighty and potentially got in the way of the missionaries' work. Berry encountered resistance from Japanese doctors at the local hospital: "The prejudice and pride of young physicians, educated in Tokio [*sic*] disincline them to cooperate with a foreigner, and their hostility to Christianity aggravates the trouble."[81] Whereas this quotation attributes the resistance Berry faced to Christianity, other sources suggest it was rooted instead in the increasing preference for German medical training among Japanese doctors. Berry had trained in the United States. Japanese doctors at the Okayama Prefectural Hospital who had studied at the University of Tokyo with professors "averse to non-German medicine" attempted unsuccessfully to have Berry dismissed.[82]

Part of the value of the missionary records is that they recorded what locals took for granted about their environment and way of life. Of course, the missionaries' concerns and beliefs shaped their appraisals. They were struck by the poverty of much of Okayama, the poor hygiene practices, the sludge in the canals, and the difficulty of accessing clean water. They pronounced the mild climate hard to tolerate and believed

77. Berry, *A Pioneer Doctor*, 120.

78. James Pettee, "A New Call from Japan."

79. *Missionary Herald* 76 (1880), 391.

80. Berry, *A Pioneer Doctor*, 105.

81. *Missionary Herald* 78 (1882), 67.

82. Fujimoto, "Women, Missionaries, and Medical Professions," 195; Tanaka, *Kindai Nihon kōtō kyōiku taisei*, 107–8.

that the vegetables lacked minerals. They yearned for more meat and milk in their diet.[83] To be sure, their records provide valuable insights and shed light on the complexity of the cross-cultural encounter. However, my focus here remains on the Japanese networks while the foreigners remain mostly in the background.

Networks and Gender

This book investigates how local networks of women and men shaped Okayama's modernity by creating new movements and organizations.[84] However, each chapter focuses on an individual or a set of individuals (the exception is chapter 3, which centers around a political association). Some may find this method to be at odds with my overall emphasis on networks, and yet the sources lend themselves to this approach, providing a window onto the larger Okayama networks. My method also stems from my interest in gender history. Guided by Kathleen Canning's call to study the "relentless relationality" of gender, I attempt to analyze men and women together whenever possible.[85] In doing so, I have found that using a smaller scale and focusing on individuals and small groups proves conducive to teasing out gender relations: women's lives are usually less documented than men's and may escape attention when the view is too broad. A closer view allows us to see patterns that may otherwise go missing, such as the prominence of lifelong single women in the Okayama networks. In a reversal of usual historical practice, I grant female actors more attention than men, except in chapter 1, where I focus on Nakagawa. However, I do explore the activities of several men, notably Nakagawa's good friend Nishi Kiichi, minister Abe Isoo, and activist and lawyer Ishiguro Kan'ichirō (1854–1917).

These networks operated on a smaller scale than the networks that historical studies have examined to illuminate trade or communication

83. Berry, *A Pioneer Doctor*, 108–9.
84. On some of the problems with defining "networks," see Davison, "Early Modern Social Networks," 475–76.
85. Canning, *Gender History in Practice*, 62.

patterns.[86] The Meiji networks had their roots in what Eiko Ikegami has called "the Tokugawa network revolution."[87] Ikegami focuses on Tokugawa aesthetic networks and the multiple "publics" they nurtured, developments grounded in a flourishing print industry and expanding infrastructure. Many of these networks included women and men—in other words, they were heterosocial. Ikegami shows the ties between the Tokugawa and Meiji networks, discussing how the *haikai* poetry circles of the late Tokugawa period laid the groundwork for the Freedom and People's Rights Movement in the first two decades of the Meiji period.[88] Such connections are evident in Okayama in the case of former samurai men. For example, Nishi Kiichi, a leader in the People's Rights Movement, had formerly taught many of the young male activists at the domainal school.[89] Other preexisting networks certainly played a role, though they are usually not recorded and may have included ties based on *kō*, early modern credit cooperatives and various kinds of religious associations.[90]

How should we characterize the types of ties that structured these networks? Ikegami suggests that the Tokugawa aesthetic networks promoted horizontal forms of association in a society shaped by hereditary status.[91] Similarly, the networks I study were characterized less by hierarchical patron-client relationships and more by horizontal ties. But it is not always possible to determine the exact nature of a relationship given the extant sources. Consequently, the notion of "association" is key to the analytical work in this study because of its power to suggest the many possible configurations and types of interaction that can occur within a network—even when there is much we cannot know.[92]

86. See, for example, Edelstein et al., "Historical Research in a Digital Age." On the perils of network analysis, see Davison, "Early Modern Social Networks," 475–76.

87. Ikegami, *The Bonds of Civility*, 3–18.

88. Ikegami, *The Bonds of Civility*, 213.

89. *Okayama-ken shi*, 10:149.

90. On *kō*, see Najita, *Ordinary Economies in Japan*, chap. 3. See also essays in Gramlich-Oka et al., *Women and Networks*.

91. Ikegami, *The Bonds of Civility*, 157.

92. Shiba's discussion of networks built by daimyo wives reveals a case where networks were clearly hierarchical because of the women's high status. It is not hard to imagine gradations in relationships that were neither completely horizontal nor vertical. Shiba, "Building Networks on the Fly."

Structure of the Book

Overall, this book advances three distinct but related arguments. The first is that local networks of men *and* women in Okayama shaped Japan's modernization. Often preexisting, these networks allowed people to mobilize quickly and advocate for reform. Thanks to the presence of missionaries and the movement of people nationally and internationally, networks were never just local but had a transnational dimension.

Second, I contend that although the early Meiji networks were heterosocial, associational life increasingly divided along gender lines; for example, Okayama had separate temperance organizations for women and men. However, the content of associational activities was generally not sex-specific—both men and women concerned themselves with women's education and social reform. The exception was political rights. Even though men's and women's groups initially shared an interest in formal politics, rights disappeared from the agenda of women's groups by 1890 because of a series of restrictive laws. The rise of single-sex associational life was part of a larger process by which Meiji Japanese built modern civilization around gender differences.

My third argument is that although the Meiji period did not completely break from the past, the space that opened following the decline of the old order and the rise of a new one allowed some men and women to craft new identities. The abolition of the status system, new economic opportunities, and new forms of social organization all set the stage for personal reinvention. We see this in the story of Nakagawa, who was able to cast himself as a reformer and eccentric, as well as in the experiences of Sumiya Koume, Ōnishi Kinu, and Kajiro Yoshi—three single women who had careers in institutions outside of the household. To be sure, there were precedents for such work in the Tokugawa period because a number of women ran schools and worked as teachers, especially in Edo but also in Okayama, as I have noted.[93] However, in the Meiji period, the single women I analyze worked with schools and other institutions as

---

93.   In the late Tokugawa period, one could support oneself on a teacher's salary. Seki, *Edo kōki no joseitachi*, 36–37.

individuals rather than as someone's wife, mother, or sister and did not reside in traditional households.

In analyzing both women and men, I question the tendency to conceive of activism as occurring in separate gendered spheres. In fact, women sometimes played leadership roles in networks, although such roles are often buried under androcentric documentation. An example can be found in Miyazaki Fumiko's work on Fujidō, a popular late Tokugawa–era religious organization in which women played leadership roles.[94] Similarly, Helen Hardacre has identified the ways nineteenth-century new religions in Japan offered women the chance to exercise authority.[95] By highlighting relationships between and among people, I challenge the convention of treating men like Nakagawa as independent individuals, without mentioning their wives and children, while conceiving of women only in terms of their relationship to men. For example, the family of Nakagawa's wife, the Ōnishi, played a pivotal role in local networks, though most sources do not mention this.

Chapter 1 addresses the life and work of Nakagawa Yokotarō, a former samurai and Meiji bureaucrat whose prodigious memory compensated for his near illiteracy. We saw earlier that he was the individual who invited the first foreign missionaries to Okayama. Nakagawa reinvented himself in the Meiji period by drawing on ideas old and new; he cast himself as a reformer who simultaneously cultivated the early modern role of the eccentric (*kijin*). For much of the 1870s and 1880s, he played two roles typically understood as distinct—prefectural official and local notable. He engaged in all the activist networks under discussion. The reason I introduce him first is that he serves as a kind of guide through the networks and the broader Tokugawa–Meiji transition. He left a mark on the local landscape through his building of schools. Nakagawa sought to enlighten the populace by giving speeches—he encouraged people to adopt "civilized" haircuts, to practice modern hygiene, and to build up-to-date infrastructure. He and his friend Nishi Kiichi labored to help former samurai adjust to the new world after they lost their stipends and status.

---

94. Miyazaki, "Networks of Believers in a New Religion."
95. Hardacre, *Kurozumikyō and the New Religions of Japan*, 192. See also Ambros, "Nakayama Miki's."

Both men were involved in the local Freedom and People's Rights Movement and are central to the Okayama networks. From a wider angle, Nakagawa's colorful story sheds light on the fate of the former samurai in the Meiji period and the important roles they played in local modernization projects. Above all, Nakagawa functioned as what networks studies scholars call a "go-between," or a "structural hole," a person who "connect[s] people who would otherwise be separated."[96]

Chapter 2 illuminates the trajectory of Sumiya Koume, a former geisha who worked as Nakagawa's concubine for about a decade after he bought out her contract. She was transformed by her education at Kobe College, an institution founded by Protestant missionaries in the 1870s. After less than a year under the tutelage of the missionaries, Sumiya returned to Okayama, broke up with Nakagawa, and converted to Christianity. She was a skilled networker who later ran the Okayama Orphanage and played a central role at the Okayama Church while working as a Bible Woman, a salaried employee of the missions. Using records from the American Board archives as well as those written by her Japanese acquaintances, I argue that she served as a leader at the Orphanage along with founder Ishii Jūji, but her work there and in the wider community has been obscured in the historical record because of stereotypes about women's work and leadership roles. Sumiya herself did not wish for her work to be known; her reluctance may have stemmed from the early modern notion of women performing work in the interior (*ura*).[97] Respectable women were not to be named publicly.[98] At the same time, religious modesty may also have played a role. Above all, I show that as with Nakagawa, the Meiji period offered Sumiya a new start and a chance for self-reinvention—to live as a single woman who commanded authority.

Chapter 3 introduces the Okayama Women's Friendship Society (Okayama joshi konshinkai, hereafter OWFS), likely the first political organization for women in Japan and a model for others. The Meiji period saw the rapid rise of women's associations in Okayama and around the country. The OWFS was active at the height of the People's Rights Movement from 1882 to 1884. This story of the OWFS illuminates the

---

96. Davison, "Early Modern Social Networks," 466.
97. Walthall, "Closing Remarks," 28; Roberts, *Performing the Great Peace*.
98. I thank Anne Walthall for this point.

initial opening up and eventual closing off of formal political life for women in Meiji Japan over the 1880s. I explicitly compare the OWFS documents with those of the all-male San'yō Liberal Party (San'yō jiyūtō), a local political party affiliated with the People's Rights Movement, to demonstrate how much the groups shared as well as where they diverged. Many of the male members were the husbands, sons, and brothers of the OWFS women. I posit that the OWFS served as a proving ground for the gendered activism that women took up in subsequent decades. Even after the OWFS's demise, former members used networks to continue to act in public, working for temperance, monogamy, and women's education.

Chapter 4 turns to the multifaceted activism of a married couple and two lifelong single women. I interrogate existing understandings of activism that focus on individual men or sometimes women—usually young single women who went on to marry—and offer new perspectives on activism. First, I introduce the married couple Ishiguro Kan'ichirō and Ishiguro Orio, who were active in the local Freedom and People's Rights Movement. I ask how political life was gendered, by placing their lives in the same frame to investigate where men's and women's political lives intersected and where they diverged. It is my contention that the political lives of this husband and wife have more in common than we normally appreciate.

I then analyze the work of lifelong single women Ōnishi Kinu (Nakagawa's cousin and sister-in-law) and Kajiro Yoshi. These women played central roles in girls' education at San'yō gakuen school. (Because of various circumstances, however, they did not participate in the more overtly political activities of the OWFS, covered in chapter 3.) Much like Sumiya Koume, they were self-supporting leaders at a time when, according to most scholarship, women were merely "good wives and wise mothers" (*ryōsai kenbo*).[99] I suggest that single women may have had a better chance of making it into the historical record than married women unless they were overshadowed by a male relative, which is what happened to Ōnishi Kinu.

The epilogue concludes by reflecting on the significance of these local networks and their evolution over time. What does "history on the diagonal" reveal that would otherwise escape notice? To answer this question,

---

99. See, for instance, Koyama, *Ryōsai kenbo to iu kihan*. For a useful background, Sekiguchi, "Confucian Morals."

I trace the paths of key individuals, some of whom were Tokyo-bound, while others remained in Okayama.

Although Meiji-era networks included men and women, the situation would change by the 1930s, when the networks themselves became single-sex and the government increasingly co-opted women's groups. The large women's organizations of the 1930s were all coordinated by government ministries. The trend toward heightened gender differentiation across society continued as the modernizing process obscured the Meiji moment where men and women acted together.

A final note: running through the pages is a consideration of the archives themselves, their inclusions and omissions. When scholars study nondominant groups, we must ponder silences and gaps in the records and the androcentric biases that generated much of the material in the first place.[100] Indeed, male writers often did not even mention women. As Anne Walthall has pointed out, "Women have always written within the context of their relations with men, but men often write in a homosocial context that has nothing to do with women at all."[101] Historian Adele Perry has also written provocatively about this topic in her work on the British colonial archives. Perry discusses what the archives feature and what they leave out, observing that in her sources, "Men speak with more frequency, detail, and volume," a description that applies to the people I analyze here.[102] Perry's analysis sharpens our awareness of how the archive shapes our understanding of history, erasing a good deal in the process. I have attempted to provide a fuller picture of women's and men's interconnected lives by casting a wide net, drawing not only on newspapers and local histories but also missionary archives and personal records, especially those concerning the lives of single women written down by friends and acquaintances. In these ways, I have attempted "history on the diagonal" even as much remains ultimately unknowable.

---

100. Luke Roberts has pointed out the challenges of studying samurai women "because the patriarchic bias of surviving documentation has obscured most of their activities." Roberts, "Women's Roles in Men's Narratives," 21.

101. Walthall, "Women and Literacy from Edo to Meiji," 216.

102. Perry, *Colonial Relations*, 8; Burton, *Dwelling in the Archive*, chap. 1; Stoler, *Along the Archival Grain*.

CHAPTER I

Nakagawa Yokotarō—A Samurai Reborn in Meiji Japan

I n one corner of the Okayama Castle moat, one encounters a towering
stone monument to Nakagawa Yokotarō, a bureaucrat (*meibōka*) and
local notable (*yūshisha*). The monument is inscribed with his pen name,
Kenbōsai, referring to one who "distinguished himself, forgot his accomplishments and hard work, and was not proud." Rather, Nakagawa had
"a graceful, refined temperament."[1] Erected by his friends eight years after
his death in 1911, the memorial is unique among others in Okayama
because it is dedicated to an individual. Nakagawa was a former samurai
and mostly illiterate bureaucrat with a prodigious memory, and the era
afforded him the possibility for self-reinvention. Embracing ideas old and
new, he became a modern reformer who promoted hygiene and education while also adopting the pose of a Tokugawa-era eccentric. Nakagawa
serves as an important gateway to the period because he engaged in all
the activist networks under discussion and shaped local modernization
in concrete ways by building institutions and spreading ideas.

Nakagawa relished being at the center of attention. He delighted in
strolling around Okayama wearing Western suits, conspicuously taking
out his pocket watch and popping candy into his mouth.[2] The novelty of
the watch and Western-style pockets captured local peoples' attention.
But Nakagawa was not interested merely in attention for its own sake.

1. Hōgō, *Okayama no kijin*, 121.
2. Hōgō, *Okayama no kijin*, 123; Kume, *Kenbōsai itsuwashū*, 66–68.

His actions usually served a greater purpose: to enlighten the populace. Nakagawa thoroughly embraced the project of civilization and enlightenment of the 1870s and early 1880s.[3]

Nakagawa's life illuminates how the Meiji project played out at the local level. The national government in Tokyo relied on prefectural officials like Nakagawa, and he served in the bureaucracy in the 1870s and early 1880s. However, Nakagawa was more than a bureaucrat—as mentioned, he was also a local notable, a group valued highly by the new Meiji state.[4] State ideologues envisioned such men as bearers of the government message: they were "conduits through which civic information passed unimpeded to its intended audience."[5] But the reality was often quite different, and local officials like Nakagawa actively shaped policy.[6]

The historical record offers little about Nakagawa's story in the late Tokugawa period but plenty after the Restoration. After 1868, he took on an identity as a reformer for the remainder of his life. His life challenges what Brian Platt has called the "common plotline" for narrating modern Japanese history as "the loss of Japanese values in the face of Western influence."[7] As Platt suggests, we can tell the story in other ways. Indeed, in Nakagawa, we see example of an individual who was far from disappointed by the new world. He welcomed some changes and built on others, even as he occasionally lamented the passing of older practices.

Nakagawa's personality sparkles and practically jumps off the page, giving form and a face to the often abstract and faceless modernizing process. In his attempts to reform his world, we see his humor and his abiding interest in the local. The surviving sources reveal his understandings of modernity, which he envisioned primarily in local terms, though usually in the service of the new nation. Nakagawa additionally sheds light on the fate of the former samurai: he worked to stabilize local revolts and helped former samurai adjust to the new world after they had lost their stipends and privileged hereditary status.

---

3. See Howland, *Translating the West*; Howell, *Geographies of Identity*, chap. 7.

4. Platt, *Burning and Building*; Waters, *Japan's Local Pragmatists*; Craig, "The Middlemen of Modernity"; Gluck, *Japan's Modern Myths*, 69.

5. Gluck, *Japan's Modern Myths*, 12.

6. The distinction between the officials and the people more generally was not always clear. Platt, *Burning and Building*, 11.

7. Platt, review of *Isami's House*, 422.

This chapter introduces Nakagawa's life and explores his position as a central figure in activist networks in Meiji-era Okayama. I suggest he operated as a "go-between" in these networks, bringing people together who otherwise may not have met. Although the concept of the "go-between" usually applies to servants, couriers, and others of a lower social standing, I believe it suits Nakagawa.[8] Although he was a local elite, he moved around society in unusual ways, connecting and engaging with people from different walks of life, including former outcastes and Western missionaries. As we shall see, his participation in a dense web of networks enabled him to advocate effectively for several causes.

I contend that the changes following the Meiji Restoration gave Nakagawa, a former samurai with excellent connections, a fresh start and the chance to create a new identity as a reformer. No one questioned his legitimacy. The new national media bolstered his presence beyond his locale. At the same time, Nakagawa carried forward interests and habits from the preceding Tokugawa era.[9] He participated in a modern bureaucracy and pushed for reformist goals, all the while adopting the Tokugawa literary persona of an eccentric.[10] His posture allowed him to attract considerable attention, generating a substantial record that sheds new light on how the processes of social change unfolded. Nakagawa's trajectory offers a nuanced view of changes and continuities across the 1868 divide in the case of a major figure in the Okayama-based networks.

Beginnings

Nakagawa was born in 1836 to a samurai family in the Okayama domain, part of the old province of Bizen and what would later become Okayama Prefecture. His family had served the Ikeda lords as Confucian scholars for centuries. Nakagawa's father, Kamenoshin, excelled at horsemanship, and young Yokotarō followed in his footsteps, teaching horseback riding

---

8. Davison, "Early Modern Social Networks," 466.

9. For the first mention of Nakagawa in English, see Suzuki Norihisa, "Nobuta Kishimoto," 161.

10. I thank Brian Platt for this formulation.

to the samurai youth of the domain.[11] Kamenoshin died in 1863, and Nakagawa inherited his father's stipend of ninety *koku*, along with an appointment to serve in the stables.[12] At the time, he was twenty-eight years old. Nakagawa's childhood name was Kinji or Kaneji, but following common practice, he changed it at the age of thirty-one.[13] The story goes that he did not get along with his neighbor Morishita Tachitarō, a situation that provided the inspiration for his new name—Yokotarō. In contrast to the *tachi* character, meaning "upright," that constituted the first half of "Tachitarō," Nakagawa selected *yoko*, which means "sideways," for his own name.[14] Such humor would surface at other points in his life.

Given that his ancestors had served as Confucian scholars, Nakagawa was expected to excel at book learning—or at least possess some proficiency. However, he did not. Descriptions vary, but he referred to himself as *mugaku monmō*, or "unlearned and illiterate." That phrase is misleading. Yet the upshot is that he never learned to read and write with ease. Nakagawa's true gift was "ear learning," and his memory was phenomenal—he memorized the entire text of the third-century BCE Chinese classic text *Han feizi*, a work of political philosophy.[15] His friend Nishi Kiichi recalled him explaining, "Whereas my ancestors' learning came from their eyes, mine comes from my ears."[16] His memory allowed him to compensate for his lack of facility with book learning. To be sure, historians cannot engage in the business of "diagnosing" Nakagawa, yet one can assume he had dyslexia.[17] Surviving letters suggest that he could

11.   San'yō shinbunsha, *Okayama-ken rekishi jinbutsu jiten*, 694–95.

12.   Katō, "Kenbōsai Nakagawa Yokotarō," 11. His title was *koshōgumi umayaku*. *Koshōgumi* were "regular" samurai. Jansen, *The Making of Modern Japan*, 104–5. *Koku* was a measurement for rice, approximately the amount required to feed an adult male for a year. Stipends were calculated in *koku*.

13.   Katō, "Kenbōsai Nakagawa Yokotarō," 11; Matsumura, "Ōnishi Sōzan," 71.

14.   Later, his rival Tachitarō changed his name to Kagenao and became the governor of Ōita Prefecture. Hōgō, *Okayama no kijin*, 121.

15.   On Han Feizi, see Katō, "Kenbōsai Nakagawa Yokotarō," 9. See also Nishi, *Nakagawa Yokotarō-kun ryakureki*, 4–5.

16.   Nishi, *Nakagawa Yokotarō-kun ryakureki*, 5; Nakagawa and Yoshimoto, *Bunmei saidai genso*, 1–5.

17.   Modern research on dyslexia sheds light on the particular strengths of the dyslexic brain. Some of the stories about Nakagawa appear to overlap with these findings, specifically what he called "ear learning." Other qualities include "the ability to see the

write only at a basic level. According to Ōta Ken'ichi, Nakagawa's hand-writing looks like that of "an elementary school student" and features few Chinese characters, at a time when elite adult males were expected to demonstrate proficiency. Despite such deficiencies, the content of his letters is sophisticated.[18] For longer works, Nakagawa relied on scribes. He did so, for example, in his speeches and his two published books, for which he appears as the editor or coauthor: *On Desire: The Greatest Essence of Civilization* (*Bunmei saidai genso zaiyokuron*; 1882) and *Speeches and Introduction Composed on the Departure of Dr. Kiyono* (*Igakushi Kiyono-kun sōkokubetsu enzetsu narabini jo*; 1889).[19]

Several anecdotes suggest Nakagawa's various strategies for coping with his reading and writing challenges. He once received a letter from an admirer, the bureaucrat Enomoto Takeaki (1836–1908), to which Nakagawa replied by "writing down squares, triangles, and circles on a paper. An observer stated, 'That looks illegible,' to which Nakagawa responded nonchalantly, 'Never mind, I didn't understand his letter. So we are even!'"[20] A similar tale unfolded when official Itō Hirobumi (1841–1909), future author of the Meiji Constitution, spent time in Okayama in 1884–1885 and wished to meet the extraordinary Nakagawa and sent him a letter. Nakagawa later went to the inn where Itō was staying, dressed in the attire of a Buddhist priest, and handed a letter to a maid. The roll of paper contained nothing but lines. Itō declared, "This is the first time I have met you, and I do not know the meaning of your letter." Nakagawa

---

gist or essence of things or to spot the larger context behind a situation or idea; multidimensionality of perspective; the ability to see new, unusual, or distant connections; inferential reasoning and ambiguity detection; the ability to recombine things in novel ways and a general inventiveness; and greater mindfulness and intentionality during tasks that others take for granted." Eide and Eide, *The Dyslexic Advantage*, 42. See also Wolf, *Proust and the Squid*.

18. Ōta, "Nakagawa Yokotarō to Sumiya Koume," 286–87.

19. Ōta, "Nakagawa Yokotarō no enzetsu," 73–81. Kiyono was the first director of Okayama Prefectural Hospital.

20. Hōgō, *Okayama no kijin*, 123. Enomoto, born the same year as Nakagawa, also had a notable career. A *bakufu* loyalist, Enomoto attempted to create an independent state in Hokkaido in 1868 and, as a consequence, spent three years under house arrest. He was later rehabilitated and served the Meiji government in several bureaucratic positions including minister of the navy. Wert, "Tokugawa Loyalism," 438–39; Ravina, *To Stand with the Nations*, 125–27.

replied, "Yes, I did not understand your letter either so I came to see you!"[21] The two men shared a laugh. These are the types of anecdotes that circulate about Nakagawa. Such stories also bring to light his connections with well-known Meiji government officials and provide concrete examples of the links between the central and prefectural governments.

How can we write the history of a man who left so few records? He frequently wrote letters to his friends using a set of symbols that meant things such as "Come for a meal" or "I need to borrow money" or "Let's meet at Okayama Station."[22] The historian must supplement Nakagawa's own writings dictated to scribes along with anecdotes written down by friends and acquaintances as well as American Board missionaries. Local newspapers reported on his actions.[23] During his lifetime, Nakagawa's good friend Nishi Kiichi wrote letters in support of Nakagawa's fundraising campaigns.[24] After Nakagawa's death in 1903, Nishi and other friends, along with local scholars and boosters, collected and compiled anecdotes to keep his memory alive. In the 1930s, another local author named Kume Ryūsen published a compilation that would bolster Nakagawa's memory at a time when the central government invested in efforts to promote local history.[25]

A Local Bureaucrat

Nakagawa was in his early thirties around the time of the Meiji Restoration. Major changes were under way in the 1860s and early 1870s as the country modernized rapidly. He implemented important new policies as a bureaucrat in the newly-established Okayama Prefecture. At the time, local bureaucrats were appointed by prefectural governors who themselves

21. Hōgō, *Okayama no kijin*, 123. For a longer version, see Kume, *Kenbōsai itsuwashū*, 75–78.

22. Kume, *Kenbōsai itsuwashū*, 78.

23. On the national press, see Huffman, *Creating a Public.*

24. For one example, see San'yō gakuen, *San'yō gakuen hyakunenshi*, 41–42.

25. Kume, *Kenbōsai itsuwashū.* On Kume's informants, see Ōta, "Nakagawa Yokotarō no enzetsu," 73. Postwar biographers Katō Shōzō and Hōgō Iwao relied on Kume's collection together with Nishi's biography. On 1930s efforts to nurture local history projects, see Young, *Beyond the Metropolis*, chap. 4.

had been chosen by the central government. Nakagawa's first appointment in 1871 put him in charge of school affairs and hygiene.[26] It is not clear how he managed this particular work, but we know he relied on his concubine Sumiya to read to him and on scribes to write down his thoughts. In 1873, he and Nishi dealt with the violent revolts against military conscription in nearby Mimasaka, part of neighboring Hōjō Prefecture.[27] The rioters attacked government buildings but also focused their ire on newly-liberated former outcastes. The men were successful in subduing the uprisings, and as a result, in 1875 the governor Takasaki Itsumu appointed Nakagawa as a *gondaizoku*, a mid-level appointment, in spite of his professed illiteracy. The governor needed Nakagawa's help— along with that of Nishi Kiichi and local business magnate Nozaki Bukichirō—in implementing the contentious new land tax.[28] Nakagawa rejected the initial prestigious appointment and successfully negotiated for a smaller portfolio.[29] Nishi later declared that Nakagawa's powers of persuasion helped smooth the introduction of the tax.[30]

In these ways, Nakagawa and his friends provided support to the new Meiji state as it faced extremely intense protest around the country. But Nakagawa's main passion, as we shall see, lay in the reform work he engaged in outside of the government.

On Nakagawa as an Eccentric

Before proceeding further, I want to elaborate on my characterization of Nakagawa as an "eccentric." This is not my label, but rather a term that nearly all sources use and one he actively cultivated. Biographer Hōgō Iwao observes that the notion originally comes from the Chinese Daoist

26. Hōgō, *Okayama no kijin*, 120–22.
27. Hōjō, formerly the Tsuyama domain, merged with Okayama Prefecture in 1876. On the riots, see Jaundrill, *Samurai to Soldier*, 128–29; Howell, *Geographies of Identity*, chap. 4.
28. San'yō gakuen, *Ai to hōshi*, 23.
29. He asked to be a *gonshōzoku*. On Meiji bureaucratic positions, see Baxter, *The Meiji Unification*, 63.
30. Nishi, *Nakagawa Yokotarō-kun ryakureki*, 42; Kume, *Kenbōsai itsuwashū*, 22; San'yō shinbunsha, *Okayama-ken rekishi jinbutsu jiten*, 694–95.

text the *Zhuangzi* (fourth century BCE), which reads: "Strange people are seen as strange to human beings but are equal to Heaven."[31] In the preceding Tokugawa period, some male literati styled themselves as "eccentrics," including the haiku poet Matsuo Bashō (1644–1694).[32] In this culture, W. Puck Brecher explains, eccentrics were "commonly associated with Zhuangzian values like detachment, playfulness, and useful uselessness (*muyō no yō*)."[33] The term "strange," then, suggests an exalted status.

Although Nakagawa embraced the label, those who wrote about him after he died sought to stress Nakagawa's accomplishments beyond mere eccentricity. Nishi outright rejected the label *kijin* throughout a 1903 lament for his friend, written a few days after Nakagawa's sudden death. This hagiographic treatment sought to make Nakagawa into a model citizen and should, of course, be viewed critically. Similarly, in a postscript to his 1937 compilation of anecdotes from Nakagawa's life, Kume explains that "he was known as someone who said and did eccentric things, but really he used eccentric words and acts as a method to build culture."[34] Two decades later in 1959, Nakagawa's biographer Katō Shōzō, would also reject the label, emphasizing that "everything he [Nakagawa] did was for others."[35]

Debates about Nakagawa's legacy aside, he successfully cultivated a public position as both a reformer and an eccentric, garnering a degree of notoriety and attention within and beyond Okayama. Based on the anecdotes about changing his name to Yokotarō, he appears to have adopted the *kijin* posture well before 1868, and news of his actions spread through social networks. But the Meiji era amplified his audience— through newspapers, word of Nakagawa circulated beyond the prefecture. Locals seized proudly on cases where famous Meiji statesmen mentioned Nakagawa. For example, Kume begins his 1937 account, noting proudly that when famous industrialist Shibusawa Eiichi (1840–1931) and

---

31.   Rendered in Japanese as "kijin naru mono wa, hito ni kishite, ten ni hitoshii." Brecher translates *kijin* as "oddball." Brecher, *The Aesthetics of Strangeness*, 10.

32.   Brecher, *The Aesthetics of Strangeness*, 98.

33.   Brecher, *The Aesthetics of Strangeness*, 10.

34.   Kume, *Kenbōsai itsuwashū*, 107.

35.   Katō, "Kenbōsai Nakagawa Yokotarō," 27.

oligarch Ōkuma Shigenobu (1838–1922) traveled to Okayama in the early twentieth century on business, they commented, "Nakagawa died, didn't he. What a pity."[36]

The Challenges of the Meiji Restoration

As noted earlier, Nakagawa and the other samurai faced multiple challenges following the Restoration. In the early 1870s, the government abolished the hereditary status system. Of course, status categories did not disappear overnight and the new term for former samurai, *shizoku* ("warrior families"), made their background evident to all.[37] In 1876, the cash-strapped government converted the hereditary stipends the former samurai had received into interest-bearing bonds. Some former samurai negotiated these changes with aplomb, while others suffered.

One of the projects Nakagawa took on was helping former samurai find suitable occupations, a process known as "rehabilitation."[38] To this end, he worked with his biological half-brother Sugiyama Iwasaburō (1836–1913) to reclaim land in nearby Kojima Bay and to start the Okayama Spinning Mill. The area, including nearby Kurashiki, would become a textile center in the 1880s. Nakagawa and Sugiyama formed a society called the Biryokusha (Society of little power) to support other former samurai. Members of the society traveled to Tokyo to request support from central government officials for their projects including two textile mills. Such efforts bolstered the state goal of rapid industrialization, a policy that succeeded but ultimately at a great cost to rural farmers, the urban poor, and female textile workers.[39]

Nakagawa's half-brother Sugiyama was a prominent figure in Okayama in his own right. These two brothers were born the same year to different

---

36.   Kume, *Kenbōsai itsuwashū*, 17.

37.   Howell translates this term as "gentry." Howell, *Geographies of Identity*, 67. See also Yokoyama, *Meiji ishin*.

38.   See Harootunian, "The Economic Rehabilitation."

39.   On the Biryokusha, see Kume, *Kenbōsai itsuwashū*, 25–26. On poverty in Meiji Japan, see Huffman, *Down and Out*; Tsurumi, *Factory Girls*.

mothers.[40] Because Sugiyama was the second son and would not inherit the Nakagawa family headship, he was adopted into the Sugiyama family and became its head in 1859. This was a common practice for second sons and a welcome outcome under the circumstances because he would now gain a position and an inheritance. Sugiyama served in the imperial army in the years leading up to the Restoration in an 1868 campaign to punish the nearby Bitchū-Matsuyama domain for its support of the Tokugawa government. After the Meiji regime was established, Sugiyama received several bureaucratic appointments in the new prefectural administration, first in Okayama and then in nearby Shimane Prefecture. Later, Sugiyama moved away from government service. He helped former samurai through projects centered on land reclamation, moneylending, and the spinning industry. He founded a bank and served as the first president of the Chūgoku railway in 1895. For all these reasons, Sugiyama was central to modern industrial development in Okayama. Locals referred to him as the "Saigō of Bizen," a reference to Saigō Takamori (1828–1877), a prominent hero of the Meiji Restoration with high moral standing and one of Sugiyama's acquaintances.[41] Like many elite Meiji men—and some women—Sugiyama also traveled to Europe and the United States for three years beginning in 1887.[42]

Nakagawa and Sugiyama enjoyed stature on the local stage and a reputation for their distinctive personalities. In 1886, the local newspaper *San'yō shinpō* held a contest for "Outstanding Men of Okayama." In the end, Nakagawa was elected the "comedian," and Sugiyama received the less exciting title "commercial law expert."[43] The brothers liked to joke with each other, but Kume's account hints that they also irritated each other. Sugiyama had a reputation for seriousness and business acumen unlike his eccentric half-brother.[44] They stood on opposite sides of the Freedom and People's Rights Movement—Nakagawa was a supporter and

40. The genealogy does not say who Sugiyama's mother was—she was probably a concubine.
41. San'yō shinbunsha, *Okayama-ken rekishi jinbutsu jiten*, 546. On Saigō, see Ravina, *The Last Samurai*.
42. San'yō shinbunsha, *Okayama-ken rekishi jinbutsu jiten*, 546.
43. Matsumura, "Ōnishi Sōzan," 75.
44. Kume, *Kenbōsai itsuwashū*, 63.

Sugiyama helped fund the opposition—which may have exacerbated tensions between them.[45] It is possible these different views may have been tied to the brothers' different positions within the family, which channeled them into different paths for advancement.[46]

Marriage and Family Networks

Nakagawa married his first cousin Yuki, an act that was not unusual at the time. The match, following common practice, was surely arranged by relatives rather than the couple themselves. No one bothered to write down Yuki's birth date, but given that she was seventy-two at the time of her death in 1906, she was born in either 1834 or 1835, and was slightly older than her husband.[47] Her natal family, the Ōnishi, were prominent in Okayama, and her father had served as an administrator representing the domain in Kyoto.[48] Yuki was the eldest of four children—she had two sisters, Kimata Kayo (1838–1901) and Ōnishi Kinu (who appears in chapter 4), and a brother, Sadamichi (n.d.–1877), who died in the Satsuma Rebellion of 1877, an uprising by discontented former samurai that challenged the new regime. Together, Yuki and Nakagawa had two sons, Tateichi (1865–1914) and Naname (1868–1902).[49] As with Nakagawa's own chosen name, Yokotarō, he applied humor and an obsession with directions to the naming of his sons: Tateichi means "vertical," and Naname means "diagonal." The names grew out of Nakagawa's goal to "view the world from all angles."[50]

Yuki, her mother Hide (1814–1899), and her sisters Kinu and Kayo all converted to Protestant Christianity in the late 1870s and helped found

45. San'yō shinbunsha, *Okayama-ken rekishi jinbutsu jiten*, 581.
46. I thank an anonymous reviewer for this point.
47. It is not clear if people reckoned Yuki's age using the traditional method of *kazoedoshi*, in which a child is one year old at birth and gained an additional year after each New Year.
48. Matsumura, "Ōnishi Sōzan," 66.
49. Kume's genealogy suggests the couple lost a baby girl in 1865.
50. Hōgō, *Okayama no kijin*, 121.

the Okayama Church in 1880.[51] Yuki was baptized shortly thereafter. Together with her sisters and mother, Yuki helped fund a new building when the Church moved. (Nakagawa's soon-to-be former concubine Sumiya Koume also belonged to this community.) People at the Church apparently regarded Yuki highly for her charitable works.[52] She and her sons also supported the Okayama Orphanage.[53] Former minister and socialist Abe Isoo would later recall that Yuki was the matriarch of the Church.[54] Yuki's descendant Matsumura Midori similarly praised her forbearers: "The Ōnishi girls were blessed with unusual resources. As women of that generation, they made their mark and deserve attention."[55] The sisters' embrace of novel ideas may have come from their mother, who was herself a trendsetter. After turning seventy, Hide reportedly turned her back on the expected fashions for women—she cut her hair, let her eyebrows grow out, and stopped blackening her teeth.[56]

Whereas Nakagawa and Yuki flourished, their two boys faced challenges. First son Tateichi struggled throughout his life. He studied Western art in Tokyo and later went to study in Italy. Nakagawa sent him to Doshisha University in Kyoto, but he left without graduating.[57] Later, when Tateichi succeeded the family headship, Nakagawa decided to set up a separate household; he left the ranks of the former samurai, and became a commoner.[58] Tateichi held various positions teaching art, specializing in portraiture. His 1883 painting of his mother, held by the

51. On the development of Kumiai churches, see Moriya, "Auto sutēshon kara sutēshon e," 99–100.

52. Matsumura, "Ōnishi Sōzan," 71.

53. Ōta, *Zusetsu Okayama, Bizen, Tamano no rekishi*, 159.

54. Abe, *Shakai shugisha*, 142.

55. Matsumura, "Ōnishi Sōzan," 73.

56. Nakai, "Ōnishi," 46. See also the description of the women in Nihon kirutokyōdan Okayama kyōkai, *Okayama kyōkai hyakunenshi*, 38–39.

57. Moriya, "Auto sutēshon kara sutēshon e," 103; Kume, *Kenbōsai itsuwashū*, 104. According to one source, Tateichi was baptized in 1880 along with his mother. Nihon kirutokyōdan Okayama kyōkai, *Okayama kyōkai hyakunenshi*, 37.

58. Nishi, *Nakagawa Yokotarō-kun ryakureki*, 4. This move may perplex readers as *shizoku* status increasingly had little meaning in modern Japan. Another example of someone leaving the samurai ranks is future prime minister Hara Kei (1856–1921). Although Hara is generally considered the first commoner prime minister, he was born to a samurai family. Thanks to David Howell for this information. See also Najita, *Hara Kei in the Politics of Compromise*, 13–14.

Okayama Prefectural Museum of Art, is one of his few surviving works.[59] He drank heavily and retired early after suffering from a stroke. He died in 1914 at the age of forty-nine.[60] Second-born Naname was never of strong constitution and died young. Local people attributed the boys' problems to inbreeding, given that Nakagawa and Yuki were first cousins.[61]

Nakagawa's children with women other than his wife fared better than Tateichi and Naname. Not only did Nakagawa have a concubine (Sumiya Koume) for a time, but he took up with another woman after she left him. The full name of the other woman is not known, but descendants referred to her as the "widow Watanabe."[62] Nakagawa had a daughter Toyo (1877–n.d.) with Sumiya and a son Shigeru (1888–1959) with the widow Watanabe. Half-siblings Shigeru and Toyo maintained close connections with each other, and Shigeru lived with Toyo and her family during his college days in Tokyo.[63] He graduated from the University of Tokyo School of Law and worked at Meiji Seitō Confectionary, later becoming the president of Meiji Seika, a confectionary founded in 1916. Toyo had six children, five boys and one girl, with her adopted husband, Aoki Yōkichi.[64] She kept up ties with her father, and letters in her beautiful flowing cursive script are preserved in the Okayama Prefectural Archives.

On Christianity and Missionaries

In the mid-1870s, at the same time he worked as a prefectural bureaucrat, Nakagawa and his family's lives were transformed by encounters with Western doctors and Protestant missionaries. Fascinated by all things

---

59. An image of the portrait can be found in the Okayama Prefectural Museum of Art's collections database: http://jmapps.ne.jp/okayamakenbi/det.html?data_id=1887 (accessed 15 February 2019).

60. San'yō shinbunsha, *Okayama-ken rekishi jinbutsu jiten*, 693–94.

61. Matsumura, "Ōnishi Sōzan," 76.

62. Matsumura, "Ōnishi Sōzan," 76.

63. Matsumura, "Ōnishi Sōzan," 76.

64. Matsumura, "Ōnishi Sōzan," 75.

novel, Nakagawa developed an interest in Western medicine and Christianity after the ban on the foreign religion was lifted. As we saw in the introduction, he invited the first Western missionaries to Okayama beginning with Dr. Taylor in 1875 and the group who established the mission station in 1879.

Also in those years, Nakagawa began inviting Japanese Christians to the area, including Kanamori Michitomo, who later became Okayama Church's first pastor. Nakagawa also summoned Niijima Jō (1843–1890) whom he had met in Kobe. Niijima occupies a key place in the history of Christianity in Japan and deserves a brief introduction. In 1864, before the Restoration, Niijima stowed away on a Western-style ship and sailed from the treaty port of Hakodate to the United States. While in Massachusetts, Niijima converted to Christianity in 1866 and graduated from Amherst College in 1870, along with future Okayama Station missionary Otis Cary. Niijima returned to Japan and was active in establishing a mission station in Kyoto, where he also founded what is now Doshisha University in 1875.

Niijima visited Nakagawa in 1880 during a trip to Okayama to see friends. He wrote to his wife Yae that both he and Nakagawa delivered sermons in surrounding areas.[65] During this time, Nakagawa held religious services at his house every Sunday and sponsored prayer meetings on Tuesdays. At Niijima's urging, Nakagawa sent several Okayama boys to Doshisha, including Tateichi and two nephews—one of Sugiyama's sons and Ōnishi Hajime (pen name Sōzan; 1864–1900), who later became a famous philosopher.[66]

Relations between Nakagawa and the Christians frayed over time for multiple reasons. Although Nakagawa was responsible for bringing Christian missionaries to Okayama, and spent considerable time with them initially, in the end, his concubine Sumiya left him after hearing the missionary message. "Jesus stole my mistress," he exclaimed.[67] His friends observed that he subsequently lost his "pluck" (*iki*).[68] Although writers

---

65. *Niijima Jō zenshū*, 169–73.

66. Hajime was the son of Yuki's sister Kayo, but Kinu adopted him as her heir.

67. Hōgō, *Okayama no kijin*, 122. Kume could not confirm that Nakagawa in fact said this and noted that one would need to ask locals. Kume, *Kenbōsai itsuwashū*, 28.

68. Kume, *Kenbōsai itsuwashū*, 99.

connected Nakagawa's separation from Sumiya with his move away from the Christian missionaries, we should bear in mind that sex can be used to cover other kind of disagreements, including political and cultural ones.

Indeed, Nakagawa later expressed irritation with aspects of the faith, notably the missionaries' focus on temperance. On one occasion, he engaged in a debate about the merits of temperance, which was recorded in a local journal. He suggested that if sake harmed the body, even more people were harmed by encounters with women. He wondered rhetorically how it would be to open an association that opposed women just as temperance advocates opposed alcohol. Such a group would lead to the end of humanity.[69] He invited those who had "complaints" to visit him at his home or offered to call on them if they provided an address. Nonetheless, later in life, he gave up alcohol, based on his conviction that one must ultimately choose either women or wine.[70]

Nakagawa's disagreements with Christianity notwithstanding, it was true that Sumiya left because of her own acceptance of the Christian message. In spite of this, Nakagawa did not harbor a long-term grudge toward Christianity. Summing up Nakagawa's views on religion, Nishi's hagiography explained, "He lamented the corruption of customs and the stagnation of religion. With impartiality he surveyed Shinto, Buddhism, and Christianity and took what he wanted and believed what he did. It was all in order to correct the ills of the world and guide people."[71] Missionary Julia A. E. Gulick memorably wrote in a report back home, "Like Noah's carpenters, he continues outside of the ark himself."[72]

Different perspectives and audiences led to very different assessments of Nakagawa. Missionary views on Nakagawa ranged widely depending on the person and the time period. Initial impressions of him by the missionaries in 1879 were warm. Missionary James Pettee saw Nakagawa as providing valuable assistance to the missionaries as they began their work. Pettee explained to the American Board: "Our most powerful ally was

69. Yoshizaki, "Nakamura Shizu," 3.

70. Kume, *Kenbōsai itsuwashū*, 78–80.

71. Ōta, "Nakagawa Yokotarō no enzetsu," 73; Nishi, *Nakagawa Yokotarō-kun ryakureki*, 3.

72. Julia A. E. Gulick, "Bible Women's Work in Okayama Station," (1900), American Board of Commissioners for Foreign Missions archives, ABC 9.5.1 (7). By permission of the Houghton Library, Harvard University.

Mr. Nakagawa, a wealthy, influential citizen and an earnest disciple of Christ. He was the general of the whole campaign," who played an important role introducing the missionaries to local people.[73] Nakagawa made sure the foreigners were treated well. This was much to their surprise, for they had not expected it. Pettee confessed, "It quite upset all our former theories of the actual treatment of missionaries on the part of rich men and rulers."[74] In point of fact, Nakagawa does not seem to have been wealthy, as his fundraising activities (which I discuss later) make clear. It appears that the missionaries mistook his influence and stature for wealth.

Missionary records offer evidence of Nakagawa's penchant for public speaking. On one trip to a village, Pettee observed that Nakagawa waited until business was over, then took over:

> [Nakagawa] preached an extempore sermon on the existence of God, taking for his text the views of certain atheistic professors, as well known in Japan as they are in America, and working far more injury here than there. As he closed he gave opportunity to any to present counter arguments and offer questions, when a gray haired physician, the venerable father of the village, quietly replied, "What you have said is the truth," and not a dissenting voice was heard.[75]

This anecdote may reveal more about power dynamics in the village than Nakagawa's rhetorical prowess or the appeal of Christianity to local people. But it serves to showcase Nakagawa's stature—as well as, of course, what James Pettee wanted people back home to know about the mission.

Over time, politics complicated the relationship between the missionaries and Nakagawa. Missionaries found themselves in a situation where the group of men who had welcomed them to Okayama were themselves in a feud over the growing local Freedom and People's Rights Movement. Nishi and Nakagawa and others in Okayama supported the movement, whereas the governor Takasaki Itsumu vehemently opposed it for it challenged the new Meiji state. Although the missionaries initially tried to stay on good terms with both parties, historian Tanaka Tomoko argues

73. James Pettee, "A New Call from Japan."
74. James Pettee, "A New Call from Japan."
75. James Pettee, "A New Call from Japan."

that ultimately, the missionaries distanced themselves from men like Nishi and Nakagawa, concluding there was nothing to be gained by being in the middle.[76] Tanaka's explanation challenges the usual assumption that Nakagawa initiated a parting of ways with the missionaries because of his anger over the loss of his concubine.[77]

It is difficult to piece together the exact chronology for the years 1879–1881 because so much happened at once and the surviving records do not always illuminate the exact course of events. Several tensions bubbled to the surface. Governor Takasaki had already suffered for his support of the missionaries, inviting them and giving them lodging (one suspects he was most drawn to the medical knowledge brought by missionary doctors like Berry). Otis Cary wrote that the governor's initial support had smoothed the path for the missionaries with local people, but Cary also registered the ridicule Takasaki endured from the Japanese newspapers. Commentators mocked the governor for his apparent embrace of the foreign faith, which they saw as a blatant and insincere attempt to curry favor with the populace.[78] Takasaki gave Christian services "the same privileges accorded to Buddhist and Shinto lectures" and delivered an order to local officials not to stand in the way of Christian gatherings, which no doubt irritated some.[79] Indeed, cases of anti-Christian sentiment occasionally pop up in the records of the American Board missionaries, demonstrating how the Christian presence disrupted the workings of local society.

Belle Pettee, James's wife, had a negative view of Nakagawa. We do not know what she initially thought of Nakagawa in 1879. But years later, in 1897, she wrote about him in an article devoted primarily to his former concubine Sumiya. In the article, Belle Pettee took Sumiya's side in all things. Belle Pettee gave Nakagawa no credit for bringing missionaries to Okayama. She allowed only that a book Nakagawa had received

76. Tanaka, *Kindai Nihon kōtō kyōiku taisei*, 106.

77. Hōgō, *Okayama no kijin*, 122.

78. Cary recorded that "a comic paper published in Tokyo contained a picture that represented the Governor of Okayama as an acrobat balancing on his forehead a cross upon which was a pole labeled 'Popular Favour.' Underneath was the inscription 'The Governor of Okayama hopes to gain favour by becoming a Christian.'" Cary, *A History of Christianity in Japan*, 146.

79. *Missionary Herald* 76 (1880), 393.

from Niijima inspired Sumiya to become a Christian.[80] Pettee commented disparagingly on Nakagawa's supposed illiteracy, noting that Sumiya served as his secretary "as he was unable to read or write."[81] In Belle Pettee's eyes, Nakagawa was a roadblock to Sumiya's salvation. Pettee suggested that Nakagawa engaged in deception in his dealings with Sumiya: he held Sumiya back from baptism, urging her to wait "and they would be baptized together."[82] However, there is no evidence that Nakagawa ever intended to be baptized. Even the fact that Nakagawa eventually relented and surrendered custody of their daughter Toyo to Sumiya did not endear him to Pettee: "For two years, she [Sumiya] bore persecution, poverty, and trial, and entreaties from the child's father to return; but at last he yielded, less for her than for the sake of the little one [Toyo], who pined and fretted for her mother."[83]

After both Nakagawa and Sumiya had died, Belle Pettee wrote about their relationship again in a short undated pamphlet about Sumiya's life: "Geisha Girl to Bible Woman: The Story of Koume Sumiya."[84] The text contains a number of assertions about Sumiya and Nakagawa found nowhere else in the historical record. Pettee asserted that Nakagawa had moved Sumiya's things to his house at the beginning of their relationship "without her knowledge or consent," at a time when she had been caring for his ailing young son.[85] He caused trouble when Sumiya decided to go to Kobe College. Pettee allowed that although Nakagawa thought highly of missionary and college founder Eliza Talcott, he needed a pledge, a kind of guarantee from Talcott, when he sent Sumiya off to Kobe:

80.   Belle Pettee, "Two Personalities," *Life and Light for Woman* 27, no. 9 (1897), 396.

81.   Belle Pettee, "Two Personalities," 396. Others likewise chose concubines for their literary skills rather than merely for sex appeal. One example is Tokugawa Tsunayoshi's (1646–1709) chief advisor Yanagisawa Yoshiyasu (1659–1714). He encouraged his concubine, the daughter of a court noble, to write a memoir modeled on the Heian-era *A Tale of Flowering Fortunes* (*Eiga monogatari*). I thank an anonymous reader for pointing this out.

82.   Belle Pettee, "Two Personalities," 397.

83.   Belle Pettee, "Two Personalities," 398.

84.   Belle Pettee, "Geisha Girl to Bible Woman: The Story of Koume Sumiya," no date, American Board of Commissioners for Foreign Missions archives, ABC 77.1 (58:13). By permission of the Houghton Library, Harvard University.

85.   Belle Pettee, "Geisha Girl to Bible Woman," 3.

In true samurai spirit he asked from Miss Talcott a pledge, something she valued, which he might keep while his loved Koume was in her care. She gave him a gold pencil, a precious keepsake of a dead brother, and this same pencil he never would give up, but carried it with him till his death, years later, and gave orders it should be buried with him in his coffin.[86]

This last detail about the golden pencil, meant to show Nakagawa's greediness, cannot be corroborated by any other source but reveals that in Belle's eyes, he was a petty and vengeful man.

Belle and James lived in Okayama much longer than any of the other Western missionaries who set up the station—over thirty-five years—and have thus shaped how Nakagawa has been remembered in English. Unlike his wife, James Pettee appears to have stopped writing about Nakagawa after distance grew between the missionaries and the People's Rights advocates.

Nakagawa and Associational Life

Nakagawa joined men's associations—though scholars rarely call them that—in contrast to women's associations, which are always marked in gendered terms. Along with his friend and neighbor Nishi Kiichi, Nakagawa participated in the Okayama branch of the Freedom and People's Rights Movement. Nishi was a leader in the movement. Years earlier, he had taught many of the young men who were the movement's core activists at the domainal school. Nishi led the school in the early 1870s and oversaw its transition to a Western-style curriculum after he had briefly traveled to Shanghai to study English.[87]

Sometime after the Satsuma Rebellion, Nakagawa and Nishi traveled to Tokyo to converse with prominent politicians and public intellectuals about the state of the country including Fukuzawa Yukichi, Katsu Kaishū (1823–1899), Soejima Taneomi (1828–1905), and Nakamura Masanao

86. Belle Pettee, "Geisha Girl to Bible Woman," 4.

87. *Okayama-ken shi*, 10:149–50; San'yō shinbunsha, *Okayama-ken rekishi jinbutsu jiten*, 741.

(1832–1891). The two friends then headed to Kōchi Prefecture where the People's Rights Movement flourished to learn more about the Risshisha (Free thinkers society) from leader Itagaki Taisuke (1837–1919).[88] After their return to Okayama, Nishi and Nakagawa formed a regional organization in 1879 to push for the creation of a constitutional government. The first part of the organization's name "Ryōbisaka sangoku" referred to the three areas that participated by their abbreviated old provincial names: Bizen, Bitchū, and Mimasaka. Previous efforts to advocate change within the prefectural legislature had been shut down by the governor.[89]

By the late 1870s and early 1880s, Okayama was a hotbed of People's Rights activism, and Nishi led the some seven hundred activists of Ryōbisaka sangoku, who sent a petition demanding the opening of a national Diet the same year. Nishi also chaired the meeting where the first of several petitions was drafted.[90] The petition garnered twenty-five thousand signatories, an accomplishment some attributed to the energetic leadership of former samurai like Nishi and Nakagawa.[91] This energy culminated in the founding of a local political party in 1881, the San'yō Liberal Party, which was connected to the national Liberal Party (Jiyūtō), founded the previous year. Nakagawa liked to be at the center of everything, so his involvement is not surprising. But unlike Nishi, he did not assume a leadership position in the People's Rights Movement. Moreover, in contrast to other men of his background in similar circles, he never stood for political office. Nishi was elected to the national diet twice. Yet his career in national politics was not a resounding success. During his first term, Nishi gave an excessively "abstract speech" regarding the budget on the floor of the Diet that proved deeply embarrassing.[92] In the end, Nishi does not appear to have been suited for high office and resigned in 1893.

Above all, Nakagawa was drawn to activism that allowed him to act on his own and attract a crowd. Although he participated in networks and in some associations, his actions were usually solo affairs, frequently

88. *Okayama-ken shi*, 10:151.

89. Maus, "Ishii Jūji," 183–84; San'yō shinbunsha, *Okayama-ken rekishi jinbutsu jiten*, 741.

90. San'yō shinbunsha, *Okayama-ken rekishi jinbutsu jiten*, 741.

91. San'yō gakuen, *Ai to hōshi*, 25; *Okayama-ken shi*, 10:135–86. Nishi also formed a political organization (the Jikkōsha) with Kobayashi Kusuo (1856–1920). Kido, *Nihon teikoku kokkai giin seiden*, 225.

92. San'yō shinbunsha, *Okayama-ken rekishi jinbutsu jiten*, 741.

involving speeches. His primary concerns centered on social reform rather than high politics in the narrow sense. By his own account, his main interests after retirement in the early 1880s were education and hygiene, a list to which he later added raising cattle.[93]

Nakagawa's Causes

I have suggested that Nakagawa's identity was bound up with reform of all types during the Meiji period. The dramatic way he carried out his efforts left an impression on his local audience. How exactly did Nakagawa go about advocating for his projects, all of which were tied to the networks in which he participated?

EDUCATION

In 1885, Nakagawa got into the business of founding a women's group, an organization called the Gensenkai (Origin association).[94] This act was in contrast to what appears to have been Nakagawa's limited involvement in men's groups. This interest in women's edification is not something we normally associate with local notables, though Buddhist men founded women's groups to compete with Christian women's groups.[95] The group invited male speakers to enlighten its female members. As with so many Meiji-era groups, little information survives, but Yoshizaki Shihoko has pieced together valuable evidence. A letter to the editor of the local paper suggests that the group was dominated by men and collapsed within a year.[96] Women were the objects of reform rather than subjects. To be sure, Nakagawa regarded the populace in general as in need of instruction, in line with his Confucian upbringing that dictated the obligation of those above to enlighten those below.

Nakagawa remained committed to education despite his personal challenges with literacy. His achievements in this arena defy easy summation.

93. Hōgō, *Okayama no kijin*, 124.
94. Yoshizaki, "Nakamura Shizu," 2.
95. Kōchi shiritsu jiyū minken kinenkan, *Meiji no joseishi ten zuroku*, 54; Sotozaki, *Kōchi-ken fujin undōshi*, 45–46.
96. Yoshizaki, "Nakamura Shizu," 2.

We already saw that his first appointment in the prefectural administration in the 1870s set him on routes around Okayama where he inspected schools and promoted hygiene. This work familiarized him with the state of education.[97] He constantly preached the virtues of modern education and threw himself into the establishment of several private schools, notably Kanzei gakkō and San'yō gakuen, and the revitalization of Shizutani gakkō.[98] Together with Nishi Kiichi, he formed a society to rebuild Shizutani.[99] Nishi later presided over the school in the 1890s after resigning from the Diet, and Nakagawa visited every week.[100] The two men also set up the Ikeda school with money from the former domainal lord. The school convened at Nakagawa's home.[101] Nakagawa also founded a hospital, a medical school, and a school for midwives. His work in training midwives and nurses stood out: as a result of his efforts, Okayama Prefecture was able to send nurses to the front during the Sino-Japanese War of 1894–1895.[102]

Nakagawa dedicated himself to promoting girls' education, especially at San'yō gakuen school, a girls' school founded by Japanese Christians in 1886 with extensive ties to the Okayama Church. For him, as for many Meiji individuals, educating women was critical to building a modern society. Anecdotes about Nakagawa and education for girls abound. Teacher and future principal Kajiro Yoshi recalled an impromptu song that students sang for Nakagawa after he unexpectedly showed up at the school with a large mackerel to share for lunch. He insisted the children eat it and joined them at the table. "Everyone, let's welcome Uncle Nakagawa who has brought his famous sushi . . . without hesitation, let's eat." The song continued: "This is Nakagawa's unexpected treat with bamboo shoots, dried gourd, and mushrooms. We are so thankful. We gratefully receive it."[103] In stark contrast to Belle Pettee's impressions of him as selfish and

---

97.   Hōgō, *Okayama no kijin*, 121.

98.   "History," *Tokubetsu shiseki kyū Shizutani gakkō*, accessed 9 December 2016, http://shizutani.jp/#history.

99.   For one explanation, see San'yō shinbunsha, *Okayama-ken rekishi jinbutsu jiten*, 741.

100.   Katō, "Kenbōsai Nakagawa Yokotarō," 22.

101.   Moriya, "Auto sutēshon kara sutēshon e," 108. For the diary of a student who attended his school for midwives, see Ōta and Takeuchi, *Aru Meiji jogakusei nikki*.

102.   Hōgō, *Okayama no kijin*, 122.

103.   Katō, "Kenbōsai Nakagawa Yokotarō," 19–21. Katō visited Kajiro and interviewed her when she was eighty years old.

dishonest, Nakagawa emerges in this account as charming and magnani-
mous, someone given to acts of spontaneity. Such differences can be attributed in part to the very distinct audiences for each of the texts. Belle
Pettee wrote for an audience of North American Christian women, while
the story of Nakagawa's gift was recorded in a volume dedicated to local
history.

Nakagawa believed passionately in the importance of cultivation as
a part of education.[104] On one occasion, to convey the importance of hu-
mility, he compared human beings to ears of rice: "Good rice ears bend
to the side, and bad ones do not."[105] He also borrowed from Buddhist
philosophical ideas that stressed the importance of tranquility in all situations: "Those with cultivation are like a bottle full of water that does
not slosh. Those who are noisy do not have enough cultivation."[106] Such
anecdotes made their way into English-language records. James Pettee related a similar tale about Nakagawa to the American Board in 1879:
"Our general [Nakagawa], ever on the alert for an opportunity of enforc-
ing a lesson in morals, took a teacup in his hand and compared it to the
human heart, its value depending on its contents."[107]

In prefectural histories and websites devoted to local history, Nakagawa today gets the bulk of the credit for building Okayama's schools,
sometimes together with Nishi.[108] Yet Nakagawa surely did not conduct his pursuits alone. The details, by and large, may be lost, but his
activities took place in the context of local networks—and he was
helped by many others, including male friends, female relatives, and
scribes.

HAIR, HYGIENE, AND ELECTRICITY

Nakagawa relished speaking in public, and speechmaking remained a
constant practice throughout his life. He spoke on street corners and in
theaters. He delivered at least one speech while traveling on horseback

104.   Katō, "Kenbōsai Nakagawa Yokotarō," 25.

105.   Katō, "Kenbōsai Nakagawa Yokotarō," 25. See also Kume, *Kenbōsai itsuwashū*,
74–75.

106.   Katō, "Kenbōsai Nakagawa Yokotarō," 26.

107.   James Pettee, "A New Call from Japan."

108.   For example, see the chronology on San'yō gakuen's website: http://sanyogakuen
.net/history/story (accessed 4 November 2019).

through the city.[109] Sometimes, he brought vegetables like radishes or bur-
dock root (*gobō*) to use as props, although exactly how he deployed these
items is not typically recorded.[110] Otis Cary wrote that on one occasion,
Nakagawa used cherry blossoms "in his apt way of taking illustrations
from anything that happens to be at hand."[111]

Japan did not have a tradition of public speaking before the Meiji
period, and the 1870s saw elite efforts to translate Western volumes on
the craft and nurture the skill in schools.[112] Records suggest that Nakagawa carefully observed the techniques exhibited by visiting speakers to
Okayama as well as Okayama Church pastors such as Abe Isoo. He then
incorporated what he learned into his own speeches.[113] One wonders if
Nakagawa's penchant for public speaking was part of what drew him to
Christianity in the first place. Cary recorded in 1879 that Nakagawa
turned up on a quiet Sunday morning when the missionaries, who had
just arrived in town, hoped to rest and keep visitors at bay. Cary elaborated
that "Nakagawa came in with one of his friends to whom he wished to
preach a sermon. This is a common practice with him, and we have learned
to sit quietly while he takes us for a text."[114] Records from the following
year also feature Nakagawa delivering several popular speeches.[115]

Nakagawa promoted new hairstyles in the 1870s when many local
men still wore the old top knot.[116] During the Tokugawa period, men's
hairstyles indicated their social status. The abolition of status in the early
1870s made the reform of hairstyles urgent.[117] Henceforth, reformers urged
short haircuts, which they saw as more enlightened as well as econom-
ical.[118] In an 1871 speech on hairstyles, Nakagawa informed audiences that
he worried if he cut his hair, women would not like it. In fact, they loved
it: "I was told you have pluck [*iki*]." He went on to advise his audience,

109. Kume, *Kenbōsai itsuwashū*, 60–61.
110. Kume, *Kenbōsai itsuwashū*, 61.
111. *Missionary Herald* 75 (1879), 298.
112. Tomasi, *Rhetoric in Modern Japan*, chap. 3.
113. Kume, *Kenbōsai itsuwashū*, 48, 52, 88.
114. *Missionary Herald* 75 (1879), 298.
115. For example, *Missionary Herald* 76 (1880), 19.
116. Hōgō, *Okayama no kijin*, 123.
117. Howell, *Geographies of Identity*, 164–66.
118. Yamakawa, *Women of the Mito Domain*, 7.

FIGURE 3. Photograph of Nakagawa Yokotarō, circa 1890. Courtesy of the Okayama Prefectural Archives.

"You, too, should cut your hair."[119] At first, central government officials assumed that since short hair was a "rational" choice, men would naturally cut their hair. However, because men did not rush to adopt the new styles, "it was primarily on more local initiative, both official and individual, that short hairstyles spread throughout Japan in the mid-1870s," according to Suzanne O'Brien.[120] Nakagawa thus offers a strong example of local initiative in action (fig. 3).

119. Hōgō, *Okayama no kijin*, 124; Kume, *Kenbōsai itsuwashū*, 19–20.
120. O'Brien, "Splitting Hairs," 1325.

Nakagawa used humor to spread ideas about new customs and hygiene practices—he even obtained a storytelling license from the police. His popularity with audiences grew over time. He used the proceeds from his speeches at the local Asahi Theater to make rice porridge, which he sold at a discount to impoverished people, no doubt contributing to his popularity.[121] When his favorite *rakugo* troop came through town, he made a special guest appearance using the performance name Higemaru.[122] Given Nakagawa's love of speechmaking on busy streets, one of his biographers likened Nakagawa to a modern-day Nichiren (1222–1282), the medieval Buddhist prophet and founder of the Lotus sect of Buddhism. Nakagawa spoke next to a banner that proclaimed his identity as "Kenbōsai [his pen name], believer in the Mahavairocana Buddha and in hygiene and education."[123] In these ways, he played with names and symbols to great comic effect in his quest to promote reform.

One of Nakagawa's banners is still extant and is held in the Okayama Prefectural Archives (fig. 4). It features a portrait of educator and journalist Fukuzawa Yukichi together with sayings from Fukuzawa, Nakagawa's friend Nishi, Okayama Medical School professor Katsurada Fujirō (1867–1946), and two religious texts in an original combination curated by Nakagawa and written down by Nishi.[124] The quotation by Fukuzawa is the most prominent: "Working with an independent will and subsisting without the help of others is the essence of an independent life; it follows that a person of independence and self-respect must be an independent worker and a bread winner."[125] Nishi's contribution reads: "Hygiene is the foundation of strong soldiers and the source of the country's wealth. Without it, there is no religion." The banner continues by invoking a

---

121. Hōgō, *Okayama no kijin*, 124.

122. *Rakugo* is a form of storytelling featuring comic dialogue. Hōgō, *Okayama no kijin*, 124.

123. Hōgō, *Okayama no kijin*, 124. On his banners, see San'yō gakuen, *Ai to hōshi*, 29.

124. San'yō gakuen, *Ai to hōshi*, 29–30. The banner was apparently never used. Katsurada had studied in Germany and was an advocate of public hygiene; he was best known for his research on parasites.

125. The phrase comes from Fukuzawa's Moral Code (Shūshin yōryō), Article 3, written for Keio University students. The text is available on Keio University's website: https://www.aozora.gr.jp/cards/000296/files/47063_32088.html (accessed 3 June 2021). For an English translation, see Sale, "The Moral Code of Fukuzawa Yukichi," 326.

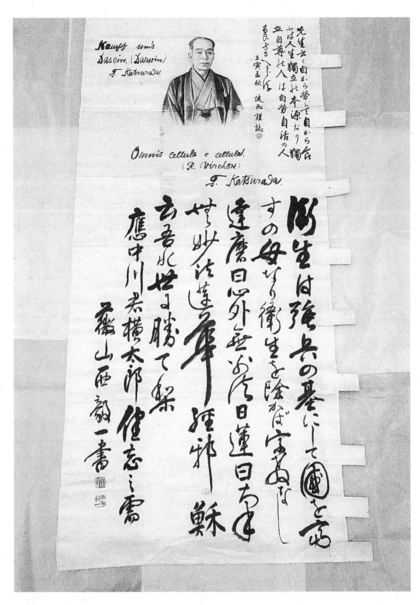

FIGURE 4. Banner of Nakagawa Yokotarō, circa 1890. Courtesy of the Okayama Prefectural Archives.

saying of the monk Bodhidharma (fifth or sixth century): "Apart from the mind there is no dharma," followed by a mantra associated with the *Lotus Sutra*, "Glory to the law of the Lotus Sutra" and a quotation from the Gospel of John: "Jesus said, 'I have overcome the world.'"[126]

The eclectic combination of sources stands out and matches Nakagawa's personality. The quotations also reflect Nakagawa's broad range of interests: his advocacy for civilization and his passion for science, public health, and religion, all concerns that were familiar to village elites. Nakagawa agreed with Fukuzawa on the importance of independence and self-sufficiency, but his convictions did not prevent him from working to alleviate poverty. For instance, he paid for and attended the funeral of a rickshaw driver, expressing a concern for common people that his friends found remarkable.[127]

After retiring from his position in the bureaucracy in the 1880s, Nakagawa moved to the countryside. He advocated drinking cow's milk, a new practice in Meiji Japan associated with civilization. To support the cause, he opened a dairy and set up a store to sell the milk.[128] He believed in order to fight contagious diseases, individuals must strengthen the body, and drinking milk constituted an important part of that project. Ultimately, strong bodies served the state.[129] On the occasion of his move to the countryside in 1886, his change of address announcement, in the *sōrōbun* literary style proclaimed, "I have become impoverished as of late, therefore I am moving to the village of Kitagata. In order to ensure a long life, I will run a pasture and live a modest life. I would be pleased if those who pity me and who wish to visit me would come to Kitagata, Section 180."[130] The village, we should note, was less than three miles from the center of Okayama and thus his commute was not arduous.

126. Matthew Hayes helped translate Bodhidharma's phrase. "Dharma" here refers to Buddhist teachings. *Lotus Sutra*, trans. Watson. John 16:33, English Standard Version.

127. Kume, *Kenbōsai itsuwashū*, 84.

128. Katō, "Kenbōsai Nakagawa Yokotarō," 21. On the milk store, see Ōta, "Nakagawa Yokotarō to Sumiya Koume," 292; San'yō gakuen, *Ai to hōshi*, 28. On the introduction of milk and beef in the 1870s, see Miyachi, *Meiji jidaikan*, 98.

129. San'yō gakuen, *Ai to hōshi*, 29.

130. The change of address announcement appeared in the *San'yō shinpō*. Hōgō, *Okayama no kijin*, 124; Kume, *Kenbōsai itsuwashū*, 80.

Nakagawa's idiosyncratic habit of wearing a Buddhist stole (*kesa*) captured attention. On meeting bureaucrat Gotō Shinpei (1857–1929) at a hygiene conference, Nakagawa asked Gotō for directions since he could not read the signs. Confused by the question, Gotō inquired among the other attendees: "Who is the large, strange man from Okayama who cannot read and wears a Buddhist stole?"[131] In general, Nakagawa liked to experiment with clothing, and once he wore a Japanese-style jacket over Western garb. After locals got over their initial shock, they warmed to the hybrid style.[132]

Alongside his interest in Christianity, Nakagawa maintained a deep interest in Buddhism, which may explain why he so often wore a stole. He attempted to become a disciple of the Fuju fuse sect of Buddhism. This sect, a form of Nichiren Buddhism, had been deemed heterodox for much of the Tokugawa period but was made legal in the 1870s.[133] In the end, the local priest rejected Nakagawa because he tended to fall asleep when meditating even though the priest repeatedly stuck Nakagawa with a stick. Perhaps Nakagawa's jokes also rubbed the teacher the wrong way. When asked if he had achieved enlightenment, Nakagawa replied that he was "enlightened" about how poor the barley served at the temple tasted compared to rice, his normal fare.[134]

Regardless of his retirement to the country, Nakagawa maintained a public presence, appearing in the city from time to time when he felt compelled to enlighten his fellow citizens. In 1894, when electric power arrived in Okayama, Nakagawa went to work to advertise it. At the time, the cost of electricity was prohibitive for all but the wealthy. He dressed up in a festive straight-sleeved coat (*happi*) with Japanese-style trousers and beat a drum while explaining the issue to audiences. He was similarly moved to act during a cholera outbreak, wearing a demon mask and high-platform clogs as he expounded on the importance of proper hygiene.[135]

131. Kume, *Kenbōsai itsuwashū*, 70.
132. Kume, *Kenbōsai itsuwashū*, 71–73.
133. Kume, *Kenbōsai itsuwashū*, 35–36.
134. Kume, *Kenbōsai itsuwashū*, 35–36.
135. Hōgō, *Okayama no kijin*, 124–25.

Managing diseases like cholera posed a great challenge to the Meiji state, as it had to the Tokugawa authorities before it. In early Meiji Okayama, sludge filled the canals, and clean water was difficult to access, a situation that contributed to the spread of cholera. Men like Nakagawa urged for sewers to be built to control the spread of the disease.[136] His work advocating for modern infrastructure—together with the efforts of the wealthy Nozaki family—meant that by 1900, Okayama led on this front, compared with neighboring cities including Hiroshima, Hyōgo, and Sakide.[137] So great was the progress that when the Western missionaries had to move to the center of the city in the 1890s, they were quite comfortable. James and Belle Pettee's daughter Anna recalled, "Because now the city had a modern water supply system and sewage was more competently disposed of, we had no objection" to living there.[138]

Lastly, Nakagawa urged people to use mosquito nets. He planned a speech on the topic. However, the advertisements for the speech used the incorrect Chinese characters for "mosquito nets" (*kachō*). Instead of "mosquito net," the sign featured the characters for "flower and bird" (also pronounced *kachō*), referring to a style of painting. Listeners registered surprise at the actual content, though given what they knew of Nakagawa, the error could not have been entirely unexpected.[139]

INTERACTIONS WITH FORMER OUTCASTES

Nakagawa's desire to enlighten people extended to former outcastes (*burakumin*, sometimes *eta* and *hinin*, both pejorative terms)—a status that was formally abolished in the early Meiji period but lived on in the appellation "new commoners" (*shinheimin*).[140] In the 1870s, seeking to elevate his employees and educate his peers, Nakagawa invited employees of his Minamigata pasture to attend sermons at his home and seated them

---

136. Ōta, "Nakagawa Yokotarō no enzetsu," 77. On efforts to fight the disease, see Johnston, "Buddhism Contra Cholera."
137. San'yō gakuen, *Ai to hōshi*, 28–29.
138. Sugiyama, "Untitled Speech."
139. Kume, *Kenbōsai itsuwashū*. 82.
140. Howell, *Geographies of Identity*, 28–29, 85. The origins of the outcastes are not clear. Members engaged in activities that non-outcastes considered polluted, including conducting executions and dealing with human and animal corpses.

alongside former samurai, shocking locals accustomed to the status system which prohibited samurai and outcastes from mixing.[141] He brought missionaries to the former outcaste village Takeda-mura in 1878. Together with a pastor, Nakagawa worked to ease relations between *buraku* and non-*buraku* community members, which had become strained after the violence of the Mimasaka riots against universal conscription five years earlier.[142] James Pettee confirmed in 1879 that Christian services were "also held regularly among the Etas [outcastes], the lowest class of people in the Japanese social scale, there being a colony of these people in one of the suburbs of the city," though he did not provide further details.[143] An 1878 Christian journal *Shichiichi zappō* reported that at a gathering where Nakagawa spoke, "old commoners" (*kyūmin*) by which Nakagawa meant non-*burakumin* "were giving new commoners (*shinmin*) [in other words, *burakumin*] their seats in a humble way. We have not seen anything like it elsewhere. It made one think of the explanation of the first chapter of the Gospel of John, verses 12 and 13. The men of the village who had before used the derogatory term 'eta' now stopped using it."[144] The writer refers to a passage where the apostle John explains that all people are children of God, a sentiment that in the author's telling transformed local relationships, rendering them more harmonious and egalitarian.

These efforts by Nakagawa and church leaders to elevate the former outcastes bore some fruit. The founding members of Okayama Church included four members of outcaste background, though the integration of former outcastes caused some strains in the community.[145] (To be clear, Nakagawa did not help found the Church, but his wife and her natal family did and were extensively involved in it.) The Church, whose members were mostly people of status and means like Yuki, developed a reputation for its work with the former outcaste community.[146] Still, we should be wary of understanding this engagement as unqualified social progress or liberation from old shackles, for as David Howell has pointed

---

141. Matsumura, "Ōnishi Sōzan," 72. Matsumura claims that the Ōnishi and Kimata families followed suit.

142. Mizuuchi, "Hyakunen mae," 44–45.

143. James Pettee, "A New Call from Japan."

144. Mizuuchi, "Hyakunen mae," 44–45.

145. Matsumura, "Ōnishi Sōzan," 72. On the strains, see Berry, *A Pioneer Doctor*, 105.

146. Maus, "Ishii Jūji," 178; Tomoyose, "Okayama no hisabestu buraku to kirisutokyō."

out, modernity brought a "delineation of a realm of discrimination that was in many ways more focused and hence more pernicious."[147] Modern ideas about race and hygiene—rather than simply liberating former outcastes—reshaped understandings of this group with complex consequences. The Meiji era homogenized what had once been a range of identities, and modernity took away the economic privileges and autonomy outcaste groups had once possessed.[148] We cannot understand this period in terms of simple progress or regression.[149]

In the 1930s, long after Nakagawa had died, one former outcaste recalled to one of Nakagawa's biographers that when he was young, Nakagawa had come to his village along with pastor Kanamori Michitomo. Nakagawa told villagers, "You have been discriminated against for a long time. But discriminatory treatment is banned by the Charter Oath [Gokajō no seimon] and by an order from the High Council [Dajōkan] . . . We are all brothers. We all drink tea. We all eat. Come to my house and eat, please." And when the man came to eat with Nakagawa, his wife Yuki and his sons joined them, just as if they were relatives.[150]

Nakagawa continued this work with former outcastes even after his close association with the missionaries ended. He did so despite some relatives' disapproval of his efforts with this stigmatized community.[151] Yet days after Nakagawa's death, Nishi wrote a lament singling out Nakagawa's work with former outcastes as especially noteworthy. In Nishi's explanation, Nakagawa attempted his outreach efforts with this group because he was interested in reforming customs. Nakagawa lamented the "corrupt customs" (*fūzoku taihai*) of society's upper ranks. In his estimation, focusing on helping former outcastes was a worthwhile endeavor, whereas he was unable to exert direct influence on elites.[152] It is not en-

147. Howell, *Geographies of Identity*, 154–55.

148. Like all status groups in Tokugawa Japan, outcastes largely regulated themselves, practicing "the principle of internal autonomy." Howell, *Geographies of Identity*, 33.

149. Timothy Amos points out that there are not always links between pre-Meiji outcaste groups and modern *buraku* communities and argues that modernity brought unprecedented marginalization. Amos, *Embodying Difference*.

150. Kume, *Kenbōsai itsuwashū*, 90–92. The 1868 Charter Oath announced a new direction for the state and promised that matters would be decided based on public discussion.

151. Kume, *Kenbōsai itsuwashū*, 90–91.

152. Nishi, *Nakagawa Yokotarō-kun ryakureki*, 5.

tirely clear why Nakagawa viewed the situation this way—he seems to have viewed former outcastes as more amenable to guidance and persuasion through socializing together. No doubt former outcastes themselves were more appreciative of his efforts to end discrimination.

In the absence of more sources and context, I find it difficult to evaluate Nakagawa's outreach efforts to the outcaste community. What looked enlightened to commentators in the early decades of the twentieth century seems problematic and elitist in hindsight. The politics swirling around the *burakumin* liberation movement also impact our study of the past.[153] Yet even in the face of these complicated factors, the surviving records indicate that Nakagawa strove to correct past wrongs, part of his attempt, however imperfect, to rectify the world. His actions reflected both his enlightenment reformist zeal and his Confucian background.

FUNDRAISING AND THE FUNERAL

Nakagawa lived surrounded by Christians. His wife, cousins, and mother-in-law attended Okayama Church, along with his former concubine Sumiya, and he supported San'yō gakuen. His cousin and sister-in-law Ōnishi Kinu ran the dormitory and the finances, as we shall see in chapter 4.

Nakagawa raised funds for the school, sending around a letter titled "Expanding Girls' Education in Okayama" to his friends in 1897. He highlighted the importance of women's education to the state. Women's education, in his view, was tied to "wealth and prosperity" at both the local and national level—here, the two levels flow together seamlessly. He urged acquaintances not to neglect it.[154] In fact, girls' education remained as essential to modern civilization as sewers and proper hygiene. He emphasized the struggles surrounding the construction of the Okayama Girls' Higher School, referring to details now lost to us, but concluded that supporters worked hard, and the school was eventually completed. He declared that a similar set of circumstances had contributed to the founding of San'yō gakuen, and he supported the building of schools

153. Michael Abele noted to me in April 2019 how the emphasis on outcaste struggle above all has shaped the historical record, especially what gets reprinted in volumes of source materials.

154. San'yō gakuen, *Ai to hōshi*, 30–32.

throughout the prefecture, declaring, "I dedicate my old body [*rōkotsu*] to girls' education; this will be my service in old age."[155] In 1890, Nishi suggested to a potential contributor that since Nakagawa was dedicating himself entirely to the cause, the least the supporter could do was pay up![156]

The following year, Nakagawa began traveling to see his acquaintances with a bag for donations, complete with a ledger that featured a letter from Nishi Kiichi.[157] Nishi's appeal urged recipients to eat at home rather than at a restaurant and donate the money saved to the school.[158] Nakagawa's many efforts on behalf of San'yō gakuen led the school to invite him to serve on the board of trustees, but he declined, an act that the school officials attributed to his "modest temperament."[159]

Nakagawa's public performance on behalf of San'yō merits close attention. Beginning in 1899, he hatched a plan to save the school from financial disaster. At the time, the school faced pressure on several fronts. The 1899 Girls' Higher Education Law (Kōtō jogakkō rei) mandated the creation of a higher school for girls in each prefecture, which meant San'yō gakuen faced more competition to attract students. Early in the decade, an increasingly nationalistic atmosphere less open to Western influences—and embodied in the conservative 1890 Imperial Rescript on Education (Kyōiku chokugo)—led the school to drop the two-character compound *eiwa*, or "English-Japanese," from its name. The institution moved away from its original mission to provide English-language education and faced financial pressures as it sought to expand the campus.[160] Matsumura suspects that Nakagawa may have felt especially tied to the school because of his cousin Ōnishi Kinu's position there.[161] He placed the following an-

155. San'yō gakuen, *Ai to hōshi*, 31–32.

156. Ōta, "Nakagawa Yokotarō to Sumiya Koume," 293.

157. See the letter from Nishi to Nozaki Manzaburō from 1890 in Ōta, "Nakagawa Yokotarō to Sumiya Koume," 293.

158. For Nishi's letter, see San'yō gakuen, *San'yō gakuen hyakunenshi*, 41–42.

159. San'yō gakuen, *San'yō gakuen hyakunenshi*, 40.

160. Okayama joseishi kenkyūkai, *Kindai Okayama no onnatachi*, 80; Ōta, "Nakagawa Yokotarō to Sumiya Koume," 295. On the funding of the school, see San'yō gakuen, *Ai to hōshi*, 36–37; Ōta, "Nakagawa Yokotarō to Sumiya Koume," 295.

161. Matsumura, "Ōnishi Sōzan," 76.

nouncement together with his will (*yuigon*) in a local paper. Newspapers in Osaka and Tokyo subsequently picked it up. It read:

> Although I am fond of meddling and have gotten involved in things without regard to private or public, now there is something I realize. On the twenty-seventh at 2 p.m. at Kunitomi Shōrinji Temple, I will die for a time. I will not deal with any tasks thereafter apart from education, hygiene, and raising cattle. Please bring as much incense money as possible [customary for funerals]. Please bear in mind that the more, the better.[162]

In the will, Nakagawa noted that he needed at least four pallbearers who would switch off during the ceremony because he was such a large man. He also required someone to carry a banner. He reiterated his request that the incense money brought as a funerary offering be given to the school, though we do not know how much he actually collected. Nakagawa explained he had reached old age and was giving up his pursuits, but San'yō gakuen school was having a difficult time making ends meet and he needed to act.[163]

On the day of the event, Nakagawa appeared in fine form, as his many chroniclers relate, though the precise details of their accounts vary.[164] He hired geisha to give him the ritual bath for corpses. At the beginning of the ceremony, he stood naked in front of the washtub in a crowded room with standing room only. He drew himself up to full height and adopted a stern, imposing stance (*niōdachi*) while geisha dried him and dressed him in white burial clothes. He then entered the coffin. After the coffin was shut, monks processed in front of it ringing bells. The service went on as usual as the priest intoned sutras. From time to time, a voice came from the coffin urging the priest to "hurry up," prompting the crowd to erupt in laughter. The priest ignored the disruption and proceeded with the rituals.[165]

---

162. Hōgō, *Okayama no kijin*, 125; San'yō gakuen, *San'yō gakuen hyakunenshi*, 42–43.

163. The will is reproduced in Ōta, "Nakagawa Yokotarō to Sumiya Koume," 294; Ōta, "Nakagawa Yokotarō no enzetsu," 75–76.

164. The accounts of the funeral by Ōta, Hōgō, and Kume all vary slightly.

165. Ōta, "Nakagawa Yokotarō no enzetsu," 75.

Near the end of the service, Nakagawa suddenly yelled from the coffin, "It's cold, and I can't stand it!"[166] He emerged from the coffin and stood up, staring at the laughing audience out of the corner of his eye. He walked to the waiting room. When he appeared later, his Buddhist funerary garb was gone, replaced by Western clothing, reflecting his multiple interests and identities. He proceeded to deliver a disjointed speech (*shiri metsuretsu*), his specialty. The speech is no longer extant, but Ōta Ken'ichi has uncovered an earlier draft, from around 1894, that was the basis for his monologue.[167]

Throughout his monologue, Nakagawa highlighted the need to invest in schools and infrastructure. In addition, he stressed the importance of public hygiene and proper sewage treatment to prevent the spread of cholera and typhus and to protect the health of the local economy and its inhabitants. If the surviving script is any clue, he punctuated his rambling address with memorable declarations. For instance, at one point, Nakagawa exclaimed, "Representative government may not care about hygiene or rotting brains, but I, the illiterate Yokotarō, do."[168] In his view, building up infrastructure at the local level offered a way to serve the country, though in this case, he suggested that the central government did not care as much about the local level as he did. Like Nishi, Nakagawa also advised people to stop spending money on pleasure and instead donate to the school.[169] His efforts on behalf of the school moved the audience. Kajiro Yoshi, a teacher at the school and its future principal, was reported to have wept—she was overwhelmed by his generosity.[170]

Although precedents existed for mock funerals in the Tokugawa period, such events were unusual in Meiji Japan.[171] W. Puck Brecher introduces the case of eccentric Yamazaki Hokka (1700–1746), who in 1739

166. Another account records Nakagawa jumping out of the coffin and proclaiming that he had "died so the school did not have to." Katō, "Kenbōsai Nakagawa Yokotarō," 18. Kume states that Nakagawa walked alongside the coffin en route to the temple. Kume, *Kenbōsai itsuwashū*, 59.

167. Ōta, "Nakagawa Yokotarō no enzetsu," 76.

168. Ōta, "Nakagawa Yokotarō no enzetsu," 80.

169. San'yō gakuen, *Ai to hōshi*, 29.

170. Hōgō, *Okayama no kijin*, 126. Kajiro became principal in 1908.

171. Brecher, *The Aesthetics of Strangeness*, 60–61. I thank Laura Nenzi for the reference.

held his own funeral, which similarly included jumping out of the coffin. Yamazaki then held a party for his friends, though the event was not a fundraiser. Writing about Nakagawa in 1937, biographer Kume showed awareness of the early modern living funerals, but he pointed out the difference in what Nakagawa had done, with his efforts to fundraise.[172] In Nakagawa's funeral performance, as in other parts of his life, he combined old and new ideas.

Nakagawa died in 1903 at the age of sixty-seven, four years after his spectacular staged funeral. At the time, he was away at the Osaka Industrial Exposition investigating the training of horses for the imperial army. He maintained a lifelong interest in horses—after all, he had worked closely with horses in his youth.[173] His 1903 funeral, held at Kokuseiji Temple, drew more than two thousand attendees, including a number of students from the schools he had supported. His friends erected the stone monument in 1911, now located near the castle moat.[174] Its position next to the castle—with the modern city as a backdrop—seems fitting for a man who straddled old and new.

Endings

How should we understand Nakagawa and his role as a central node in Okayama networks? Nakagawa undoubtedly brought people together and contributed to the strength of local networks. Biographer Kume regarded him as an "architect of culture" in the region. Meanwhile, Nakagawa's good friend Nishi portrayed him as a "true patriot of the realm," "a rare person who lamented the state of Japan and dedicated his life to making it a great country."[175] Both tried to make sense of him in all his fascinating complexity, sometimes resorting to hagiography. Nakagawa demonstrates

172. Kume, *Kenbōsai itsuwashū*, 58.
173. San'yō shinbunsha, *Okayama-ken rekishi jinbutsu jiten*, 695.
174. A 1926 photograph of the monument is available through the Okayama Prefectural Library: http://digioka.libnet.pref.okayama.jp/mmhp/kyodo/kento/T15/si/T15 -shi-syasintyo-jpeg-37.htm (accessed 11 July 2018). It is unclear when the monument was moved to its current site, most likely after World War II.
175. Kume, *Kenbōsai itsuwashū*, 107; Nishi, *Nakagawa Yokotarō-kun ryakureki*, 1.

that the possibilities for a new start after the Restoration did not mean a wholesale rejection of the past, nor did he express a sense of overwhelming loss as Japan modernized. He embraced everything new, perhaps a bit too quickly when it came to Christianity.

From a wider angle, Nakagawa's advocacy of hygiene and electricity reflected new trends in leadership around the world that attended the rise of modern nation-states. As Charles Maier writes of modern states more generally,

> the authorities we routinely aggregate as the state did become more ambitious about shaping the everyday attributes of the societies they governed in the late nineteenth and early twentieth centuries. They envisaged a more encompassing and interventionist agenda, and the results they sought entailed a different sense of mission. The good ruler in the eighteenth century might define his objective in terms of felicity or happiness or the preservation of order. The good bureaucrat in the late nineteenth century might think in terms of energy or hygiene.[176]

Nakagawa's interest in hygiene and energy fits Maier's description although as we have seen, he was hardly a conventional "good bureaucrat."

Unlike Nakagawa, most Meiji bureaucrats were highly literate. The media tended to portray these men as dour and silly. In stark contrast to Nakagawa, they did not quite know how to act in a world where everything was in transition. Newspaper accounts lampoon them for sporting Western swallowtail coats while also incongruously bowing deeply in the older manner.[177] Nakagawa, on the other hand, exhibited style, humor, and a commanding presence. The anecdote where he paired a Japanese jacket with Western clothing suggests he was a trendsetter. Time and again, we see how he brought people together: foreign missionaries, former samurai acquaintances, family members, and former outcastes.

Nakagawa did not inhabit established categories. Consequently, he offers new perspective on the changes and continuities that characterized the Meiji moment. He associated closely with Christians but himself was

176. Maier, *Leviathan 2.0*, 158.
177. Gluck, *Japan's Modern Myths*, 95.

not one. He lived part of his life under Tokugawa rule. Although he respected and at times clung to certain practices from the past—such as keeping a concubine—he simultaneously embraced the post-Restoration reforms. Sometimes he moved ahead without hesitation, brimming with a zeal for reform. He made his mark in Okayama with his embrace of modern hygiene, medicine, and education. No doubt ordinary people remembered him more for the way he strode around the city in a Buddhist stole delivering speeches on street corners. He occupies a key place in histories of Meiji Christianity in Okayama, bringing the first non-Japanese and later Japanese Christians to the prefecture. Of course, his relationship to the faith remained complicated after Sumiya departed and relations with the missionaries grew strained over the People's Rights Movement.

Nakagawa's advocacy of education straddled elements old and new. He hailed from a scholarly family and valued education despite his own struggles with it. He supported schools, including those dating from the Tokugawa period as well as more "modern" institutions tied to Christianity, including girls' schools.

Some aspects of Nakagawa's identity—his charisma and penchant for performance—do not surprise and remind us of other eccentric figures in Tokugawa history.[178] What may be most striking to modern readers as it was to his contemporaries is the amount of emotion Nakagawa expressed. For example, those around him registered surprise by how demonstrative he could be. Nishi's daughter Tsuyako later recalled his "huge tears." She remembered provoking him to cry when she was a child during his weekly visits to Shizutani because she was so intrigued by and unaccustomed to the site of a large man, a former warrior, sobbing. She recalled how he seemed like an overgrown child who delighted in activities like running to catch dragonflies with a net.[179]

Nakagawa's incredible charisma would have made him stand out in any age. What would have happened to him if the Tokugawa period had continued? Nakagawa no doubt would have found a place for his

178. For other examples, see the sketches in McClellan, *Woman in the Crested Kimono*, 35–36.

179. Kume, *Kenbōsai itsuwashū*, 83–85, 97.

idiosyncratic personality as an eccentric, but not as a bureaucrat, a reformer, and a local personality with a national reputation. He achieved his position through his participation in the Okayama networks—by giving speeches, engaging in fundraising, and bringing people together. Meiji Japan offered Nakagawa a new beginning, a chance to restyle himself as a reformer *and* an eccentric. He seized the chance and sought to make the world anew.

CHAPTER 2

Sumiya Koume, From Concubine to Activist and Hidden Leader

Sumiya Koume, despite being a diminutive woman under five feet tall and weighing less than eighty pounds, proved to be persuasive, persistent, and prolific in her role following the Meiji Restoration. She helped to found a school, lead the Okayama Orphanage, serve the Okayama Church, and work as a Bible Woman and evangelist.[1] Those who wrote about Sumiya often mentioned her asthma, which gave her a chronic cough. But her condition did not prevent her from working tirelessly to spread the gospel, regardless of the wealth or poverty of her audience.[2] As we saw in the introduction, Sumiya had served as a geisha for three years until Nakagawa Yokotarō bought out her contract in 1870 and installed her as his concubine. After almost a decade at Nakagawa's house, Sumiya left him, became a Christian, joined a political organization, and worked as an activist and reformer for the rest of her life.

This chapter explores Sumiya's life, focusing on the period after she left Nakagawa. What kind of roles did she play in the Okayama reform networks? What opportunities were possible for a single woman? Specifically, I analyze her association with the Freedom and People's Rights

---

1. Yoshizaki, "Meiji no shijuku Fujin eigakusha ni tsuite," 28. On the Okayama Orphanage in English, see Hastings, "A Christian Institution"; Maus, "Ishii Jūji." Maus discusses Sumiya briefly in chap. 3.

2. Okayama danjo kyōdō sankaku suishin sentā, *Jidai o hiraita Okayama no joseitachi*, 17.

Movement, her role at the Okayama Orphanage, and her work as a Bible
Woman and evangelist. Sumiya was a consummate networker—she knew
how to bring people together. Taking Sumiya as a case study, I argue that
more was possible for women than previous scholars have generally considered because of stereotypes, both in Sumiya's own time and since, about
women's roles as assistants.

To supplement the limited record, I analyze how Sumiya was received
by individuals around her, including Japanese activists, writers, and Western missionaries. I suggest she was an activist and a leader at the Orphanage and in the larger Christian community but that her work has
been obscured by an androcentric record that highlights male leadership
in institutions and networks. China historian Zheng Wang has suggested
that a focus on male leaders has concealed women's contributions to the
People's Republic of China in its formative decades.[3] I think a similar
point holds true for scholarship on Meiji women's activism. Many of the
sources characterize Sumiya's work as an "assistant" to men and highlight
her maternal and religious qualities. When women work in the company
of men, it may be harder for scholars to see women's contributions—and
they end up buried in the historical record. Nevertheless, some acquaintances wrote about what Sumiya did in depth, and these accounts allow
deeper insights into her contributions.

Sumiya's story sheds new light on the possibilities for women to act
and to lead during a period of large-scale social transformation. Her life
also illuminates how former samurai women supported their households
during this transitional moment.[4] Although I wish to highlight Sumiya's
leadership, I intentionally do not characterize her as "independent," as
scholars have sometimes done for single women in missionary circles.[5]
Such a notion would not have made sense to her, nor the other single
women I address in chapter 4. Rather, she performed a leadership role
within the context of overlapping networks alongside men and women.
Her life provides a window into the interdependence of women's and
men's lives in associational activity and institution building (fig. 5).[6]

3. Zheng Wang, *Finding Women in the State.*
4. Matsuzaki, "Meiji ishinki no jendā kenkyū," 55–56.
5. Hamada, *Kadota kaiwai,* 86.
6. Walthall, review of *The Problem of Women in Early Modern Japan,* 91.

FIGURE 5. Photograph of Sumiya Koume, circa 1910. Courtesy of Houghton Library, Harvard University and United Church Ministries.

Background

Sumiya was born in 1850 to a lower-level samurai family in the Nodaya-chō district of Okayama. Her mother died soon after her birth. Her father worked as a temple administrator not far from Okayama Castle, but he, too, died when she was six—likely in a cholera epidemic. Sumiya's maternal grandmother and uncle, who bore the surname Aoki, raised the orphaned girl. She started learning to dance and to play the shamisen when she was five, and by her late teens, she was an accomplished teacher who had several students. Sumiya also likely had some formal education at a temple school during her youth. Her district had two academies, including one run by activist Fukuda Hideko's family.[7] Her grandmother died in 1868, the year of the Meiji Restoration, and she needed to support her uncle for reasons that remain unclear. That same year, out of necessity, Sumiya became a geisha at the Matsu-no-e restaurant, where she was known for her beauty, talent, and skills as a teacher of *nagauta*, a form of Japanese classical music; her training as a geisha also likely included reading and writing.[8] It is possible that had the Restoration and the surrounding upheavals not happened, she would not have become a geisha: her uncle would have been in better financial shape and probably would have adopted a husband for her to continue the Aoki line.[9] In this hypothetical scenario, the adopted husband would have received a stipend and been able to support the household.

However, the Restoration did happen, and circumstances compelled Sumiya to join the ranks of entertainers at Matsu-no-e. Nakagawa Yokotarō met her at the restaurant. Three years later in 1871, he bought out her contract and made her his concubine, thus stabilizing the finances of the Aoki household. She began living with Nakagawa and his wife Yuki and, in 1877, Sumiya gave birth to her daughter, Toyo. She

---

7. Yoshizaki, "Hōshi suru onnatachi," 105–6.
8. Okayama danjo kyōdō sankaku suishin sentā, *Jidai o hiraita Okayama no joseitachi*, 14.
9. Okayama danjo kyōdō sankaku suishin sentā, *Jidai o hiraita Okayama no joseitachi*, 17.

also served as Nakagawa's secretary and read books aloud so that he could memorize them.[10]

Sumiya was exposed to Christianity through sermons at Nakagawa's home beginning in 1875, when he brought the first Western missionary to Okayama. She learned about the schools that Protestant missionaries were establishing around the country for women and girls. In 1878, she went to study at one such school set up by the American Board: Kōbe eiwa jogakkō, known subsequently as Kōbe jogakuin or, in English, Kobe College. Nakagawa likely paid her tuition at the school, where her status as a concubine-student would have been unusual. However, Sumiya's time in Kobe was short-lived, and sometime in 1879, she was called back to Okayama by Nakagawa, who sent a telegram stating falsely that her adopted father was critically ill.[11] Apparently, he could not bear to be without her for long—Sumiya came home to Okayama and did not return to Kobe. If she stood out among her Kobe College classmates as a concubine, in dropping out she fit right in, as it was not uncommon for students to leave women's colleges without graduating.[12]

Perhaps the most important legacy of Sumiya's time in Kobe lies in the nurturing ties formed with Eliza Talcott, a missionary and cofounder of her college. Sumiya learned that Talcott and the other missionaries abhorred concubinage.[13] Talcott herself was less interested in teaching at a school and more committed to spreading the gospel, and around this time left Kobe College to devote herself full-time to missionary work. Talcott would meet with Sumiya again in Okayama the following year.

When Sumiya returned to Nakagawa's home sometime in early 1879, she no longer wished to be a concubine.[14] In her coming to this view, her

10. Okayama danjo kyōdō sankaku suishin sentā, *Jidai o hiraita Okayama no joseitachi*, 14, 17.

11. Yoshizaki, "Hōshi suru onnatachi," 107. Yoshizaki is listed as the author of this section of the edited volume *Kindai Okayama no onnatachi*. I list her here to highlight her pioneering scholarship.

12. Noriko Ishii, *American Women Missionaries*, 17. The 1906 Kobe College alumnae bulletin *Megumi* lists Sumiya as a past student and Toyo as her daughter. The record erroneously states that Sumiya was a student in 1880; in fact, she left the previous year. I thank Noriko Ishii for providing me with this source.

13. Noriko Ishii, *American Women Missionaries*, 92.

14. Belle Pettee, "Two Personalities," 395–98; Okayama danjo kyōdō sankaku suishin sentā, *Jidai o hiraita Okayama no joseitachi*, 14–15.

encounter at Kobe College with Christian ideas decrying concubinage
was important, but she may also have been influenced by contemporary
debates in the press about the rights of concubines. Such women had previously held legal standing, but they lost this status by 1882.[15] During
this period, Sumiya agonized about her situation and her daughter.
Nakagawa insisted that if she left him, Toyo must stay. It was a common
practice at the time, but Sumiya did not want to leave Toyo behind. In
1880, Sumiya began attending the newly-founded Okayama Church but
held back from baptism. One source claims her reluctance stemmed from
her status as a concubine.[16] In contrast, Belle Pettee attributed Sumiya's
decision to Nakagawa instructing her to hold off until they could be baptized together.[17] That same year, Talcott came to work with the missionaries at the Okayama Station and helped Sumiya finally leave Nakagawa.[18] Extant materials explain that for Sumiya, the decisive push came
from encountering the words "No cross, no crown" at church.[19] The phrase
came from the title for a 1669 religious treatise by Quaker leader William
Penn (1644–1718) in which he asserted that only by bearing the cross could
one enter the kingdom of God. This message proved transformative and
moved Sumiya to act decisively. She left Nakagawa in 1880, and the following year, Sumiya was baptized at the Okayama Church.

The Church attracted well-off local people, many of whom were former samurai. Sumiya worshiped there with many of Nakagawa's female
relatives, including his wife, cousin, and mother-in-law, all central figures at the Church. (The Ōnishi women funded a new building for
the Church in 1885.)[20] Sumiya was struggling financially after leaving
Nakagawa, but she was not alone. Some other members were poor and of
lower status, including a number of outcastes as I have mentioned. The
mixing of social groups impressed potential converts. Otis Cary noted how

15. Mackie, *Feminism in Modern Japan*, 17.
16. Okayama danjo kyōdō sankaku suishin sentā, *Jidai o hiraita Okayama no joseitachi*, 14.
17. Belle Pettee, "Two Personalities," 397.
18. Missionary records suggest that Nakagawa trusted Talcott. Belle Pettee, "Two Personalities," 397.
19. Belle Pettee, "Two Personalities," 397; Yoshizaki, "Hōshi suru onnatachi," 108.
20. Okayama joseishi kenkyūkai, *Kindai Okayama no onnatachi*, 65.

surprised local people were when wealthy members served as pallbearers at the funeral of an indigent congregant.[21] This example should not suggest that all Kumiai churches were equally open to people on the margins. Rather, Emily Anderson has observed that in contrast to other Protestant denominations, the Congregationalists allowed for more autonomy on the part of individual congregations.[22]

After leaving Nakagawa, Sumiya was in a precarious situation since she lacked the means to support herself. Moreover, her uncle relied on her for support. Scholars disagree as to what happened next but concur that she went to Kobe for a short time.[23] Upon returning to Okayama, she taught at the Kyokutō Sunday School (Kyokutō nichiyōbi gakkō) which was connected to but not under the jurisdiction of the Okayama Church. She lived in poverty for two years.[24] Her financial situation improved in 1883 when she was hired by a local missionary's wife, Belle Pettee, as a translator to help spread the gospel. Sumiya also taught Pettee the Japanese language. The situation improved on other fronts as well— that same year, Nakagawa relented and handed over custody of Toyo to Sumiya.

Throughout these difficult transitions, Sumiya relied on emotional support from Talcott, who had remained in Okayama. The two women were extremely close throughout their lives. James Pettee, writing after Talcott's death, described the nature of their relationship in familial terms, observing that "Mrs. Sumiya, the efficient Bible woman, whose personal life story is so full of dramatic incidents . . . always thought of Miss Talcott

21. Cary, *A History of Christianity in Japan*, 161.
22. Emily Anderson, *Christianity and Imperialism*, 6. On the status background of the Okayama Church members and those of other area churches, see Moriya, "Auto sutēshon kara sutēshon e," 101.
23. One source claims Sumiya attended Kobe Women's Bible Training School (Kobe joshi shingakkō) to receive training as a Bible Woman. Okayama danjo kyōdō sankaku suishin sentā, *Jidai o hiraita Okayama no joseitachi*, 14. However, Talcott wrote that Sumiya never attended the school. Given their close relationship, I find Talcott more reliable. Talcott, "The Work of Bible Women in Japan," *Life and Light for Woman* 27, no. 3 (1897), 100. Julia Gulick claimed that Talcott trained Sumiya "as there was no training school for Bible-women" at the time. Gulick, "Bible Women's Work in Okayama Station." I am grateful to Noriko Ishii for this reference.
24. Belle Pettee, "Two Personalities," 398.

as her mother."[25] Leaving aside the question of whether Pettee was correct, his claim points to the limited possibilities for conceptualizing relationships among women outside of familial relationships. Most notably, he overlooked the possibility of friendship.

Politics, Education, and the Work of Bible Women

One of the first things Sumiya did after leaving Nakagawa was to become involved in 1882 with the OWFS, a local women's political group loosely affiliated with the Freedom and People's Rights Movement (see chapter 3). How exactly Sumiya came to join the group remains unclear, although the overlap in local networks of Christians and of People's Rights activists played a role.[26] The men involved in the movement held their initial meetings at the Matsu-no-e restaurant, where she had worked as a geisha years earlier.[27] It is also possible that Sumiya knew about the group because she had grown up in the same district as some of the other members, including Fukuda Hideko and Fukuda's mother Ume. The following year, at the age of thirty-three, Sumiya delivered a speech to the OWFS titled "The Cherry Blossoms in the Valley" (Tanima no sakura) at a local temple. The event was not religious but rather made use of an available public space, a common practice during the People's Rights era. Even though we do not have the text of her speech, based on speeches by other women during this period, we can assume that Sumiya likely called for raising women's status and discussed natural rights.[28]

We know few details about Sumiya's initial time teaching Belle Pettee in the years 1883 to 1885. In 1886, Sumiya worked with local missionaries to open a school in Okayama called the Fujin eigakusha (Women's English school). Sumiya filed the application with the local authorities and identified the school's aim as educating interested women of all ages

25. James Pettee, "Work in Chugoku," *Mission News* 15, no. 3 (15 December 1911), 49.
26. On these links, see Isshiki, "Kirisutokyō to jiyū minken undō."
27. *Okayama-ken shi*, 10:137.
28. San'yō shinbunsha, *Okayama-ken rekishi jinbutsu jiten*, 559.

and boys under the age of fifteen.[29] Belle Pettee later explained how Sumiya managed to fit the Bible into the curriculum so that no one could avoid it: "The daily Bible lesson was put in the middle of the one session. If it came at the beginning the pupils were late; if at the end, they left early; in the middle they heard willy-nilly the gospel message."[30] The school remained open until 1890 and had ninety students registered at one point, including a sixty-year-old widow. It closed in the midst of a wave of anti-Western sentiment that swept the country in the 1890s.[31] Even though the school was not around for a long time, it had an impact: according to Belle Pettee, some former students went on to become leaders in the "woman's work" of Kumiai churches.[32]

In addition to running the school, Sumiya worked as a Bible Woman. Bible Women were local salaried mission employees who supported the work of Western female missionaries to further the missionary cause around the world in the late nineteenth and early twentieth centuries. Even though scholars acknowledge the importance of Bible Women, we know little about them for the records are scarce.[33] Bible Women enjoyed considerable autonomy and did not need to write reports—making an accounting of their role difficult for the historian. Bible Women most often worked with individual missionaries rather than larger organizations (though in this case, Sumiya was employed by the Okayama Mission Station). Historian Sakamoto Kiyone notes that missionaries often wrote about Bible Women using only their personal names and omitting their surnames. As a result, it is nearly impossible for scholars to determine what became of the women once the missionaries left Japan. Limited archival records aside, Sakamoto contends that the work of Bible Women was critical to spreading Christianity in Japan since Western missionary movements were restricted until the late nineteenth century.[34]

29. Saitō, "Meiji-ki Okayama-ken," 1–2; Yoshizaki, "Meiji no shijuku Fujin eigaku-sha ni tsuite," 28.

30. Belle Pettee, "Geisha Girl to Bible Woman," 6.

31. Yoshizaki, "Hōshi suru onnatachi," 111–12; Onoda, *Tsuikairoku*, 20.

32. Belle Pettee, "Geisha Girl to Bible Woman," 6.

33. Sakamoto, "Ūmanzu bōdo to Nihon dendō," 142; Lublin, *Reforming Japan*, 190n33.

34. Sakamoto, "Ūmanzu bōdo to Nihon dendō," 141–42.

Bible Women spread the gospel primarily through home visitation and could access Japanese homes in ways foreigners and Japanese men could not. Moreover, Westerners struggled with learning the Japanese language, as we have already seen.[35] Records confirm the success of specific Bible Women. For instance, Eliza Talcott mentions one parish outside of Okayama facing serious financial troubles. The church employed a pastor and a Bible Woman but needed to trim expenses; one of the employees therefore had to go. In this case, Talcott explains that "the Christians said if they must give up one of their Christian teachers they must at all events retain the Bible woman."[36] A similar case occurred in Hiroshima, where Gulick notes that a certain woman named Shibata performed extremely valuable work even though Gulick thought her crude. Gulick knew Shibata from her time assisting at the Kobe Women's Bible Training School (Kobe joshi shingakkō), a school dedicated to educating future Bible Women, which Shibata had attended. Shibata-san, Gulick observed, "is the same coarse, loud mouthed woman as before, quite the opposite of the ideal Japanese lady, and yet Mr. Pettee tells me that for downright personal work, he thinks the people value Shibata San more than their pastor. Partly as a result of her faithful labor, women quite outnumber men in that church."[37]

What Bible Women did was not necessarily obvious to Western readers who supported the missionary project. However, Eliza Talcott explained the labor of Bible Women and the many skills they offered to readers of *Life and Light for Woman*, the Protestant missionary magazine published by the Woman's Board of Missions in cooperation with the American Board:

They go into a community, get acquainted with as many people as possible, and by their lives and words win the people to listen to the story of what Christ has done for them. Often they teach the women to read intelligently; they labor to remove prejudices and jealousies, and to rouse the women of the church to a sense of their privilege and responsibility to reach out beyond their own homes. Usually, they learn while in the Bible school

---

35. Sakamoto, "Ūmanzu bōdo to Nihon dendō," 141–42.
36. Talcott, "The Work of Bible Women in Japan," 98.
37. Gulick, "Bible Women's Work in Okayama Station."

to read the simple music of the Christian hymns, and if the Christian community to which they go is a proud possessor of a baby organ, they play the tunes, and thus lead the singing in the public services.[38]

Missionary records confirm Sumiya's considerable success as a Bible Woman. Eliza Talcott highlighted Sumiya's "efficiency," listing Sumiya's many contributions to the cause, beginning with the Japanese-language instruction she gave Mrs. Pettee.[39] Talcott's words were based on experience: she and Sumiya worked together closely many times while negotiating difficult circumstances. Belle Pettee later stressed the trials Talcott and Sumiya had endured while they spread the good news. She recalled with typical dramatic flair: "Those were days of persecutions, of perils by land and sea, of perils from exasperated fathers and mothers who even threatened the life of the devoted missionary and her helper."[40] Talcott particularly valued Sumiya's flexibility and keen ability to connect with people across rank: Sumiya "can enter with equal ease the home of the governor of the province and the cottage of the humblest peasant."[41] Her social graces likely came from her training as a geisha.

But Sumiya was more than an assistant to the Westerners. Talcott relates an anecdote that draws attention to Sumiya's considerable influence and social standing as she used her skills as a master mediator to bring together a deeply divided congregation outside of Okayama. Church members had broken into two groups over "practical issues in the conduct of their work." Into the deadlock came Sumiya: "Mrs. Sumiya visited the church and became acquainted with both parties. She felt she was sent of God to heal the dissension, and her faith and love triumphed. Proud men and women yielded, and the church was reunited, and has worked harmoniously together ever since."[42] In general, Talcott held Bible Women in high regard, calling them "intelligent, earnest women, whose counsel and cooperation were of great service to the missionaries at a time when their ignorance of customs and modes of thought of the

38. Talcott, "The Work of Bible Women in Japan," 98.
39. Talcott, "The Work of Bible Women in Japan," 100.
40. Belle Pettee, "Geisha Girl to Bible Woman," 5.
41. Talcott, "The Work of Bible Women in Japan," 100.
42. Talcott, "The Work of Bible Women in Japan," 102.

people was as great a hindrance to successful work as was the lack of ability to use the language skillfully."[43] In Talcott's account, Bible Women seem to have accomplished far more than the missionaries did initially.

A 1900 report by missionary Julia A. E. Gulick, titled "Bible Women's Work in Okayama Station," echoes and amplifies Talcott's comments. Gulick, who served in Okayama in 1885–1886, affirmed that the missionaries held Sumiya in the highest regard.[44] Gulick described Sumiya's labor in detail, apparently in response to a request from the Woman's Board of the American Board for more information about what Bible Women did and who some of them were. The request appears to have irritated Gulick, leaving her defensive. She wrote back that those who "undertake the support of Bible-women in Japan should be prepared for frequent changes, for they are much like Methodist preachers in this respect. This is partly on account of their disposition, of the people, and partly because many of them are not thoroughly furnished enough to work successfully in one place very long at a time." Sumiya, however, was not typical: she was "a native of the place, of natural ability, great tact, and more education than most of her age."[45] Gulick discussed Sumiya's work in depth:

> She visits the sick, and where occasion requires remains with them days and nights, looks after the poor of the church and those who have no friends, reminds those who are likely to forget, of the regular meetings for women which she conducts, gives personal notice of special meetings to those who would not hear or heed a general notice. She also does much house to house visiting, is *practically the assistant pastor* as well as an evangelist [emphasis mine]. On the Sabbath she teaches a class in the Church Sunday School and another at the Orphan Asylum; and she is the trusted friend and advisor of Mr. Ishii the head of that institution, and secures many contributions for the Asylum by personal solicitation.[46]

43. Talcott, "The Work of Bible Women in Japan," 98.
44. Moriya, "Auto sutēshon kara sutēshon e," 106. Gulick arrived in Japan in 1874.
45. Gulick, "Bible Women's Work in Okayama Station."
46. Gulick, "Bible Women's Work in Okayama Station." Gulick's parents were missionaries, as were some of her seven brothers. On her parents, see Putney, *Missionaries in Hawai'i*. On nephew Sidney, see Hollinger, *Protestants Abroad*, chap. 6; Taylor, *Advocate of Understanding*. Missionaries at the time referred to the Okayama Orphanage as an "asylum."

Gulick's account attests to the wide range of activities Sumiya carried out as a Bible Woman. In particular, the observation that Sumiya served as "practically the assistant pastor" constitutes the closest evidence yet of Sumiya's leading role and draws attention to her authority among the wider Christian community.[47]

Gulick also includes invaluable information on Bible Women's salaries. Sumiya's ($4.50 or 900 yen) was a bit higher than that of the other Bible Women and was supplemented by a "missionary friend" because what the mission offered was "not enough for her to live on comfortably."[48] For Sumiya, then, this work enabled her to support herself—though that does not seem to have always been the case for other Bible Women.

Sumiya engaged in other kinds of labor. In 1887, Sumiya began assisting Ishii Jūji with the Okayama Orphanage. She had met Ishii a few years earlier, and they became close. She provided emotional and financial support for him and his wife Shina: he called her "his angel" and "the mother of his faith."[49] Sumiya played a central role in running the Orphanage. She wrote fundraising letters.[50] She traveled and spoke on the institution's behalf. Ishii Jūji's diary reveals that he wanted Sumiya to turn the Fujin eigakusha over to Nakamura Shizu, another female activist and church member.[51] It seems likely that he wished to free Sumiya up to devote more of her time to the Orphanage.

Sumiya also adopted a more informal role as an evangelist for the Church. *Remembering Sumiya Koume* (*Sumiya Koume-shi tsuikairoku*, hereafter referred to as *Tsuikairoku*), a collection of reminiscences published two decades after her death, particularly emphasizes this work, calling her a "born evangelist" (*tensei no dendōsha*).[52] Sumiya was passionate and persistent in her evangelical work. One acquaintance recalled, "If

---

47. Gulick, "Bible Women's Work in Okayama Station."

48. Gulick, "Bible Women's Work in Okayama Station."

49. James Pettee, *Mr. Ishii*, 54. Hosoi, *Ishii Jūji to Okayama kojiin*, 318. An example of networks in action: Niijima's writings inspired Ishii when he founded the Orphanage. Hamada, *Kadota kaiwai*, 61–62.

50. Yoshizaki, "Hōshi suru onnatachi," 113; Okayama danjo kyōdō sankaku suishin sentā, *Jidai o hiraita Okayama no joseitachi*, 15; Yoshizaki, "Sumiya Koume nitsū no shokan ni tsuite," published in two parts (of which the second is "sono ni").

51. Yoshizaki, "Nakamura Shizu," 2.

52. Onoda, *Tsuikairoku*, 100.

Sumiya had her sights on you, you could not run away."[53] After Sumiya's death, Belle Pettee elaborated on the source of Sumiya's success: "She was a sunshine-carrier wherever she went, the friend of old and young, rich and poor alike."[54]

"I Recommend against Becoming a Geisha or Concubine"

Sumiya left few sources in her own hand, mostly letters to Ishii and fund-raising letters to potential donors to the Orphanage. Also extent are a transcription of a speech she gave in 1900 on the Orphanage's behalf in Tokyo as well as an essay titled "The Necessity of Faith" (Shinkō no hitsuyō). The longest work is an essay she wrote for *Jogaku zasshi* (Women's education journal) in 1893.[55] *Jogaku zasshi* aimed to enlighten educated men and women about the importance of women's education and also encouraged activism opposing prostitution and concubinage.[56] We know what public intellectuals, government officials, and female reformers thought about concubinage, but to the best of my knowledge, Sumiya's 1893 essay "I Recommend against Becoming a Geisha or Concubine" (Geisha to tekake to ni susumezu) is the only source written by someone who had actually worked as a concubine. I have analyzed the essay extensively elsewhere, so I shall limit myself to mentioning the highlights here.[57]

Sumiya's main interest lies in delineating proper roles for women. Time and again, she stresses women's natural role as wives and mothers and states that "becoming a concubine goes against women's nature."[58] Sumiya declares, "In the world, women's roles are as follows: to be good wives and good mothers; to help husbands and educate the children; to

53. Onoda, *Tsuikairoku*, 9–10.
54. Belle Pettee, "Geisha Girl to Bible Woman," 7.
55. Onoda, *Tsuikairoku*, 3–8.
56. Copeland, *Lost Leaves*, 24–25.
57. Marnie Anderson, "Critiquing Concubinage."
58. Sumiya Koume, "Geisha to tekake to ni susumezu," *Jogaku zasshi* 342 (1893): 12.

run households and to help benefit the state. But there is something that damages good women, ruins households and causes confusion to the state. It is geisha and prostitutes."[59] Sumiya's mention of motherhood is noteworthy, for motherhood did not figure prominently in discussions of women's roles in the Tokugawa period. Moreover, understandings of women's roles primarily in terms of motherhood developed with full force only around the turn of the twentieth century. This shift took place in conjunction with the founding of women's higher schools and the elaboration of "good wife and wise mother" as the state policy for women's education.[60]

Readers learn that although Sumiya does not approve of geisha or prostitutes—she also displays a more general aversion to sex work—her focus is on advising such women that they should *not* become concubines. Although she recognizes that concubinage may offer an attractive option for geisha, in that it offers stability as they age, she wants to show how the practice works against social harmony and harms all concerned. Indeed, in perhaps the most memorable line of the essay designed to shock potential concubines out of their complacency, she declares, "That which kills without a knife is a concubine."[61]

Sumiya calls attention to the negative aspects of concubinage that may not be immediately evident to geisha and prostitutes considering the practice as an option. Specifically, she illuminates the problems that arise when wives and concubines live together. These problems continue even if the concubine has her own living quarters, Sumiya warns. In fact, separate quarters can make the situation worse for the wife since the distance prevents her from assessing the state of the relationship between husband and concubine. The presence of a concubine affects all members of the household negatively, including the children and the husband. Once a concubine arrives, trouble begins, although it may take a while to manifest. No one behaves well, and everyone suffers. Sumiya explains the bad behavior of all parties (husbands, wives, concubines) in terms of inevitable structural problems.

59. Sumiya, "Geisha to tekake to ni susumezu," 5.
60. Nolte and Hastings, "The Meiji State's Policy."
61. Sumiya, "Geisha to tekake to ni susumezu," 6; Marnie Anderson, "Critiquing Concubinage," 10.

Although Sumiya judges concubines quite harshly at certain moments—declaring at one point that their lives are steeped in "sin"—she expresses a degree of understanding for women who find themselves in bad situations with no other means to support themselves. "What a pity to become someone's toy," she exclaims.[62] Yet characterizing concubinage in terms of sin never becomes a dominant theme in her essay. Instead, Sumiya remains sympathetic to all parties. She even allows for some good intentions, stating that a concubine may initially not wish to cause trouble for the wife—although that is surely what will happen, for the presence of a concubine inevitably interferes with the husband-wife relationship.[63] To imagine otherwise is to deceive oneself.[64] Despite her generally sympathetic view, Sumiya expresses no compassion in cases where concubines maneuver and become the main wife, in effect stealing other women's husbands.[65]

Most of the time, Sumiya separates the situation that produces concubinage from the individuals involved. She recognizes the full variety of human beings—deceptive concubines, concubines with good intentions, foolish wives, and wives who terrorize concubines when their husbands are absent. All individuals, although not without fault, are caught up in an untenable system, no matter the arrangements and intentions of those involved. The only other group that Sumiya targets unsparingly, besides ruthlessly ambitious concubines, are the "parents and brothers" who sell their daughters and sisters in the first place, especially those who do not work themselves.[66] (One wonders if she had her uncle in mind here.) She notes how families and concubines invoke the language of obligation to justify the practice, but she has no patience for such logic, suggesting instead that one's livelihood need not harm others.[67]

The most surprising aspect of the essay is that Sumiya puts the burden of ending concubinal relationships on concubines or potential concubines. She exhorts these women to leave men, rather than calling on

---

62.   Sumiya, "Geisha to tekake to ni susumezu," 11; Marnie Anderson, "Critiquing Concubinage." 10–11.

63.   Sumiya, "Geisha to tekake to ni susumezu," 7.

64.   Sumiya, "Geisha to tekake to ni susumezu," 13.

65.   Sumiya, "Geisha to tekake to ni susumezu," 11.

66.   Sumiya, "Geisha to tekake to ni susumezu," 5.

67.   Sumiya, "Geisha to tekake to ni susumezu," 11.

men to stop procuring concubines or for the government to halt the practice. Even the 1882 law that stripped concubines of legal standing was unconcerned with the practice itself. Rather, the government wished to revise the unequal treaties with Western nations, and abolishing customs that Westerners perceived as "backward" was a crucial component of this renegotiation of Japan's position vis-à-vis the West. In her insistence that concubines should take the initiative and leave men, Sumiya also—whether intentionally or not—justified her own behavior in leaving Nakagawa.

Concubines, writes Sumiya, should think of the greater good and not be swayed by pressure from men to stay in the household: they "should think of other women's hearts and the future of the descendants. Even if they are despised and hated and told they do not know the meaning of obligation, concubines should leave men."[68] Although a man may start to hate his former concubine, "most people [involved in the situation] will be happy." In general, Sumiya sees it as "women's job to reform men's lustfulness and uncleanliness" for men cannot control their desires. Nor does she think that wives hold much power in the situation. In light of men's lack of self-restraint and wives' general disadvantage, she concludes that the concubine must be the one to take the initiative and leave. If women—presumably meaning both concubines and wives—can manage to clean up the household, with each group shouldering a distinct task, it will result in the "happiness of the household as well as benefit to the state."[69]

Sumiya does not shy away from denouncing the practice of concubinage itself. She ends by declaring, "There is nothing in the world that causes others as much unhappiness as becoming a concubine."[70] Sumiya's essay imparts a new view on concubinage, one less burdened by notions of sin and impurity than other Meiji critiques of the practice associated with women's groups like the JWCTU.[71] In contrast to contemporary

68. Sumiya, "Geisha to tekake to ni susumezu," 10; Marnie Anderson, "Critiquing Concubinage," 11.

69. Sumiya, "Geisha to tekake to ni susumezu," 13; Marnie Anderson, "Critiquing Concubinage," 12.

70. Sumiya, "Geisha to tekake to ni susumezu," 13; Marnie Anderson, "Critiquing Concubinage," 12.

71. Lublin, *Reforming Japan*, chap. 2.

debates among government officials and intellectuals, Sumiya's comments were directed at other women. Her essay both calls upon women to reform men—whether by leaving men or "cleaning" them up—but also limits the role of proper women to wifehood. For Sumiya, wifehood is women's destiny and the only acceptable role. On one level, this is an interesting position considering her own status as an unmarried woman. Yet on another level, her perspective is not surprising given that in late Tokugawa society, into which Sumiya was born, social norms dictated that nearly everyone should marry eventually.[72] One way to interpret her essay is that she offers women of all backgrounds a path forward. In this view, even wives have a job—to reform men. Yet the essay can be read in another way—one that sees wives as essentially powerless and possessing few possibilities.[73]

One can reasonably assume that Sumiya's views expressed in this essay reflect in part lessons learned at Kobe College and the views of Japanese Christians more broadly. However, her first-hand experience makes the essay unusual. She does not mention her past directly, but her given name Koume (Little plum blossom) would have struck readers as sounding like a geisha name.

Reactions to Sumiya

Records from Japanese men in Christian circles in the 1890s show how they understood Sumiya's work, including her essay on concubinage. Editor of *Jogaku zasshi* Iwamoto Yoshiharu introduced her text to readers by mentioning her contributions to the Okayama Orphanage; he neither referenced her past experience as a geisha nor as a concubine. The purpose of the article, Iwamoto explained, was to educate readers. Many people in the anti-prostitution movement had no first-hand knowledge of geisha and concubines, so he imagined this piece would serve as an important reference. Iwamoto's introduction is worth quoting for the way he

72. Walthall, "Masturbation and Discourse," 11.
73. I thank an anonymous reader for urging me not to be overly optimistic here.

presented Sumiya as well as for what he identified as the value of the essay:

> The essay that follows is written by Sumiya Koume, the assistant to Ishii Jūji, founder of the Okayama Orphanage. In a straightforward way, she sees the truth and cuts to the heart of it. Thanks to Sumiya's proselytizing, not a few people have stopped being concubines. I have no doubt that this message does not apply to any readers of this magazine. But there are many readers who wish to urge geisha and concubines to quit. Such people are very noble-minded but do not know the situation of geisha and concubines. . . . Reading this essay will help them understand a number of things. It would be even better if they read it and talked about it [with others].[74]

In addition to Iwamoto's sympathetic introduction portraying Sumiya as Ishii's assistant, we have access to Ishii's own observations on Sumiya from an essay one year later, on an occasion when reporters for *Jogaku zasshi* visited the Orphanage. In his interview with reporters, Ishii highlighted Sumiya's central importance to the project. Indeed, he gave her far more credit than Iwamoto did. Here is how the reporter summarized Ishii's comments on Sumiya:

> Ishii says, "If one wants to accomplish something, a sympathetic friend is absolutely necessary or one will not succeed." For him [Ishii], that person is the woman of strong faith, Sumiya Koume. When he has experienced trouble on a number of occasions but stayed firm and unmoving, it is thanks to the strength of Sumiya. As Ishii declares, "The achievements of the Orphanage are not my own, they are the achievements of Sumiya."[75]

Of all the Meiji-era Japanese portrayals of Sumiya, Ishii's remains the most glowing and revealing of Sumiya's central role in running the institution. Theirs was a relationship we seldom see in the historical record, one where Sumiya as an older woman served as a mentor to Ishii and he

74. Iwamoto, "Untitled," *Jogaku zasshi* 342 (1893), 5.
75. "Sumiya Koume joshi," *Jogaku zasshi* 390 (1894), 504.

credited her as such.[76] Ishii's declaration that the "achievements of the Orphanage" were Sumiya's is not hyperbole but confirms her pivotal role at the Okayama Orphanage, a point I return to later.

Other writers attested to her important work, though they were more muted in their praise. Even James Pettee, Belle's husband, took notice of the bond between Sumiya and Ishii. Writing in 1894, Pettee explained, "They were kindred spirits of the soul. He [Ishii] named her the mother of his faith, and aimed from that time at a spirit and consecration like hers. To this day, he goes to her for counsel and sympathy in every experience."[77] Talcott likewise observed, "She has been for years a most valued adviser of Mr. Ishii in the Okayama Orphanage, the 'mother of the Asylum,' as Mr. Ishii calls her, and far and wide her name is honored as an earnest, wise, and efficient worker."[78] At the same time, they acknowledge Sumiya's labor at the Orphanage; however, Pettee and Talcott place her in a supporting role rather than identifying her as a leader in her own right.

Not everyone was supportive or enthusiastic about Sumiya. A very negative reaction to her can be found in the miscellaneous news section of the daily newspaper *Yomiuri shinbun* in 1893. The *Yomiuri*, like other Meiji newspapers, used scandal to boost circulation.[79] The article, titled "Geisha and Concubines," summarizes Sumiya's piece in *Jogaku zasshi*. The reporter critiques her efforts and suggests she had stepped out of line. He claims that by "breaking apart the inner curtain on geisha and concubines and dissecting their subjective feelings . . . she [Sumiya] relates the immoral and impure aspects of their lives."[80] Throughout, the author aims to cast doubt on Sumiya personally by exposing her past and suggesting that Sumiya has no business relating what goes on in the lives of geisha and concubines to outsiders. In contrast to other Japanese-language representations of Sumiya from this period, the author recounts her personal history: "Now she is an assistant at the Okayama Orphanage, but

76. "Sumiya Koume joshi," *Jogaku zasshi* 390 (1894), 504.

77. James Pettee, *Mr. Ishii*, 15.

78. Talcott, "The Work of Bible Women in Japan," 100.

79. Karlin, *Gender and Nation*, 30; Huffman, *Creating a Public*, 196.

80. "Geisha to tekake," *Yomiuri shinbun*, 27 August 1893, morning edition. I assume the author was male given that female reporters were rare during this period.

in her youth, she worked in that area as a popular geisha, flirting with many customers. Later she became a concubine and was bought by a wealthy family." Although he attempts to blunt the force of her critique, his reasons for doing so remain opaque. Perhaps he meant to suggest she was hypocritical given that she had worked as a geisha and a concubine. Or perhaps he thought she had no right to judge such situations. In the end, he pronounces and dismisses her work as a form of *zange*, a term that can be "translated variously as 'repentance' or 'confession'" according to Christine Marran. Although a number of writers produced *zange* around the turn of the century, the only group of women associated with the genre were ex-convicts.[81] Sumiya did not touch on her own past in her essay—and she had no criminal record—so it is remarkable that the author chose to categorize her work in this way. To be sure, Sumiya shared with *zange* writers a distinct change in direction and the term *zange* was used in Christian discourse. But her article does *not* represent a case where "the speaking subject's self-proclaimed social rehabilitation plays an essential role."[82] Whatever the author meant by *zange*, his goal was clear—to discredit Sumiya and her critique.

Significantly, the author did not object to Sumiya's ability to leave the geisha life behind—nor her work as a geisha and a concubine. Rather, the author takes issue with the fact that she had confused gender categories by exposing details about the lives of concubines which, in this author's opinion, should not be exposed. Perhaps he objected to her lifting the veil on men's privacy as well.[83]

Sumiya, the "Saintly Concubine"

Sumiya's story reached an international audience in the 1930s after she appeared in a book by Kagawa Toyohiko (1888–1960), a famous Christian pacifist, social reformer, and labor leader. Kagawa discussed Sumiya in his 1931 *Meditations on the Cross* (*Jūjika ni tsuite no meisō*), which was

81. Marran, *Poison Woman*, 66.
82. Marran, *Poison Woman*, 67. On *zange*, see *Nihon kokugo daijiten*, 6:286.
83. I thank an anonymous reader for making this point.

translated into English in 1935. Kagawa noted her reputation as the "Woman Sage of Okayama Prefecture."[84] Today, Kagawa is largely unknown outside of Japan circles, but in the 1930s, Kagawa was "a household name and one of the best-known Japanese in the Western world," according to Mark Mullins.[85] Kagawa also served as a "reverse missionary": whereas Western missionaries went abroad to the non-West, Kagawa came on a speaking tour of the United States in 1936.[86]

Kagawa had learned about Sumiya from multiple sources, though I have not seen evidence that he actually met Sumiya (she died when he was thirty-two years old). In *Meditations*, Kagawa credits Sumiya, albeit erroneously, with being "the first person to accept the faith" in Okayama.[87] He recalls reading a 1925 book titled *A Japanese* (*Ichi Nihonjin*) by Sugiyama Heisuke wherein "one of the characters is styled 'a saintly concubine.'" Such a characterization struck him as strange, for how could such a person exist, he wonders. Kagawa continues, "At first I thought the author had imagined the character, but learned later that he had merely depicted this Koume Sumiya."[88] While traveling in Okayama, Kagawa learned that many people he encountered had been influenced by Sumiya and Ishii, including the famous artist Toyotake Roshō (1874–1930), a prominent female *gidayū* performer.[89] In coming to terms with Sumiya's impact, Kagawa draws attention to "the actual practice of love" that characterized Sumiya's life and which she passed on to others: "I cannot help but ponder upon how many people Koume, the redeemed concubine, was able to bring under the influence of Christ!"[90] For Kagawa the practice of "redemptive love" meant that one went "outside of the church to live and work with those in greatest need." In these ways,

84. Kagawa, *Jūjika*, 141. In English, see Kagawa, *Meditations*, 152.

85. Mullins, "Christianity as a Transnational," 70.

86. Hollinger, *Protestants Abroad*, 74.

87. Kagawa, *Meditations*, 152.

88. Kagawa, *Meditations*, 152.

89. Kagawa, *Meditations*, 153. *Gidayū* performance features narrative recitation with shamisen accompaniment.

90. Kagawa, *Meditations*, 153; Mullins, "Christianity as a Transnational," 77. Knowledge of Sumiya continues to circulate in the West because of Kagawa's book. In his 2007 book, Hughes Old draws on Kagawa's portrayal of Sumiya and calls her a Mary Magdalene figure. Old, *The Reading and Preaching of the Scriptures*, 583.

Kagawa draws attention to her influence and high stature. At the same time, he continues to stress her status as a former concubine, impressing on readers the power of the Christian faith and its ability to lead people to new paths. The effect on the audience is mixed: one may be both impressed by her accomplishments and personal transformation and, at the same time, continue to frame her life in terms of her background as a concubine.[91] Kagawa's approach bore more resemblance to Western missionary understandings of Sumiya than other Japanese writings, which evince less concern with Sumiya's background as a geisha. His strategy no doubt appealed to those eager for confirmation that the missionary enterprise was successful.

Foreign Women Missionaries on Sumiya

Belle Pettee wrote more about Sumiya in English than any other missionary. But her writings pose challenges for the historian because she made statements that are either incorrect or unverifiable. In contrast, other women missionaries like Talcott and Gulick adopted a more factual approach and did not single out Nakagawa for censure as Pettee was wont to do.

Belle Pettee embraced Sumiya as a model convert—Pettee was the one after all who had initially hired Sumiya to teach Japanese in the early 1880s.[92] In 1897, Pettee showcased Sumiya in an article for *Life and Light for Woman*. In that essay, Pettee highlights Sumiya's past experience as a concubine—though not as a geisha—and her escape from this life, thus showcasing the redemptive power of Christianity.[93]

Pettee had two distinct ways of portraying Sumiya. One way was to paint Sumiya as lacking agency—events simply happened to her, beginning with the death of her parents when she was still young and continuing through her departure from Nakagawa's home. She remained powerless when dealing with Nakagawa and behaved passively in her dealings

91. For references to her past in Japanese sources, see Onoda, *Tsuikairoku*, 66, 80.
92. Yoshizaki, "Hōshi suru onnatachi," 108–9.
93. Belle Pettee, "Two Personalities," 395–98.

with the missionaries. Yet Belle Pettee's other method stressed the significant influence Sumiya exerted on those Japanese people around her, specifically her impact on so many of the faithful Christian converts in Okayama. Pettee also records Sumiya's influence on religious matters over Ishii Jūji, but not Sumiya's central role at the Orphanage.[94] Here Pettee portrays Sumiya as a supporter, even an advisor on occasion, but still not a leader in her own right. She was "the right hand of the missionaries, whose true friend and helper she has been for all these years."[95] These competing images—one of Sumiya as passive, the other of her as a helpful figure for the missionary cause due to her successful relationships with local people—are never reconciled and echo throughout Pettee's subsequent writings about Sumiya.[96] One possible interpretation is that Sumiya had to be understood as passive in Pettee's view because the alternative is that Sumiya wanted to be a concubine.[97] But a third image of Sumiya—more evident in Eliza Talcott's and Julia Gulick's writings than in Belle Pettee's—is that of Sumiya as an eminently capable and competent member of the community who commanded considerable authority over others. Yet even here, Eliza Talcott portrays Sumiya as less of a leader than Julia Gulick does, though this difference may be attributed to the different audiences for their work.[98] Talcott wrote for general readers, and Gulick's account—a private report to the Woman's Board—reads as a defense of the funding for Bible Women's work in Japan. It made sense for Gulick to impress upon her audience how critical Sumiya and the other Bible Women were to their mission.

One way to complicate the various missionary writings is to place them alongside Japanese-language records. Whereas Pettee focused on the ways missionaries helped Sumiya, *Tsuikairoku* provides an interesting account, one strikingly different in its insistence that Sumiya had something to teach Westerners like Pettee: "She [Sumiya] worked to make [Belle Pettee] realize the virtues of Japanese women and encouraged her

94. Belle Pettee, "Two Personalities," 395.

95. Belle Pettee, "Two Personalities," 398.

96. Belle Pettee's "Geisha Girl to Bible Woman" is undated but was written sometime after Sumiya's death in 1920.

97. Thanks to Ellen Boucher for suggesting this point to me.

98. Talcott, "The Work of Bible Women in Japan," 98.

to learn [these virtues]. . . . [Pettee] learned Japanese without an accent and made a favorable impression on upper-class Japanese women with her gentle and charming attitude."[99] Sumiya was, in this view, crucial to the success of the missions.

The records suggest another point, which is that new religions, both Japanese and foreign, gave women opportunities to move beyond more conventional gender roles even before the social reform circles of the late nineteenth century. (To be sure, social reform circles were often related to Christianity and sometimes Buddhism.) One can think of women active in such arenas even prior to the Meiji period, such as Tenrikyō founder Nakayama Miki (1798–1887) and Matsushita Chiyo (1799–1872), a woman leader in the popular religion Fujidō, as discussed by Miyazaki Fumiko.[100] These cases should be understood as a precursor to the emergence of women in reform movements in the late nineteenth century.

Evaluating Sumiya's Work

In this chapter, we have seen that although Ishii and missionaries like Talcott and Gulick highlighted Sumiya's contributions to the Okayama Orphanage, others placed Sumiya in a subordinate position, as an assistant or a maternal figure. Recent scholarship adopts this latter approach. For instance, Hosoi Isamu writes of Sumiya's relationship to the Orphanage, "Although she did not go center stage, she was a strong supporter."[101] Hamada emphasizes her reliability and the extent to which others valued her support and assistance—important qualities to be sure, but hardly those of a leader.[102] Similarly, a 2008 *San'yō shinbun* article, announcing the discovery of her grave by researchers, calls her the "hidden strength"

99.   Onoda, *Tsuikairoku*, 23. See also Talcott, "The Work of Bible Women in Japan," 102.

100.   Ambros, "Nakayama Miki's"; Miyazaki, "Networks of Believers in a New Religion." I thank an anonymous reviewer for raising this point.

101.   Hosoi, *Ishii Jūji to Okayama kojiin*, 300.

102.   For example, Hamada, *Kadota kaiwai*, 82.

behind the Orphanage, and notes that she "continuously supported founder Ishii."[103]

Sumiya herself demonstrated awareness of gendered expectations and intentionally worked around them. One *Tsuikairoku* contributor quotes a revealing text by Ishii in which he recounts the founding of the Orphanage. In response to Ishii's plea to Sumiya for assistance, he recalls that she replied, "Of course, I will be a founder [*hokkisha*] and take responsibility. However, because I am a woman, I do not wish to put my name out in public. I ask to be an anonymous founder; as your partner, I will work tirelessly."[104] Ishii himself then elaborated, "Since that time, she has truly been the life of the Orphanage, the arms and legs."[105]

Her unusual candor here is striking, and yet her strategy was not unusual. Sumiya's words remind us how women may enter realms that are formally off limits through various strategies, including the use of non-threatening language.[106] In this case, Sumiya chose not to discuss her founding role at all. Her reluctance stemmed from the early modern legacy of samurai women performing work in the interior and the idea that respectable women should not be named in public.[107] It also likely connected to Christian ideas of modesty. So much did Sumiya dislike advertising her own work that her daughter Toyo did not approve of the publication of *Tsuikairoku* two decades after Sumiya's death. Toyo informed the editor, "Mother did not like to hear talk about what she did in front of others if it made her sound self-important—she despised it, and I was scolded about it while she was alive. I want to avoid being scolded again in Heaven, so I oppose publication."[108] Nevertheless, Toyo

---

103.   "Okayama kojiin no kage no chikara," *San'yō shinbun*, 20 October 2008.

104.   The section originally comes from Ishii's *Nisshi* and was included in Mitsunobu Yoshitami's contribution to *Tsuikairoku*. Quoted in Onoda, *Tsuikairoku*, 98–99. See also Hamada, *Kadota kaiwai*, 76–77.

105.   Onoda, *Tsuikairoku*, 99.

106.   Zheng Wang, *Finding Women in the State*, 17; Marnie Anderson, *A Place in Public*, chap. 4.

107.   Walthall, "Closing Remarks," 28; Roberts, *Performing the Great Peace*. For a case where an early modern religion challenged ideas about conventional gender roles, see Miyazaki, "Networks of Believers in a New Religion."

108.   Onoda, *Tsuikairoku*, 115.

assured the publisher that she did not plan to file a lawsuit against him, and he moved forward.

Sumiya's formal silence about her work notwithstanding, other examples serve to underscore Sumiya's vital role at the Orphanage.[109] Ishii constantly experimented with new ideas and institutional innovations, and his thinking underwent several changes.[110] He traveled often, and Sumiya ran the Orphanage in his absence.[111] From 1894 on, Ishii was frequently at the Chausubaru Settlement in Miyazaki Prefecture, leaving Sumiya to run operations in Okayama.[112] In 1906, Sumiya wrote letters to donors who supported the work of the Orphanage; she asked them to purchase tickets for a music concert, the proceeds of which would fund relief efforts for orphans from Tōhoku, an area that had been struck by famine.[113] When, in 1909, a fire destroyed a building Ishii intended to use as a base for the Orphanage's work in Osaka, Sumiya assumed charge of operations.[114] All in all, Sumiya was the steady hand who kept things running in Okayama much of the time. In her public speeches—for instance, in a 1900 fundraising speech for the Orphanage, delivered in Tokyo—she highlighted Ishii's work at the Orphanage and downplayed her own, but her actions reveal her central role.[115]

Ishii's diaries and letters constitute the major source concerning Sumiya's life from 1900 until his death in 1914, leaving the last six years of her life (she died in 1920) poorly documented. Although many of his letters to her have been preserved, only two of Sumiya's letters to him remain.[116] By 1912, the Okayama Orphanage had become an administrative office,

---

109. Hosoi, *Ishii Jūji to Okayama kojiin*, 321; Onoda, *Tsuikairoku*, 50–53; Talcott, "The Work of Bible Women in Japan," 102.

110. For example, Maus, "Ishii Jūji," 203–5, 250–51.

111. Onoda, *Tsuikairoku*, 50–53.

112. Onoda, *Tsuikairoku*, 46; Hosoi, *Ishii Jūji to Okayama kojiin*, 320.

113. Yoshizaki, "Hōshi suru onnatachi," 113–14; Okayama danjo kyōdō sankaku suishin sentā, *Jidai o hiraita Okayama no joseitachi*, 16.

114. Maus, "Ishii Jūji," 228, 232; Yoshizaki, "Hōshi suru onnatachi," 113–14.

115. For the speech, see Onoda, *Tsuikairoku*, 26–46.

116. Hosoi, *Ishii Jūji to Okayama kojiin*, 299. This book includes some of the 140 extant letters that Ishii wrote to Sumiya. *Tsuikairoku* contains five letters written by Sumiya, including two addressed to Ishii. The second letter is not listed in the table of contents but appears at the end. Onoda, *Tsuikairoku*, 111–13.

though it did not close until 1926, and most of the institution was trans-
ferred to Miyazaki Prefecture.[117] Sumiya headed up the Okayama office,
as Ishii's letters addressed to her make clear. At the same time, the networks she participated in during the 1880s and 1890s continued to occupy her, most notably those surrounding the Okayama Church. There,
she led a group for elderly women, helping sooth tensions between
mothers-in-law and daughters-in-law. She also taught at the Kyokutō Sunday School. Former Sunday school pupils, most from non-Christian
families, remembered her strict but loving instruction.[118] One former student credited the memory of her love with saving his life.[119] In spite of
her chronic asthma, which made her appear weak, her spirit proved in-
domitable. After Talcott died in 1911, Sumiya raised money for a memorial fund in Talcott's honor at Kobe College and Kobe Women's Bible
Training School. In the wake of Ishii's death in 1914, Sumiya stepped up
her efforts as a traveling evangelist.[120]

Fellow parishioner Kajiro Yoshi recalled that Sumiya attended most
church-related social events, including graduations and literary salons.
Sumiya also organized moon-viewing parties at the Pettees' home.[121]
A well-known photograph of Sumiya with businessman and Orphanage
supporter and financial backer Ōhara Magosaburō (1880–1943) and several others on the occasion of Ishii's daughter's wedding in 1913 attests to
her continuing involvement in these circles.[122] As before, Sumiya resided
in Okayama, though she traveled to Chausubaru in Miyazaki Prefecture
to visit Ishii on his deathbed.[123] His final letter—which reads like a last
will and testament—urged her to consult with Ōhara about the Okayama
Orphanage when necessary.[124] After Ishii's death, Ōhara assumed the

117.   Maus, "Ishii Jūji," 238.
118.   Onoda, *Tsuikairoku*, 84.
119.   Onoda, *Tsuikairoku*, 89–90.
120.   Okayama danjo kyōdō sankaku suishin sentā, *Jidai o hiraita Okayama no joseitachi*, 16.
121.   Onoda, *Tsuikairoku*, 71.
122.   The photo belongs to the Ishii kinen yūaisha and can be found, captioned
"Chōjo Tomo no kekkon," on the organization's website: http://www.yuuaisya.jp
/jyuuji, accessed 8 October 2019.
123.   Yoshizaki, "Hōshi suru onnatachi," 113–14.
124.   Hosoi, *Ishii Jūji to Okayama kojiin*, 318. For the letter, see Onoda, *Tsuikairoku*,
53–56.

formal directorship of the institution. That said, the letter imparts a different perspective on the leadership issue, implying that Ōhara shared responsibility with Sumiya. Ōhara, it should be noted, decided to close the Orphanage permanently in 1926.

Sumiya died in 1920 at the age of sixty-nine. Pallbearers typically hailed from the lower classes. But Sumiya's casket, Belle Pettee noted, was "voluntarily carried out by men prominent in church and city life, the last tribute they could pay to the wonderful Christian woman who had led many of them to the Light of the World."[125] In her death as in her life, Sumiya brought people together in new ways.

Conclusion

Sumiya's journey was a long one—from geisha to concubine, to social activist, evangelist, and leader at the Orphanage. Her position of authority outside a family business or household marks her as unusual, especially as an unmarried woman.

By the time the Okayama Orphanage opened its doors in 1887, Sumiya was thirty-seven years old. We have already seen that she was a central figure at the institution. Her status as an unmarried older woman gave her more freedom since she did not have to run a household for a typical family. Moreover, her role at a Christian institution imparted a status and respectability within her community that she may otherwise not have had given her unmarried state. Her standing in these roles, however, was certainly not for everyone, as seen in the scathing critique by the *Yomiuri* author.[126]

I have suggested that the extant records by Ishii and by the missionaries, especially Talcott and Gulick, indicate that Sumiya was respected within her community during her lifetime and that she was considered a leader at the Orphanage. Later portrayals of her from the 1940s in *Tsuikairoku* support this view. Former Okayama Church pastor Abe Isoo remembered Sumiya in his 1932 biography, along with Nakagawa Yuki

125.   Belle Pettee, "Geisha Girl to Bible Woman," 8.
126.   On age as a crucial variable, see Walthall, "The Life Cycle of Farm Women," 66.

and Ōnishi Kinu (Nakagawa's wife and cousin, respectively), as pillars of the Church.[127]

The records reveal Sumiya to have been a consummate networker, activist, and leader who thrived in the novel spaces opened up by the new institutions of the Church, the Orphanage, and the Okayama Mission Station that employed her as a Bible Women. She played an integral role in local heterosocial networks. And yet because of her gender and social position, she did not have access to the wide range of contacts that Nakagawa did—nor could she venture into the world of men in the way he made forays into the world of women. As we saw, he founded a women's association and brought fish to San'yō gakuen. Her sphere was necessarily more circumscribed.

How else can we understand Sumiya's trajectory? A number of factors converged in enabling her activity, including the upheaval of the Restoration, Sumiya's age, the strong networks in which she participated, and the respectability and status imparted by Christianity. Her activism occurred largely before modern gender ideals took hold, particularly that of the "good wife and wise mother." Sumiya may have been a wise mother, but she was never a wife, though she came to see wifehood as the natural role of women, reflecting both Christian influence and modern Japan's gender system. Like the other single women I discuss in chapter 4, she managed to live as a self-supporting single woman with a career.

Sumiya's household continued because her uncle's family adopted a son-in-law, Aoki (formerly Sakasai) Yōkichi (1867–1938), for her daughter Toyo to marry in 1887. At the time, Yōkichi was at student at Doshisha University. Before the two wed in 1895, he attended Yale and Columbia while Toyo was a student at Kobe College.[128] Later, Yōkichi served as the principal of San'yō gakuen from 1905 to 1906 and also worked as an entrepreneur. Together, the couple had five sons and one daughter. Their lone daughter Aiko held a position at San'yō gakuen and later converted to Catholicism, becoming a nun and joining a convent.[129] One notes the parallels of Aiko's life with her grandmother Sumiya; perhaps Aiko also

127. Abe, *Shakai shugisha*, 142. See also Onoda, *Tsuikairoku*.
128. San'yō shinbunsha, *Okayama-ken rekishi jinbutsu jiten*, 2–3; Matsumura, "Ōnishi Sōzan," 76; San'yō gakuen, *Ai to hōshi*, 24. It is not clear when Sumiya's uncle died.
129. Matsumura, "Ōnishi Sōzan," 76–77.

relished the opportunities afforded by single status, secure in the respectability imparted by religion.

To return to the question of leadership roles for women, we have seen that what was possible for Sumiya goes beyond what many scholarly texts suggest she did. A woman could exercise a leadership role so long as she did not draw attention to it—in speeches, for example—and remained content with obscurity in written sources. Sumiya had multiple accomplishments, small and large. She was hardly alone: other women and men performed important and often overlooked roles at the Orphanage and the Church. For Sumiya, the small roles are documented. The large leadership roles are more elusive in the records. To bring them to light, we have to expand our source base and locate sympathetic portrayals, as I have done with records from Ishii, Talcott, and Gulick. That we have lost sight of the range of Sumiya's roles speaks to the power of gender stereotypes that define women as subordinate to men—and in assisting rather than leading roles. Sumiya herself contributed to the tendency to adopt this view, shaped as she was by her background. Thinking about Sumiya reminds us of the indispensable role of women within heterosocial networks.

Overall, Sumiya's story calls to mind the discussions in Bonnie Smith's *The Gender of History*, a book that explores the transformation of the discipline of history in the West from an art to a science in the nineteenth century. In the process, history became a masculine domain. The consequences for women were multiple. Smith points out that much of the scholarship of nineteenth-century historians was conducted by "author teams" of husbands and wives. She supplies the memorable example of Jules Michelet (1798–1874) and his wife Anthenais Michelet (1826–1899), who conducted research, wrote, and edited work "that was published under his name."[130] After her death, Anthenais's critical role was forgotten or was the subject of derision. We can observe a similar dynamic at work with Ishii and Sumiya, though of course they were not a married couple. Even though Ishii acknowledged Sumiya's work, most of the people writing about the Okayama Orphanage, both then and now, have either overlooked her or portrayed her in a supporting role. To be sure, running an orphanage and writing professional history remain different

130. Smith, *The Gender of History*, 87.

endeavors. Yet in neither case can we take what many records say about women's roles uncritically.

How then to sum up the kinds of roles Sumiya played in reform networks in the nineteenth century? Far beyond the limited view in most historical accounts, she played a significant role in the Okayama Church, in the wider Christian community, and especially at the Okayama Orphanage. Although she may have been an exceptional woman, her case illustrates that more was possible for women than has been thought. Men and women were interdependent after all—to focus on one group without considering the other leads to an incomplete understanding. By exploring different sources, we can begin to see a clearer picture of women like Sumiya who are peripheral to traditional accounts. Yet the fact remains that the full extent of women's activities may well be impossible to document given the partial nature of the historical record.

CHAPTER 3

The Okayama Women's Friendship Society and Women's Political Life

In 1882, Murasame Nobu (n.d.), a woman from Aichi Prefecture, sent a letter to Itagaki Taisuke, the leader of the Liberal Party, and included five yen from her home business (*naishoku*) making fireworks to support the party. Murasame would go on to become one of the founding members of a local women's organization, the Toyohashi Women's Cooperative Association (Toyohashi fujo kyōkai). She later met several famous male activists and was arrested for her involvement, along with her husband, in the 1884 Iida Incident, a failed uprising against the government loosely linked to the Freedom and People's Rights Movement. Eventually, the authorities released her given a lack of evidence.[1] Five years later, she wrote a preface for the activist Ueki Emori's 1889 *Women of the East* (*Tōyō no fujo*), revealing her commitment to raising women's status and her high level of education and knowledge of history.[2] In particular, she invoked several female figures from centuries of the Japanese past, including an empress, a warrior, and several authors. She called on women to make a new society:

> Become self-respecting, even if you are not a standout like Empress Jingū [Jingū Kōgō] or brave like Tomoe Gozen, or like Ono no Komachi or Lady

1. Sotozaki, *Ueki Emori to onnatachi*, 92–93.
2. Murasame's preface can be found in *Ueki Emori shū*, 208–10. The complete text of *Tōyō no fujo* is included in *Ueki Emori shū*, 219–90.

Murasaki [Murasaki Shikibu] or Sei Shōnagon.[3] Even if you do not con-quer Korea, or take your enemy's head, or pen poetry about love, or write the *Tale of Genji* or the *Pillow Book*. Polish your womanly virtues [*shuku-toku o migaku*]. Study modesty, be chaste and faithful, believe in the gods, observe the teachings, become flowers of society, make peace, eliminate the terrible old custom of "honoring men and despising women" [*danson johi*], make a new, beautiful, equal, free society. This is the obligation you women must carry out today.[4]

Murasame's story surprises readers who are accustomed to thinking of women's political involvement as a twentieth-century tale focused on the quest for suffrage.[5] It draws attention to an earlier moment when women struggled to define a political role, a place in public. This chapter examines women like Murasame who formed local women's groups in the 1880s. The Meiji period saw the rapid rise of women's associations in Okayama and around the country, coinciding with the Freedom and People's Rights Movement.[6]

This chapter introduces the OWFS, likely the first political organ-ization for women in Japan. The OWFS was active between 1882 to 1884. Unlike the previous two chapters, I focus here on an organization as my unit of analysis. In a book about networks and associational activities, this examination of a larger group offers new perspectives on a network in operation. The story of the OWFS illuminates the initial opening up and eventual narrowing of political life for women in the late nineteenth century. By comparing OWFS documents with those of the all-male San'yō Liberal Party, I demonstrate how much men's and women's groups

3.   Empress Jingū was Japan's legendary first empress. Tomoe Gozen was a medi-eval warrior. The next three women listed were all authors of the works listed in the following sentence: Ono no Komachi wrote love poetry, Lady Murasaki wrote the *Tale of Genji* (*Genji monogatari*), and Sei Shōnagon, the *Pillow Book* (*Makura no sōshi*).

4.   *Ueki Emori shū*, 209.

5.   Women activists in Japan struggled to win the vote in the 1920s and 1930s but did not gain suffrage rights until 1946. Recent scholarship has shown the ways women were active before they got the vote: Lublin, *Reforming Japan*; Marnie Anderson, *A Place in Public*; Patessio, *Women and Public Life*.

6.   Yoshizaki, "Nakamura Shizu," 8–10.

had in common as well as where they were distinct. After the society's demise in 1884, former members continued to act in public, working for causes including temperance, monogamy, and women's education, suggesting that the OWFS was a proving ground for the activism that women took up in the following decades.

Thanks to the relatively robust documentary record and the attention of grassroots historians, we know a good deal about the OWFS. Other groups existed too. The Toyohashi Women's Cooperative Association, to which Murasame Nobu belonged, was based in Aichi Prefecture, and a third group, the Aikō Women's Association (Aikō fujinkai), hailed from Kanagawa Prefecture.[7] But less documentation is available for these other associations. One challenge this subject presents is that most of the records are newspaper articles. Rather than transcripts of what women said or wrote, we have records of what male journalists record them saying and doing. As such, these records feature an extra layer of interpretation.

Scholars have tended to understand women activists either as assistants to men or as "independent."[8] I challenge this binary and suggest that women's activism constituted a range of possibilities. Indeed, women may have begun by assisting men and then moved to a more active role. Moreover, I contend that activism was often a family affair because women were first exposed to politics at home by male relatives. Still, activism was never gender-neutral—gender roles informed what people could do and how, even before the Associations and Political Meetings Law (Shūkai oyobi seisha hō) of 1890 circumscribed women's formal political lives.

Histories of Activism

Men's involvement in the Freedom and People's Rights Movement has long been the subject of scholarly inquiry—particularly the activities of wealthy farmers who formed organizations, read Western political theory, and drew up constitutions during the heady period of the late 1870s and

7. Marnie Anderson, "Women's Agency and the Historical Record," 43–44.
8. Suzuki Yūko, "Kaisetsu," 23.

early 1880s.[9] In contrast, studies of women's activism have been limited largely to examinations of the few women who went on to become famous at the national level, such as the speaker Kishida (later Nakajima) Toshiko (1861–1901).[10] Scholars usually mention the widow and household head Kusunose Kita (1836–1920) who sent a petition to local authorities in 1878 asking why she must pay taxes when she did not have the right to vote.[11] Ōki Motoko's work demonstrates that Kishida and Kusunose were merely the tip of the iceberg. Across the archipelago, women were active—giving speeches, forming groups, and attending meetings.[12]

Women's activism predates the Meiji period. Anne Walthall has highlighted the role of women in late Tokugawa-era rice riots.[13] In the years leading up to the Meiji Restoration, female peasants joined in uprisings, and some women fought alongside men in the Restoration wars in the Aizu domain.[14] Loyalist women such as Matsuo Taseko (1811–1894) and Kurosawa Tokiko (1806–1890) worked alongside men in order to achieve their goal—restoring the emperor to what they saw as his rightful place at the center of the polity.[15] But such actions were part of larger, male-led movements, and the parameters of women's activities were circumscribed by variables including gender, status, age, and region. The situation changed with the advent of the Meiji period, when most examples of female activism occurred within the context of women-only organizations.

What, then, does the story of the OWFS reveal about the shifting opportunities for Meiji women's participation and the form that that participation took? Even though the association's actual history lasted two years, the broad range of causes members embraced and the networks they formed allowed the women to continue to act after 1884 when the group

9.   There is an impressive body of literature on men's activities: Irokawa, *The Culture of the Meiji Period*; Kim, *The Age of Visions and Arguments*. More recently, see Matsuzawa, *Jiyū minken undō*; Inada, *Jiyū minken no keifu*. On women, see Sievers, *Flowers in Salt*; Ōki, *Jiyū minken undō to josei*.

10.   On Kishida, see Marnie Anderson, *A Place in Public*, chap. 3; Mamiko Suzuki, *Gendered Power*, chap. 2.

11.   Marnie Anderson, "Women's Agency and the Historical Record."

12.   Ōki, *Jiyū minken undō to josei*.

13.   Walthall, "Devoted Wives/Unruly Women."

14.   Wright, "Female Combatants"; Nenzi, *The Chaos and Cosmos*.

15.   Walthall, *The Weak Body of a Useless Woman*, 357n34; Nenzi, *The Chaos and Cosmos*.

ceased to meet. Many engaged in activism even after 1890 when overtly political activism was blocked by means of the Associations and Political Meetings Law.[16]

The Okayama Women's Friendship Society

The OWFS began meeting when the famous female speaker Kishida Toshiko came to Okayama in 1882, the same year Murasame wrote her letter to Itagaki. Kishida, who held elite credentials as a former tutor to the Meiji empress had already established a presence on the national stage. She was known for her impeccable style—both verbal and sartorial. Her visit both inspired the Okayama women and motivated them to move forward. At the same time, the group received ample media attention due to Kishida's prominence on the national stage.

The society focused on discussing political ideas and promoting education as well as other forms of social improvement. Thirty women attended the first meeting, and at least six others joined later, possibly more.[17] Information about many of the members is limited, but we have details on twelve of them, including Sumiya Koume (chapter 2).[18] Like many late nineteenth-century women's groups around the world, the members did not discuss suffrage. At a time when most men did not have the vote, women activists focused on expanding their access to public space and their right to political knowledge.

In her 1904 autobiography, the activist Fukuda Hideko reflected on the formation of the OWFS:

> We were the first in Japan to organize such a club. We invited speakers and champions of natural rights, freedom, and equality to come and speak to us. Our aim was to work for the abolition of backward customs from the

16. Article 4 of the law barred women from attending political meetings (*seidan shūkai ni kaidō suru*), although the law contained two other articles that specifically denied political rights to women (Articles 3 and 25).

17. Okayama joseishi kenkyūkai, *Kindai Okayama no onnatachi*, 26–28; Okayama joseishi kenkyūkai, "Okayama joshi konshinkai ni tsuite," 6.

18. Okayama joseishi kenkyūkai, *Kindai Okayama no onnatachi*, 26–28.

past, which had kept women in a state of oppression. The times were pro-
pitious, and applications for membership kept pouring in and our organization continued to flourish.[19]

Members of the Okayama organization ranged in age from their late
teens to early fifties and included women who were highly skilled in
Chinese-style discourse (*kanbun*). Some were wives or sisters of People's
Rights activists, indicating the extent to which underlying social networks
were heterosocial. Like their male counterparts, they were from former
samurai and wealthy commoner families.[20]

Although Kishida Toshiko plays a leading role in most accounts of
the OWFS, closer examination reveals a more complex chronology, featuring the initiative of two local women in their forties and fifties:
Takeuchi Hisa (1830–?), age fifty-three, and Tsuge Kume (1835–1916),
age forty-eight, both former samurai.[21] The women were likely introduced to People's Rights activities through their male relatives, since
Tsuge's husband Masagorō (n.d.) was an activist.[22] Takeuchi's son Masashi (1854–1920) belonged to the Liberal Party; he was also a journalist
and politician. According to reports in a newspaper affiliated with the
People's Rights Movement, the two women had long believed that
"even women can have political thought and work for the nation." For
years, they had worked "to gain the momentum to form a women's
group."[23] In the spring of 1882, they traveled to Osaka to visit Liberal
Party leader Itagaki Taisuke after he had been stabbed by a political op-
ponent. This visit was an unusual step for two women who did not know
Itagaki personally. Shortly thereafter, they visited Kishida and her mother,

19.   For the original, see Fukuda, *Warawa no hanseigai*, 16–17. I follow Ōki in rendering the title as "hanseigai" rather than the more common "hanshōgai." For a translation, see Hane, *Reflections on the Way*, 37. I follow Hane's translation here.
20.   Okayama joseishi kenkyūkai, *Kindai Okayama no onnatachi*, 25–29.
21.   For example, see Sievers, *Flowers in Salt*, 36; Patessio, *Women and Public Life*,
151; *Nihon rikken seitō shinbun*, 9 May 1882, in *Okayama minken undōshi*, 30. For a consideration of Kishida's other speeches, see Sugano, "Kishida Toshiko," 174.
22.   Masagorō was also an adopted son-in-law whose activism was inspired by the
minken novelist Sakurada Momoe (1859–1883). San'yō shinbunsha, *Okayama-ken rekishi jinbutsu jiten*, 641.
23.   *Nihon rikken seitō shinbun*, 6 May 1882, in *Okayama minken undōshi*, 30.

who were in Osaka at the time, and invited the mother-daughter pair to visit Okayama.

Takeuchi and Tsuge thus played an active role in arranging Kishida's visit to Okayama at a time when the "spirits of Okayama women were motivated."[24] The newspaper's description of these women's activities—the reporter referred to them as "educated and elegant women" (*keishū kunsai no mi*)—includes no hint that they were in any way stepping out of place.[25] The reporter implied that women's political engagement and initiative in the form of visiting a bedridden politician, nurturing political thought, and forming a local society were appropriate and admirable.[26] To be sure, the paper was affiliated with People's Rights politics and more sympathetic to female activists than the conservative, pro-government publications of the era. However, male People's Rights activists generally did not encourage female participation, with notable exceptions such as Ueki Emori, making the press's avowal of support for the women all the more remarkable.[27]

MEETINGS: SPEECHES, GOALS, AND
REFRAMING THE PAST

The OWFS's first meeting took place on 11 May 1882, and contemporary newspaper accounts allow us to reconstruct the event. Participants met at one member's house in central Ishizeki-machi in Okayama; the meeting commenced at 7 p.m. and lasted over five hours, concluding soon after midnight. The reporter outlined the background, revealing in the process his assumptions about feminine behavior and interests: "The meeting was intended to be carried out in a graceful and ladylike way. But rather than discussing haircuts or the luster of various cosmetics, members took up politics and world affairs in a refined manner."[28] Takeuchi

24.   *Nihon rikken seitō shinbun*, 16 May 1882, in *Okayama minken undōshi*, 30–31.

25.   *Nihon rikken seitō shinbun*, 6 May 1882, in *Okayama minken undōshi*, 30. On the term "keishū," see Copeland, *Lost Leaves*, 37.

26.   This point was inspired by my reading of Ginzberg, *Untidy Origins*, 158–59.

27.   Ōki, *Jiyū minken undō to josei*, 44–64; Yoneda, "Jiyū minken to fujin mondai," 80–88.

28.   The account here is based on *Nihon rikken seitō shinbun*, 16 May 1882, in *Okayama minken undōshi*, 30–31.

began by announcing that Kishida had come to speak. Takeuchi then explained, "In the past, Eastern women have been oppressed by men and became accustomed to this situation. As a result, women do not understand anything about politics. It is time to abolish this practice, but to nurture [political] thought and eliminate this custom is no easy matter."[29] Although some early modern women did know about politics given their close association to men within households and their contacts with visitors, what makes Takeuchi's point unusual is her explicit call for the intentional cultivation of women's political consciousness.[30]

Takeuchi's cofounder Tsuge followed up by commenting on how "in our country, men have been free to serve [the country], but in the same way, women should be able to work together with men to assist [the national cause]." She invoked unnamed brave and courageous women in the national past—likely empresses, warriors, and writers, as Murasame had in her preface for *Women of the East*—in order to legitimize an active role for women in the present day. Kishida followed the two organizers with a speech, although nothing is recorded of that address. Based on other speeches she delivered, we can assume that Kishida included claims for women's right to possess political knowledge and act in the national interest.

Not surprisingly, Kishida's speech marked the highlight of the event. Together with her other appearances in Okayama, Kishida's oratory attracted publicity for the OWFS's cause and motivated members to meet every month. Fukuda Hideko later recalled, "I was beside myself with excitement when I heard her [Kishida] speak so eloquently on the principle of women's rights."[31] However, Fukuda did not attend the first meeting of the OWFS and thus could not have heard Kishida's speech there. Her account is probably based on attendance at one or both of the other

29. *Nihon rikken seitō shinbun*, 16 May 1882, in *Okayama minken undōshi*, 30–31. The concept of "Eastern women" was common in Meiji-era discourse, for example, in Ueki Emori's *Women of the East*.

30. For examples of early modern women who knew about politics, see Walthall, "The Creation of Female Networks in Exile."

31. Fukuda, *Warawa no hanseigai*, 16–17. For a translation, Hane, *Reflections on the Way*, 36. For a description of Kishida's other speeches in Okayama, see *San'yō shinpō*, 16 May 1882, in *Nihon josei undō*, 57.

occasions where Kishida spoke publicly in Okayama, alongside a lineup of male activists on 13 May and 14 May 1882.[32]

The newspaper concluded its description of the first meeting by proclaiming that for women to gather together shows that "women can be applauded as the progressive light of the East."[33] Again, the reporter does not imply that the women were behaving in a way that challenged gender norms. He may have viewed the women's activism with an element of polite condescension. Still, the article casts women's actions in a positive light.

The second OWFS meeting took place less than two weeks later, on 23 May, and featured speeches as well as the public reading of a letter that had been drafted to thank Kishida for her visit to Okayama. Uemori Misao (1858–?), who had not spoken at the previous gathering but played a central role as the group's secretary-general, delivered a lecture on the ancient past in Japan, a time when "women had been respected." Her emphasis echoed Tsuge's speech at the previous meeting. Perhaps Uemori took inspiration from contemporary British women activists, who saw the ancient past as a time of equality for women. Some Meiji men also evinced this understanding. Takeuchi Hisa followed up with a speech comparing the organization to snow. Although snow does not typically seem to be a powerful force when it falls from the sky, a large ball of snow could "knock over a fortress."[34] She discussed the need for the women to come together to form a great ball of snow and spread throughout the country.

The next speaker, Tsuge Kume, invoked the words of the Meiji emperor and government to make her case: the Charter Oath of 1868, which declared that "matters will be decided based on public discussion" and

32.   Hane's translation of Fukuda's text about Kishida's visit contains an error: "[Kishida] stayed at our house for three days and delivered public lectures." See Hane, *Reflections on the Way*, 36. There is nothing in the original text about staying at Fukuda's house; it simply mentions that Kishida stayed in Okayama for three days. For the original, see *Fukuda Hideko shū*, 16.

33.   *Nihon rikken seitō shinbun*, 16 May 1882, in *Okayama minken undōshi*, 30–31.

34.   This account comes from the *Asahi shinbun*, 31 May 1882, in *Okayama minken undōshi*, 31–32. For an instance where Meiji men drew on similar discourses, see Marnie Anderson, *A Place in Public*, 45. Chinese women adopted a similar strategy: Edwards, *Gender, Politics, and Democracy*, 36.

the government's 1875 promise to establish a constitutional government although without a firm time commitment. Having set up the context for her claim, Tsuge then demanded that women be granted the right to act in the national interest. This principle of women serving the country was based on the "just laws of the polity" (*tenka no kōdō*), she stated, paraphrasing the Oath and offering an interpretation that explicitly included women.[35] In short, women had "no reason to leave it up to men." Although it was men who had been working for the country thus far, she declared, there was nothing to prevent women from serving the country too, for such acts were "not prohibited." More generally, women activists in the 1880s and 1890s invoked the Oath, showing its appeal beyond its original narrow audience in 1868 when the emperor announced it to the "gods of Heaven and Earth" and the daimyo lords.[36] This episode also illuminates the power of nondominant groups to take up language and use it as an "authorizing discourse," even though they were not the intended recipients.[37]

When the speeches finished, the members agreed to draft a set of guidelines (*kiyaku*) before the meeting ended. The newspaper concluded its description of the second meeting by declaring, "In our country with so much weakness and powerlessness, men can look at these lively women and have nothing of which to be ashamed."[38] Women's dedication to the nation deserved admiration and support, a sentiment reflecting the widespread nineteenth-century notion that women's status served as a barometer of modern civilization. Far from challenging women's involvement in the public arena, the journalist welcomed it.

Overall, the speeches drew the attention of their audiences to women's right to play an active role and the power women possess when they band together.[39] They served to motivate women and to justify a more capacious

35.   Tsuge used slightly different language from the Charter Oath here. The original phrasing is "tenchi no kōdō," or "just laws of nature." This account comes from *Asahi shinbun*, 31 May 1882.

36.   On the oath, see Walthall and Steele, *Politics and Society*, 142. On women invoking the oath, see Marnie Anderson, *A Place in Public*, 162n51, 193n127.

37.   I am indebted to Joan Judge's work for this formulation. Judge, "Talent, Virtue, and the Nation," 765.

38.   *Asahi shinbun*, 31 May 1882, in *Okayama minken undōshi*, 31–32.

39.   Okayama joseishi kenkyūkai, *Kindai Okayama no onnatachi*, 28.

role for them. The women who delivered these addresses were engaged with current political issues, as the records attest. Yet insofar as we know, the speakers did not directly comment on women's contemporary legal status; the blunt language of oppression that Fukuda employed in her autobiography some twenty years later makes no appearance here in 1882. Speakers aimed to justify their cause by appealing both to examples of illustrious women in the past and to the logic of historical progress—that history moves inexorably forward in a progressive direction. When examined together, these two rhetorics—one focused on the past and the other on the future—did not fit together easily. Yet contemporaries felt no qualms about using both concepts simultaneously, and both could be effective in securing an expanded role for women. The OWFS meetings were not the only context in which women addressed audiences to advocate for their rights. They also spoke at "lecture meetings" for women.[40] One such event in November 1882 attracted an audience of around four hundred people suggesting that the OWFS reached a sizable group of people beyond its core membership.[41] These meetings additionally demonstrate that women activists engaged in many of the same activities male activists did, albeit on a smaller scale.

DRAFTING GUIDELINES

The reader will recall that at the end of the OWFS's second meeting, members agreed to draft a set of membership guidelines. Nearly all Meiji-era groups, whether for men or women, adopted guidelines or statutes.[42] These texts, which emphasize service to the nation, shed light on how the women understood their political identities.[43] Although "political identities" is not a concept that would have been familiar to them, I find it helpful as a tool to illuminate consciousness, especially since women navigated the political realm differently from men.

The drafting committee generated the guidelines over the summer of 1882, and the text appeared in newspapers in August of that year. The group's guidelines invoke the Charter Oath immediately: "Based on the

40. For newspaper articles covering these speeches, see *Fukuda Hideko shū*, 493.
41. *Okayama minken undōshi*, 56.
42. For other women's groups, see *Nihon josei undō*, 72–73.
43. See Ginzberg, *Untidy Origins*, 5–6.

just laws of nature [*tenchi no kōdō*], we will preserve women's chastity, expunge old customs, and clarify the principles of children's education."[44] Article 10 calls for accountability, warning that members who fail to follow the guidelines or who commit "shameless and indecent behavior" (*harenchi waisetsu*) will have their names expunged from the society's roster. But the emphasis on chastity and appropriate behavior—which may have quelled the fears of men and affirmed the group's respectability—did not figure prominently in the society's mission.

The document's references to the 1868 Charter Oath, which Tsuge had already referred to at the second meeting—"to follow the just laws of nature"—attest to the members' knowledge of important official documents. These references also suggest how members attempted to position their goals within the context of a new direction for the country. Eight of the eleven articles dwell on procedural matters for membership, elections, and payment of dues. Meetings were to be held twice a month, on the tenth and the twentieth, and last for three hours, from 7 p.m. to 10 p.m. With the exception of references to chastity, the text does not highlight gender differences between men and women, unlike the other extant documents by women's groups from Aichi and Kanagawa.[45] Perhaps this was because the OWFS guidelines were the first to be written by women and borrowed from male models; alternately, members may have felt no need to be specific about their conduct because they took status-specific gender norms for granted.

The Okayama guidelines diverge from the texts generated by the Aichi and Kanagawa women's groups in still other ways. For example, the OWFS text uses more Chinese compound words, a written form increasingly associated with masculinity during the Meiji era—but hardly surprising given that the three authors all had training in Chinese.[46] In contrast, subsequent documents by the women's groups in Aichi and Kanagawa are shorter and do not focus on procedures: they highlight

44. The Okayama guidelines can be found in *Nihon rikken seitō shinbun*, 1 August 1883, in *Nihon josei undō*, 71. Also, *Okayama minken undōshi*, 32–33.

45. *Nihon josei undō*, 72–74.

46. *Nihon josei undō*, 72–74. On the style of the guidelines, see Okayama joseishi kenkyūkai, "Okayama joshi konshinkai ni tsuite," 9–10. On Meiji-era Chinese prose (*kanbun*), see Mamiko Suzuki, *Gendered Power*, 42–47.

women's specific duties in each article and use a more feminine Japanese prose style. The Aichi and Kanagawa groups constructed their roles primarily as wives and mothers. For instance, the Aichi guidelines—on which the Kanagawa document appears to have been based—open by vowing, "We will protect our chastity and devote all of our energies to the country." Subsequent articles include calls to "instill the path of learning and seek knowledge widely" and to "console husbands" and raise "superior sons and modest daughters who will become the pillars of the country."[47] Similarly, the Kanagawa document stresses education and emphasizes the necessity of attending men's speeches and societies "as a shortcut to becoming educated."[48] Even though associational life was divided by sex, certain gathering spaces were not. Susan Mann has pointed out that in late imperial China, sex segregation "was more of a platitude than a reality in the lives of most women."[49] In Meiji Japan as well, gendered spheres were not airtight.

To be sure, all three extant guidelines by women's groups stress femininity, albeit less consistently in the OWFS case. The crucial difference is that the Aichi and Kanagawa groups positioned themselves as wives and mothers, whereas the Okayama group focused on the specific goals members hoped to achieve *as women*. The Okayama women tied their goals directly to the national interest. A Kōchi-based newspaper found the Okayama women so inspiring that it reprinted an account of their work in order to encourage local activism. Kōchi, often considered the "birthplace" of People's Rights politics, had comparatively few active women in the movement.[50]

Importantly, the embrace of a feminine role does not mean the women lacked agency. Rather, this way of carving out a space in public as women was effective and consistent with how later female activists in Japan and elsewhere secured a public role for themselves.[51] None of the women's groups expressed explicitly political goals such as acquiring the vote, working to enact a constitution, or demanding the right to stand for office.

47. *Nihon josei undō*, 72–73.
48. *Nihon josei undō*, 74.
49. Mann, *Gender and Sexuality in Chinese History*, 38.
50. Ōki, *Jiyū minken undō to josei*, 45.
51. For an earlier example, see Kelley, *Learning to Stand and Speak*, 277.

Guidelines for Men

How did the Okayama men position themselves by comparison? One way to answer this question is to review the guidelines for the all-male San'yō Liberal Party, the local chapter of the Liberal Party formed in 1881. To be sure, the men's group was a much larger regional association than the OWFS and had hundreds of members, rather than the approximately three dozen members of the OWFS.

The authors of the San'yō Liberal Party guidelines embraced concrete political goals such as the enactment of a constitution rather than the mere promise of one. They were devoted to "reforming politics and building a strong constitutional government."[52] The document stresses the importance of speech meetings and debates to carry out these goals. The list of articles, a total of thirteen, is slightly longer than the OWFS's text. The San'yō Liberal Party guidelines clarified the relationship between the regional branch and local branches of the party and proposed that the group sponsor speeches and debate meetings at regular intervals.[53]

The major difference between the San'yō Liberal Party and OWFS comes down to the fact that the men style themselves explicitly as a political party and the women as an association. At the same time, the men do not mention chastity, which of course was expected of elite women but not men. Finally, one must mention once again the difference in scale. The San'yō Liberal Party was much larger than the OWFS. This fact reflects the patriarchal political culture of the day and suggests that men had an easier time building networks.

There are, however, similarities in the aims of both groups: both were convinced of the need for social and political reform. Both discussed politics and sponsored speech meetings. Both cast their work in the national interest and aspired to broad goals—"human happiness" in the case of the San'yō Liberal Party men and making real the promise of the Charter Oath for the OWFS women. In short, gender differences mattered but not always.

52. *San'yō shinpō*, 30 September 1881, in *Okayama-ken shi*, 10:173–75.
53. *San'yō shinpō*, 30 September 1881, in *Okayama-ken shi*, 10:173–75.

Activities: Founding a School

The OWFS members prioritized girls' education. This interest demonstrates continuity with the Tokugawa period, when some women taught and ran schools. Once the Meiji era arrived, the language of enlightenment opened a space for more schools, many of which were dedicated to education for girls. A major activity for OWFS members involved founding a school, the Jōkō gakusha (for which there is no perfect translation but which one might call the Steaming rouge school). The school was run by Kageyama Ume (1826–1909), who managed the operations with the help of her daughter, Hideko (better known by her married name Fukuda Hideko), who was eighteen at this time.[54] Kageyama Ume, who had previously run another school with her husband, was deeply influenced by Fukuzawa Yukichi's famous tract *An Encouragement of Learning*, written between 1872 and 1876, with its egalitarian message and focus on the importance of cultivation and education. Specifically, Fukuzawa declares that "the question of the difference between wise and stupid is traceable to the degree of learning."[55] Although materials about the Jōkō gakusha are limited, we know that it was created in 1883, a year after the OWFS began. At the time, the law mandated elementary education for both boys and girls, but attendance rates for girls lagged significantly behind those of boys until the turn of the twentieth century. The school was open to boys age six to ten and to girls and women age six to sixty and cost much less than public schools.[56] It offered evening classes to accommodate the schedules of women who might be working during the daytime, possibly in one of the many spinning mills located in the

54. In her 1901 autobiography, Fukuda Hideko writes about the school she ran with her family's help prior to the formation of the OWFS. She does not comment on the Jōkō gakusha. *Warawa no hanseigai*, 16. For an English translation, see Hane, *Reflections on the Way*, 35–36.

55. Fukuzawa, *An Encouragement of Learning*, 3; Fukuda, "Bōbo no kinen," *Sekai fujin*, no. 34 (5 March 1909).

56. Murata Shizuko, "Hyōden," 631; Okayama joseishi kenkyūkai, "Okayama joshi konshinkai ni tsuite," 11. On tuition in Meiji public schools, see Platt, *Burning and Building*, 135–36.

area.[57] Like the temple schools of the Tokugawa period, the curriculum enabled students to advance at their own pace. The school was open on Saturdays so that students could participate in debates to hone their rhetorical skills. By 1884, the school had enrolled one hundred students and enjoyed widespread community support.[58]

Fukuda drafted the school's "statement of intention" (*shuisho*).[59] Such documents are invariably formal, but they offer insight into the central goals and principles that guided the school's leaders. The statement begins with a narrow summary of women's education throughout Japanese history, which according to Fukuda, had heretofore centered on "managing the household" with the addition of a few minor arts and skills.[60] Fukuda drew on the language of progress to point out that the world had changed dramatically in recent years, making a new kind of education for women not only desirable but imperative. Otherwise, society would look down on women and children. Fukuda and the other members not only had the education of children in mind but also hoped to make it possible for adult women to attend. Indeed, the statement reveals a nuanced understanding of how busy adult women are with household chores and children: "At night when they have a bit of time, even if they want to study, there is no school for them."[61]

The statement emphasizes that women have a right to education both for their children as well as for themselves and further states its aim to enable women to exercise this right. Fukuda treats the right to education as both self-evident and in need of justification. She points out that efforts to educate children will fall short if parents themselves are not educated. Even if children attend school, "their parents do not know how to encourage them. The children just lose themselves in play. They forget what the teacher said. When they take tests and do not perform well, they feel ashamed. How sad this is!" Lamenting the current situation, she

57.   On factories in Okayama, see Okayama joseishi kenkyūkai, *Kindai Okayama no onnatachi*, 34–35.

58.   *Jiyū no tomoshibi*, 20 September 1884, in *Fukuda Hideko shū*, 495. See also *Jiyū shinbun*, 20 September 1884, in *Fukuda Hideko shū*, 495.

59.   Fukuda, "Jōkō gakusha setsuritsu no shuisho," December 1883, 405–6.

60.   For a robust description of women's education in the Tokugawa period, see Kornicki, "Women, Education, and Literacy."

61.   Fukuda, "Jōkō gakusha setsuritsu no shuisho," 405–6.

announces the founding of the Jōkō gakusha as a step forward: "We want to improve the rotten customs of the past, enhance women's knowledge, and develop their intelligence. By doing so, mothers will have a valued place in the future."[62] Here we note the focus on educating future mothers—as well as the slippage from "women" to "future mothers." Still, the range of students' ages suggests that older women who were already mothers attended the school.

Why should one educate women? Meiji-era arguments in favor of education tended to be framed in the national interest: education would serve the nation.[63] But Fukuda only implicitly connected women's education with the national interest. The school served geisha, prostitutes, and factory workers, in accordance with the wishes of Fukuda's mother.[64] In sum, the Jōkō gakusha school aimed to educate not the emerging elite but the working class. The efforts of the OWFS, then, anticipated a trend of relatively privileged women entering public space in the name of helping those who were less well off. Their actions should also be seen as a response to local conditions, for Okayama and the nearby city of Kurashiki formed a center of the textile industry by the mid-1880s, as noted in chapter 1.[65]

Encounters with the Police and Government: The Taking the Breezes Gathering

By 1884, the People's Rights Movement had arrived at a crucial turning point. The movement's initial goal was met in 1881 when the government promised a constitution by the end of the decade. Violent uprisings in Chichibu, Iida, and elsewhere loosely associated with the People's Rights Movement rocked the country. Political groups experienced rising state repression and government scrutiny to the extent that the national

---

62. Fukuda, "Jōkō gakusha setsuritsu no shuisho," 405–6.

63. See Marnie Anderson, *A Place in Public*, chap. 4.

64. Okayama joseishi kenkyūkai, *Kindai Okayama no onnatachi*, 44–45; *Okayama-ken shi*, 10:178.

65. Tsurumi, *Factory Girls*, 37.

Liberal Party and other local parties like the San'yō Liberal Party would formally disband later that year.

To understand what happened to the OWFS in this context, we must go back to a social gathering in August 1884—before the formal dissolution of the various People's Rights parties. Members of the OWFS joined male members of the San'yō Liberal Party for an outing, a Taking the Breezes gathering (*nōryōkai*) on the Asahi River. Students from the OWFS school were also in attendance. Men and women, including a female student, gave speeches. The joint celebration of some one hundred people highlights the connections between the male and female societies and the heterosociality of social networks. Not only did both groups share a broader commitment to enhancing "people's rights" but, as noted, many were related through family and kinship ties. Exactly how the event ended remains unclear, but we do know the police arrived.

Accounts of what followed vary widely. Some scholars rely on Fukuda Hideko's 1904 description, which explains that the police intervened to shut down the gathering. Upon the appearance of a policeman, "there was a kind of furious excitement, but at the words of elderly persons in the crowd, everyone dispersed in an orderly fashion."[66] The very next day, the prefectural governor Takasaki Itsumu issued an order closing the school.[67] However, newspaper reports of the time make no reference to the police shutting down the party. One paper attributed the end of the celebration to the actions of a rival political party's members, who, in a fit of jealousy, hurled stones and other objects at the boaters.[68] Yet another article concluded with a description of the female speakers and made no mention at all of a dramatic conclusion to the evening.[69]

Although there is no generally agreed-upon account of how the evening ended, the aftermath would come into focus later. Fukuda notes that

66. Fukuda, *Warawa no hanseigai*, 17. For the English translation of Fukuda's description, see Sievers, *Flowers in Salt*, 26.

67. Fukuda, *Warawa no hanseigai*, 17. Murata writes that the order came the same day. See Murata Shizuko, "Hyōden," 629.

68. *Jiyū shinbun*, 13 August 1884, in *Fukuda Hideko shū*, 493–94.

69. *Jiyū no tomoshibi*, 14 August 1884, in *Okayama minken undōshi*, 33; also reprinted in *Fukuda Hideko shū*, 494. It is possible there was censorship, but more likely, the course of events only made sense in retrospect.

the police observed the events and punished some of the participants by closing the Jōkō gakusha school.[70] However, contemporaneous newspaper accounts suggest this did not happen immediately. The order to close the school came weeks later from Governor Takasaki, leaving the students "deeply disappointed."[71] The order did not clarify why the school was being shut down, but Fukuda's brother-in-law approached prefectural assembly members, who explained that it was because of Fukuda's and the students' participation in the boating party.[72] Historian Murata Shizuko adds that the presence of Jōkō gakusha students and teachers at a political gathering violated the conditions of the 1882 Associations Law (Shūkai jōrei).[73] The government clearly understood the event as a political one. Still, it bears emphasis that women *as a group* were not banned from most political activities until 1890.[74]

Interpretive Frameworks

In her analysis of Japanese women's movements, scholar Suzuki Yūko has identified two distinct kinds of women's activism in the People's Rights era, what she calls the "independent model" (*jiritsukei*) and the "inner assistance model" (*naijokei*).[75] In Suzuki's view, the independent type of activists gave speeches, signed petitions, and joined women's groups. Suzuki argues that the OWFS fits the independent model because the members were young and single with few burdens and "they desired to join the movement and threw themselves into it."[76] Suzuki includes in this category famous women like Kishida Toshiko and also those about whom

70. Fukuda, *Warawa no hanseigai*, 17.
71. *Jiyū no tomoshibi*, 20 September 1884, in *Fukuda Hideko shū*, 495. See also *Jiyū shinbun*, 20 September 1884, in *Fukuda Hideko shū*, 495.
72. Fukuda, *Warawa no hanseigai*, 17.
73. Murata Shizuko, "Hyōden," 629.
74. On practices that restricted women's activities across the 1880s, see Ōki, *Jiyū minken undō to josei*, 80–81; Marnie Anderson, *A Place in Public*, chap. 3.
75. Suzuki Yūko, "Kaisetsu," 23.
76. Suzuki Yūko, "Kaisetsu," 23.

less is known.[77] In contrast to the independent group, the inner assistance group provided support to men. Their work operated as an extension of women's roles as wives and included laundering clothes and providing meals for male activists. Some geisha performed a similar role at banquets, serving sake and food. Still, Suzuki observes that much research remains to be done because local women's groups represent "an undeveloped area of study."[78]

Although I find Suzuki's analysis stimulating, a closer look at the OWFS suggests that the division between the two types of activism—independent and inner assistance—is not so clear-cut. Put differently, the two types of activism did not operate exclusively. Women may well have started out as "supporters" of men who then moved on to more "independent" roles. Or they may have toggled back and forth between roles. For Suzuki, "independent activists" tended to be young and single, whereas those who offered "inner assistance" were older and married. But the OWFS included both types of women. Indeed, founders Tsuge and Takeuchi were in their late forties and fifties and married. To be sure, Suzuki acknowledges that we know little about most of the other regional women's groups. She observes the importance of family ties, especially in the case of the inner assistance model. I would add that family relationships mattered even for women who were single—for example, in the case of Kobayashi Tei (1861–?), younger sister of activist Kobayashi Kusuo (1856–1920). Another case where the binary between the independent model and inner assistance model does not work is that of activist Narita Ume (1837–?) from Miyagi Prefecture. Different texts portray her according to one or the other of Suzuki's models, but in fact, Narita seems to have straddled both.[79] In other words, Narita was simultaneously an advocate of freedom and rights *and* someone who took care of men. In a pattern we have already seen, her son was also an activist in the Liberal

---

77. Newspapers of the time mention other women activists in passing. See Ōki, *Jiyū minken undō to josei*, chap. 2.

78. Suzuki Yūko, "Kaisetsu," 23.

79. *Miyagi-ken shi*, 59; Suzuki Shizuko, *"Danjo dōkenron" no otoko*, 192. The former notes Narita Ume's advocacy of "freedom and rights," but the latter focuses on her taking care of men.

Party and involved in the People's Rights Movement. Family ties brought people into contact with the People's Rights Movement.[80] Perhaps she introduced him to politics.

One group we do not see in the OWFS record—at least in significant numbers—is married women in their twenties and thirties with children at home. This is not surprising given that the labor they had to perform would have left them with little time for political involvement.[81]

Beyond 1884

The precise details of the OWFS's demise remain a mystery. After the school closed on the orders of the governor, we read no more about it. But the end of the OWFS did not mark the end of its former members' activism. On the contrary, participation in the OWFS spurred women to pursue other activism centered on education and reform often related to Protestant Christianity.[82] We saw that Sumiya Koume founded a school and went to work for the Okayama Orphanage. Treasurer Ishiguro Orio helped found the Okayama Women's Temperance Society (Okayama fujin kinshukai) and the Okayama Women's Christian Temperance Union (WCTU; Okayama fujin kyōfūkai; see chapter 4).[83] Uemori Misao and Tsuge Kume opened schools for girls in Okayama, as did Sumiya.[84] Fukuda Hideko continued her activism in Tokyo. The following year, she was arrested and imprisoned for her role in the 1885 Osaka Incident, an abortive attempt to foment revolution in Korea. Although Fukuda did not act alone, she was the only woman involved, and the media

---

80. *Miyagi-ken shi*, 59.

81. Scholars have noted the relative freedom women enjoyed after their childrearing years. Walthall, "The Life Cycle of Farm Women." See also Walthall, *The Weak Body of a Useless Woman*.

82. Christian organizations experienced rapid growth in the period 1882–1888. Lublin, *Reforming Japan*, 44.

83. Okayama joseishi kenkyūkai, *Kindai Okayama no onnatachi*, 27, 35.

84. Okayama joseishi kenkyūkai, *Kindai Okayama no onnatachi*, 26–27. San'yō shinbunsha, *Okayama-ken rekishi jinbutsu jiten*, 641.

coverage of the event and her subsequent arrest vaulted her into the national consciousness as a lone woman among men.[85]

The OWFS stands out for its ability to attract publicity in the local papers and for the connections its founders forged with famous activists such as Kishida Toshiko and Itagaki Taisuke. Moreover, the OWFS nurtured many activists, suggesting it served as a place to test out ideas and practices that could be carried forward.

Why does the story of the OWFS matter? The question deserves consideration, in spite of the group's short existence—or perhaps because of it. First, the OWFS's activities demonstrate that the growth of political activity at the local level in Meiji Japan was not limited to men or merely a few exceptional women. The historical record shows, however, that OWFS members saw themselves as agents who had an important role to play in society, rather than as mere adjuncts to men. Journalists and members of the local Liberal Party supported their activities to a degree; indeed, the two gender-specific groups shared a good deal in common. For women to play a limited political role was not unthinkable in the early Meiji period.

Second, the OWFS complicates our assumptions about women's political involvement at the local level. Women were active in multiple ways; they were neither fully independent nor subordinate to men. Moreover, the material suggests that Meiji women's political life undoubtedly started in the home. The men in the San'yō Liberal Party were their brothers, fathers, cousins, and husbands. Sometimes, women got actively involved in politics. The women saw themselves as entitled to a role that included political knowledge, the right to assemble as a group, and the right to further their goals through social outreach, primarily in the form of speechmaking and educating the underprivileged, especially working-class women.

Third, the OWFS activists made claims for their inclusion as valuable members of society—at both the local and the national level—within the parameters of accepted gender roles. These women did not challenge the gender order so much as redefine the boundaries of those roles. They focused on accumulating political knowledge and fostering educational

85.   One text portrayed her as a Joan of Arc figure: Shimizu, *Kageyama Hide-jo no den*.

opportunities. In the process, they created a legitimate place for them-selves to act.[86] Participation in women-only groups could have what United States historian Anne Boylan calls a "dual potential": such groups could help women become more independent or, alternately, keep them "from disputing their subordinate status within the existing gender sys-tem by fortifying their sense of value and self-worth."[87]

The OWFS was the first to take up issues concerning women's roles and rights and explore them in the context of a group—they discussed issues and debated with each other. The causes these women champi-oned, notably reform and education, would be taken up in subsequent women's organizations. Such organizations are notable in part for their sheer number. Yoshizaki Shihoko has demonstrated that in the five years after the society ended, between 1885 and 1890, there were at least twenty-five women's groups founded in Okayama Prefecture alone, a striking development in women's associational life. One might be tempted to assume that women's groups were progressive, but in fact Yoshizaki notes that some organizations were devoted to cultivating elite class identities and upholding strict gender ideals.[88] Her work serves as an important reminder that women's emergence in public does not track neatly or consistently with women's liberation. Rather, women's groups with wide-ranging ideological orientations emerged at the same historical moment.

OWFS activists shared a certain level of education and the ability to devote at least some time to activities beyond household duties at a time when households were still productive units. They attended meetings and speeches. They stayed abreast of current issues, which would enable them to contribute to group discussions.[89] Of course, class and status back-ground shaped access, allowing relatively privileged women the oppor-tunity to engage in activities that women of lower classes could not. OWFS activists did not represent all women, even though they acted in the name of "women." Like their male counterparts, they behaved as

86. Okayama joseishi kenkyūkai, *Kindai Okayama no onnatachi*, 32.
87. Boylan, *The Origins of Women's Activism*, 3.
88. Yoshizaki, "Nakamura Shizu," 8–10.
89. Okayama joseishi kenkyūkai, *Kindai Okayama no onnatachi*, 28–29.

members of a particular social position, even as these categories were themselves undergoing rapid changes following the dismantling of ascriptive status and the rise of industrial capitalism. Notably, the women of the OWFS did not characterize themselves primarily as mothers, for they had been born in the late Tokugawa period, when motherhood was not highly valued and before modern discourses characterizing middle-class women primarily as mothers had crystallized.

One remaining question concerns how the women were able to mobilize so quickly and what networks may already have been in place to facilitate their mobilization. The women perhaps knew each other not just from their husbands or male family members who were involved in People's Rights organizing but also from aesthetic associations like poetry circles or *kō*, early modern credit cooperatives and religious organizations, which may have continued into the Meiji era. A shared experience attending school during the late Tokugawa or early Meiji period may also have provided an occasion for women to forge connections.[90] Founder Tsuge Kume had studied Chinese learning with member Uemori Misao's father, who operated the largest private academy in Okayama Prefecture.[91] Underlying networks stretched and evolved across time, even if the sources shed light on only a brief period of their existence.

OWFS activities in the early 1880s remind us of the rich possibilities that existed on the political landscape of late nineteenth-century Japan. This point does not deny what historian Laura Downs has called "the political problem of male domination," forcing the practice of patriarchy to "fade behind the comfortable harmonies of gender complementarity."[92] Men undoubtedly dominated Meiji political life in Okayama and elsewhere. But the OWFS's record complicates our understanding of what was possible for women.

Former OWFS members and their successors continued their activism into the early twentieth century though patriotic associations, Christian groups like the JWCTU, Buddhist groups, and other charitable

---

90. Patessio, *Women and Public Life*, 108–9.

91. San'yō shinbunsha, *Okayama-ken rekishi jinbutsu jiten*, 641; Okayama joseishi kenkyūkai, *Kindai Okayama no onnatachi*, 26.

92. Downs, "Gender History," 106.

associations.[93] They no doubt shared Takeuchi's sentiments expressed at the first meeting of the OWFS, where she lamented the oppression of women by men and women's ignorance. She called for change: "It is time to abolish this practice, but to nurture [political] thought and eliminate this custom is no easy matter."[94] Even after the OWFS had dissolved, former members continued engaging in public because they saw themselves as members of the new nation. They had always known that changing customs was "no easy matter."

93. For a partial list, Mackie, *Feminism in Modern Japan*, 29–32.
94. *Nihon rikken seitō shinbun*, 16 May 1882, in *Okayama minken undōshi*, 30–31.

CHAPTER 4

Configurations of Activism: A Couple and the Single Ladies

> Too seldom do historians of past politics recognize that their primary subjects are explicitly male, with priorities that derive from their masculine identity and social roles.
>
> —Mary Beth Norton, "History on the Diagonal"

Ideas about freedom and rights spread further in late nineteenth-century Japan than we normally assume and were not confined to elite men. One example of an educated young woman is Ishizaka Mina (1865–1942), who grew up in a household with a politically active father in the Tama region of Kanagawa Prefecture. Her life and that of her family members is beautifully told by M. William Steele, who describes how Mina's father Shōkō (1841–1906), a former village headman turned prefectural politician, held firm beliefs about natural rights that impacted his children. Ishizaka Shōkō was a prominent activist in the local Freedom and People's Rights Movement. He influenced his son Kōreki (1868–1944), who held a political study group at their home in the early 1880s.[1] The group attracted politically-engaged young men who wished to discuss ideas. In this environment, Mina absorbed what the young men and her father talked about. When she chose to marry one of her brother's friends a few years later—a match her family opposed—she drew on her father's "political creed, the call for autonomy, independence, and self-reliance, and the demand for rights and freedom, to stress her own independence," much to his dismay.[2]

---

1. Steele, "The Ishizaka of Notsuda," 63–65.
2. Steele, "The Ishizaka of Notsuda," 70. Steele notes that Protestant Christian influence also informed Mina's decision.

When scholars imagine activists in late nineteenth and early twentieth-century Japan, the default candidate is almost always a man, at least implicitly. In other words, Mina's father and brother are more likely to come to mind than Mina. To be sure, textbooks and surveys note the existence of a few exceptional women in the People's Rights Movement, including public speakers Kishida Toshiko and Fukuda Hideko. But thinking about Mina, her brother, and her father as a unit expands our understanding of activism in its social context—in this case, a family. Such an exercise shows that activism did not occur within hermetically-sealed separate spheres. Ideas circulated among family members. To be sure, gender roles shaped the ways individuals expressed themselves and occupied space, but that is not the end of the story. Mina could not join her brother's group, but she was still impacted by it. Mina's life thus points not only to the power of ideas to change the world but also how people can be inspired by ideas and act on them even when they are not the intended recipients. Her story thus both challenges and broadens our understanding of how ideas about rights and freedom circulated among family members, friends, and acquaintances during this era.

This chapter asks what activism looks like when we move away from the individual male and consider new perspectives on activism in politics, education, and social reform. It touches on key themes of this book, including the relationship between heterosocial networks and single-sex associations as well as the opportunities offered by modernity to take up new roles, in this case primarily for single women. I propose that in some circumstances, it makes sense to think of people in terms of a unit— women and men working together or a group of women—to understand how historical change happens.[3] One strategy I adopt is to explore cases in which men spent time at home and women, outside of the household, contrary to conventional expectations about gender roles. The first half of the chapter focuses on the activism of a married couple in the Okayama Freedom and People's Rights Movement and traces their subsequent involvement in politics and reform through the turn of the century. I find significant overlap in mens' and womens' political lives in the 1880s, even

---

3. I thank an anonymous reader for this formulation.

though associational life, as was society more broadly, increasingly organized around the axis of gender difference.[4]

In the second half of the chapter, I turn to two overlooked long-
term single women. I scrutinize their work and their careers at San'yō
gakuen school while also considering their activism outside of the school.
What exactly did single women do, and how were they seen? I propose
that researchers have disregarded the work of these women in part
because of the partiality of the sources themselves. People at the time
struggled to make sense of these women's roles because they were both
single and worked outside of the household, leading subsequent scholars to underestimate or mischaracterize their work. Meanwhile, it is worth
stressing that in contrast, men's marital status is almost never a concern, either for people at the time or those who retrospectively observed
their work.

One theme running through this chapter concerns how women's
labor and authority are conceived in gendered terms, both by people who
knew them and by those who have subsequently written about their lives.
Regardless of whether sources are in Japanese or English, nearly all portray women during the Meiji era as maternal or wifely figures, even though
these roles did not necessarily reflect their experiences. Women themselves
sometimes contributed to the tendency. Such examples highlight the difficulties people past and present have in writing about women in positions of authority.

The Ishiguros

Ishiguro Kan'ichirō and Ishiguro Orio were not the only married couple
involved in the Okayama Freedom and People's Rights Movement. I have
chosen them because there is more information in the record relative to
other couples, including OWFS founder Tsuge Kume and her husband
Masagorō as well as member Yamamoto Ushi, a native of Tosa domain,
and her husband Yamamoto Baigai (1852–1928), a Liberal Party member
and journalist.

---

4. Marnie Anderson, "From Status to Gender in Meiji Japan."

Here I aim to recreate the lives of the Ishiguros and what they did during the People's Rights Movement of the 1880s and in the following decades. Much is unknowable because neither Kan'ichirō nor Orio left a record explaining how they came to join the movement or illuminating anything about their family dynamics. Nevertheless, we can piece together a picture of their activism. Sometimes Orio and Kan'ichirō acted together, and at other times, they met in sex-specific spaces. Even so, they shared many of the same concerns, notably an interest in politics and the well-being of the nation.

BACKGROUND—KAN'ICHIRŌ

Kan'ichirō's story exemplifies the path a man of good background with political inclinations might follow in the Meiji period. He was born in 1854 into a samurai family in the Tanabe domain (the present-day city of Maizuru, Kyoto Prefecture). His father taught at the domainal school, but Kan'ichirō went to Edo for his education. After the Restoration, Kan'ichirō returned home and attended a military academy in Osaka. However, he withdrew from the school for reasons that remain unclear and turned to studying the law. In 1876, he was among the first group of people in Japan to pass the new legal examination, receiving his license as a *daigennin*, a precursor to modern lawyers, or *bengoshi*, a term coined in the 1890s. Two years later in 1878, he moved to Okayama, where he set up a legal practice and joined the vibrant political scene. Many activists had a similar background. Former samurai and wealthy commoners comprised a significant percentage of People's Rights activists, for as Kyu Hyun Kim has pointed out, those with money had access to People's Rights politics.[5]

Politics captivated Kan'ichirō. In 1879, Kan'ichirō sent an editorial to the *San'yō shinpō* on "The Ways to Petition for a National Diet," suggesting that supporters should consider multiple strategies for appealing to the government, including contacting the emperor, the prefectural governor, and the local assembly.[6] He joined the national Liberal Party in 1881. Shortly thereafter, he helped found the local branch of the party,

5. Flaherty, *Public Law, Private Practice*, 215, citing Kim, *The Age of Visions and Arguments*, 194–95.
6. *Okayama-ken shi*, 10:146.

the San'yō Liberal Party, along with Nishi Kiichi, Nakagawa's close friend. Kan'ichirō was an active speaker, putting himself at risk at a time when the government was committed to suppressing People's Rights activism. At least one of his speeches violated the 1882 Associations Law, and he was fined and ordered to refrain from delivering speeches for a year.[7] Today, people at San'yō gakuen, which he helped found, remember him as a "typical People's Rights activist."[8] Overall, Kan'ichirō fits a pattern identified by Darryl Flaherty in which legal advocates, mostly former samurai, played a central role in People's Rights politics and spearheaded the formation of local political parties throughout the country.[9]

Kan'ichirō enjoyed a few moments on the national stage because of his connections with the famous outspoken lawyer, politician, and provocateur Hoshi Tōru (1850–1901) but was not well known beyond the region.[10] As a result of his connections to Hoshi, Kan'ichirō took part in events on the national stage that are familiar to students of the era, notably the Osaka Incident, and the Unity Movement (Daidō danketsu) of 1886–1890, an effort to reinvigorate People's Rights politics after the initial movement had waned following the government's promise of a constitution in 1881.[11] Kan'ichirō traveled to Osaka in late 1885 to defend his friend, Okayama native Kobayashi Kusuo, who had been arrested in the Osaka Incident along with several others, including Fukuda Hideko.[12] Kan'ichirō worked alongside Hoshi on the defense; his skill in crafting arguments drew praise from colleagues.[13]

---

7.   Mitsunaga, *Ishiguro Kan'ichirō no enzetsu hikki*, 13.

8.   See "Gakuen no sōsōki" on San'yō gakuen's website: http://www.sanyogakuen .net/history/story (accessed 7 February 2017).

9.   Flaherty, *Public Law, Private Practice*, 217. On Okayama politics, see Terasaki, *Meiji Jiyūtō no kenkyū*, 62–66.

10.   Both Ishiguros are mentioned in the existing literature, although their names are rendered incorrectly in English. Patessio calls Orio "Obi." Patessio, *Women and Public Life*, 151. Flaherty refers to Kan'ichirō as "Hakoichirō" in *Public Law, Private Practice*, 226.

11.   Siniawer, *Ruffians, Yakuza, and Nationalists*, 46–47; Steele, *Alternative Narratives*, 158–67. Matsuzawa Yūsaku sees 1884 as the end of the People's Rights Movement. Matsuzawa, *Jiyū minken undō*, 204.

12.   On the Osaka Incident, see Siniawer, *Ruffians, Yakuza, and Nationalists*, 44–45.

13.   I draw on these sources in an attempt to provide as full a picture of him as possible. Mitsunaga, *Ishiguro Kan'ichirō no enzetsu hikki*, 13.

In 1887, Kan'ichirō and Hoshi worked to protest the terms of Foreign Minister Inoue Kaoru's (1836-1915) negotiations with the Western powers for treaty revision. The negotiations were conducted in secret, but word got out that the proposed concessions would permit foreign justices to serve on Japanese courts. Outraged, Kan'ichirō and Hoshi printed and circulated memorials opposing the concessions, all part of a larger opposition movement.[14] One document Kan'ichirō circulated was foreign legal advisor Gustave Emile Boissonade's memo defending Japanese sovereignty. As the politician Ozaki Yukio (1858–1954) later explained the situation:

> Not only in the capital but throughout the country opinion flared in overwhelming opposition to Inoue's proposed revisions. There were many secret publications. Submissions . . . as well as a draft constitution, were printed in secret and disseminated nationwide. There was no man of consequence who did not possess them. These subversive documents, to use contemporary terms, littered the country, and a flustered government dispatched secret agents in an attempt to control the situation.[15]

Government agents arrested several men and banished over five hundred party leaders from Tokyo in December 1887 for violating the Peace Ordinance (Hoan jōrei).[16] The police arrested Kan'ichirō in Osaka in 1888 once the government discovered his involvement in the leak, and he was sentenced to a year in prison on the charge of "secret publishing." The government released him early as part of the general amnesty of 1889 that followed the Meiji Constitution's promulgation. One contemporary source reported that Kan'ichirō immediately re-devoted himself to the Unity Movement and headed to Tokyo to protest the new foreign minister's efforts at treaty revision.[17]

---

14. Sims, *French Policy Towards the Bakufu*, 268.

15. Ozaki, *Autobiography of Ozaki Yukio*, 88.

16. Jansen, *The Making of Modern Japan*, 428; Flaherty, *Public Law, Private Practice*, 245–46.

17. Mitsunaga, *Ishiguro Kan'ichirō no enzetsu hikki*, 14. On treaty revision, see Jansen, *The Making of Modern Japan*, 428.

In 1890, Kan'ichirō stood for election to the Lower House of the Diet. A transcription of a speech he delivered while campaigning is still extant, together with a biography that establishes his credentials as a longtime member of the opposition.[18] His decision to run for office was typical for men of his background—many legal advocates ran for election in 1890. In fact, that year marked a dividing line in Meiji politics, and men like Kan'ichirō tried to "shed their outsider status and move into official positions of power and influence."[19] But in the end, Kan'ichirō lost his first bid as well as a subsequent attempt in 1892. While continuing to practice law in Okayama, he persisted in his quest for elected office, and in 1898, he finally won election to the Lower House, successively winning reelection three times.

Kan'ichirō's life had other dimensions besides his engagement with Meiji high politics. A devoted Christian, Kan'ichirō dedicated time to serving local institutions connected to the Okayama Church, notably the Okayama Orphanage and San'yō gakuen. In fact, Kan'ichirō served as the school's first principal.[20] The local paper *San'yō shinpō* offers evidence of Kan'ichirō's involvement in a local men's temperance society—he delivered a speech on the cause of temperance in 1887.[21] Okayama Orphanage founder Ishii Jūji mentions traveling with Kan'ichirō in his diary.[22] These commitments and evidence of local ties are striking, given that Kan'ichirō was physically absent from Okayama much of the time from late 1885 to 1889. He missed San'yō gakuen's opening ceremony in 1886 because he was away protesting the proposed revisions to the unequal treaties.[23] I suspect that his wife, Orio, in fact nurtured many of the connections and carried out certain obligations in his stead, a point I return to later.

18.   Mitsunaga, *Ishiguro Kan'ichirō no enzetsu hikki*, 14.

19.   Flaherty, *Public Law, Private Practice*, 251; Inada, *Jiyū minken no keifu*, 141.

20.   Ōta, "Nakagawa Yokotarō no enzetsu," 74.

21.   Yoshizaki, "Nakamura Shizu," 4. On the central role of Japanese men in promoting temperance, see Yasutake, *Transnational Women's Activism*, 75.

22.   Ishii Jūji, *Nisshi*, 1887 (Meiji 28), 10.

23.   "Gakkō hōjin San'yō gakuen hyakusanjūshūnen kinen shikiten o okonaimashita," *San'yō joshi kōshiki burogu* (blog), 1 November 2016, http://sanyojoshi.jugem.jp/?cid=9.

ORIO

As is the case with many Meiji women, Ishiguro Orio's life is much less documented than her husband's. Unlike the other women I address here, she left nothing in her own hand. Most of what we know about her comes from newspaper articles in the *San'yō shinpō*. Ten years younger than Kan'ichirō, Orio was born in 1864, near the end of the Tokugawa period. We do not know her status at birth, but we can assume that her family had means, given her marriage to Kan'ichirō and her apparent level of literacy. It was not at all unusual for elite daughters to be literate.[24] The couple had two daughters. Younger daughter Taki married the entrepreneur Yamamoto Tadasaburō (1873–1927), younger brother of Aoki Yōkichi (husband of Toyo, who was the daughter of Sumiya Koume and Nakagawa Yokotarō), demonstrating just how interconnected the Okayama networks were.[25]

Newspaper articles record that Orio joined at least three women's groups in the years between 1880 to 1890, an era that saw a sharp increase in the number of women's groups in Okayama.[26] Orio was eighteen years old when she joined the OWFS in 1882.[27] She was one of the younger members. Like Orio, many of the participants had ties to male People's Rights activists, whether spouses or siblings. After the OWFS ended in 1884, Orio continued to engage in activism. Two years later, in 1888, she joined the Okayama Women's Temperance Society.[28] Over time, this group transformed, becoming the Okayama WCTU in November 1889; Orio was a founding member. Initially, the Okayama WCTU had fifteen members, including the group's leader Nakamura Shizu (1850–1909), Sumiya Koume, Ōnishi Kinu, and Orio. Nakamura Shizu was a widow and the daughter of Ishizaka Kensō (1814–1899), a famous doctor from nearby Kurashiki who discovered the flukeworm.[29]

---

24. Gramlich-Oka and Walthall, "Introduction," 7.

25. Yamamoto become wealthy during World War I and donated generously to San'yō gakuen. San'yō gakuen, *Ai to hōshi*, 24; Ōta, "Nakagawa Yokotarō no enzetsu," 74.

26. Yoshizaki, "Nakamura Shizu," 10.

27. Okayama joseishi kenkyūkai, *Kindai Okayama no onnatachi*, 27, 35.

28. Yoshizaki, "Nakamura Shizu," 4.

29. Yoshizaki, "Nakamura Shizu," 1. The national Japanese WCTU was founded in 1893.

Following a typical practice, the group drafted a statement of intention. Suffused with the language of social reform and women's rights, the document proclaimed:

> We women have formed the Okayama WCTU to break apart our country's evil customs and habits and reform them.[30] Our Japan [*waga Nihon*] has gradually become more enlightened, and women's rights have progressed; at this favorable moment, there are many projects we women must undertake. . . . We should take our own evil customs as well as the undesirable aspects that have come from the West—things that should be feared—and expel them and instead create a foundation for beautiful customs. This is our most urgent task.[31]

Significantly, members emphasize that they do not welcome all Western influence, a point that should be understood as part of the rising distrust of foreign ideologies, including anti-Christian sentiments.[32] The statement discusses monogamy, the immoral nature of geisha and prostitutes, and the need to eliminate ideas and laws that respect men and despise women. The authors decry laziness, indulgence (presumably meaning sexual indulgence, including men's visits to brothels), the use of alcohol, and the "atmosphere of interaction" that prevails within households.[33] This latter section is vague, but the document's overall purpose is to advocate for an enhanced status for women, one tied to clean living in the Protestant interpretation.[34]

The Okayama WCTU also petitioned the Okayama prefectural assembly to abolish licensed prostitution, a move that occurred in Gunma Prefecture the same year.[35] Members delivered a memorial (*kengi*) to the

---

30. The Japanese name was Kyōfūkai, or "Reform Society." Japanese founders did not include temperance in the group's formal name. On this decision, see Lublin, *Reforming Japan*, 31.

31. *San'yō shinpō*, 17 November 1889, in *Okayama-ken shi*, 30:224–26.

32. Pyle, "Meiji Conservatism"; Fujimoto, "Women, Missionaries, and Medical Professions," 195.

33. *San'yō shinpō*, 1889 November 17, in *Okayama-ken shi*, 30:224–26.

34. On this topic, see Yasutake, *Transnational Women's Activism*, 32.

35. Fujime, "The Licensed Prostitution System," 149–50, 152; Kovner, *Occupying Power*, 100. If connections existed between developments in Gunma and Okayama, they do not appear to have been documented.

Okayama legislature in December 1889. The document portrayed prostitution as the root of all social ills and garnered fifty-nine signatures—of thirty-five women and fourteen men—an impressive number considering that at the time the group was a month old, with only fifteen members. Not all signatories were formal members of the group; this included the men.[36] Members also worked to publicize their cause through lecture meetings. They took out an advertisement in the local paper in April 1890, inviting interested parties to join them. The advertisement clarified that their group was dedicated to social reform, *not* to the expansion of Christianity, and that all were welcome.[37] Although networks overlapped, the causes—social reform and Christianity here—were understood as distinct. This separation may have enabled members to appeal to a broader range of people interested in reform but not necessarily Christianity.

In addition to women's groups, Orio joined the Okayama Church, though it is not clear when she became active; neither she nor Kan'ichirō appears on the list of founding members.[38] She became part of the OWFS in 1882, and we see overlap between the membership of the People's Rights–affiliated groups and the Okayama Church.[39] Readers are left with a picture of Orio's life as one devoted to activism and navigating a situation where the contours of what was possible for women remained in flux.

1884 Activists Together in Public

Kan'ichirō's and Orio's individual stories inform their life together as a couple. It is a probable assumption that Kan'ichirō and Orio joined other male and female People's Rights activists who came together in public protest. To consider that possibility, we turn now to the OWFS's final act before the governor shut it down.

36. *Okayama-ken shi*, 30:202.

37. Yoshizaki, "Nakamura Shizu," 7–8. On this issue, the Okayama WCTU differed from the Tokyo WCTU, though both groups were founded at roughly the same time.

38. Nihon kirutokyōdan Okayama kyōkai, *Okayama kyōkai hyakunenshi*, 37.

39. Maus, "Ishii Jūji," 189–90; Isshiki, "Kirisutokyō to jiyū minken undō," especially 137.

In August 1884, members of the all-female OWFS joined members of the all-male San'yō Liberal Party for a social outing, a gathering on the Asahi River mentioned in chapter 3. It is quite possible that the Ishiguros were present given that Kan'ichirō belonged to the San'yō Liberal Party and Orio to the OWFS.

Attended by over one hundred people, the gathering featured a party of riverboats festooned with lanterns. Red and white flags fluttered in the breeze, and one of the lanterns was emblazoned with the characters for "freedom" (*jiyū*).[40] One boat held twenty-seven members of the OWFS and students from its school. They entertained the crowd by singing "People's Rights" ballads set to lute music.[41] Later, some individuals—both women and men—gave speeches. Fukuda Hideko delivered a lecture on how men should not be left to work for important matters of state alone. One of her students, eleven-year-old Kawaguchi Ume, followed with a speech about her desire to work for the country, fulfilling her duty "as an Okayama woman." The press reported that Kawaguchi's speech moved the crowd and met with considerable applause; some people hit the sides of the boats to demonstrate support. A journalist for the pro-People's Rights newspaper *Jiyū no tomoshibi* (Lamp of freedom) commented with obvious local pride, "How promising are the young women of the San'yō region; how regrettable that the women of Tokyo are [comparatively] ill at ease."[42]

As we saw in chapter 3, the police intervened to shut down the event. During these years, the government used various tactics to squelch political activism. In this case, the presence of Jōkō gakusha students and teachers at a political gathering violated the 1882 Meetings Law.[43]

Not until 1890 were women formally banned from political meetings, although the remainder of the 1880s brought mounting restrictions on women's public political life. Family conversations would no doubt continue about politics and other matters. And women would engage in what British historian Leonore Davidoff has called the "separate semi-

40. *Jiyū shinbun*, 13 August 1884, in *Fukuda Hideko shū*, 493–94.
41. This description is based on *Jiyū no tomoshibi*, 14 August 1884, in *Okayama minken undōshi*, 33, and in *Fukuda Hideko shū*, 494. See also *Jiyū shinbun*, 13 August 1884, *Fukuda Hideko shū*, 493.
42. *Jiyū no tomoshibi*, 14 August 1884.
43. Murata Shizuko, "Hyōden," 629.

public realm of 'the social.'"[44] They would advocate for ostensibly non-political reform and at times endeavor to shore up their class interests. But the overtly political activities with women present including the Taking the Breezes gathering ceased.[45]

What We Write about When We Write about Men

What happened to the Ishiguros after 1884, a low point when political parties like the Liberal Party and its local chapters disbanded and the Unity Movement had not yet coalesced? From 1885 to 1890, Kan'ichirō was away from Okayama much of the time. He traveled to defend clients and served time in jail. Orio ran the household while her husband was absent, a form of invisible labor that is expected of wives but not of husbands. During this period, she participated in the Okayama Women's Temperance Society and later the Okayama WCTU. Her ties to better-known members of the same groups—for example, activists Sumiya Koume and Okayama WCTU leader Nakamura Shizu—indicate that Orio belonged to a circle of remarkable women based at the Okayama Church. In his autobiography, former pastor Abe Isoo reflected on his time at the Church: "Especially among the women, there were many extraordinary figures who shown like stars."[46] Abe specifically praised both the intelligence of male and female members of the Church, mentioning Ishiguro Kan'ichirō, Sumiya Koume, and Nakamura Shizu by name and calling them all "representative." The people Abe named were in their thirties and forties, his "parents' generation," as he put it. He noted the presence of many outstanding young people as well. Perhaps he had Orio in mind, but the women he mentioned explicitly were unmarried apart from church "matriarch" Nakagawa Yuki. Married women may have been "represented" by their husbands in his mind.[47]

44.　Davidoff, "Regarding Some 'Old Husbands' Tales,'" 257.

45.　This right would not be restored until 1922. Ōki, *Jiyū minken undō to josei*, chap. 3.

46.　Abe, *Shakai shugisha*, 142.

47.　For example, the prominent reformer Fukuzawa Yukichi turned down his wife Kin's invitation to join the JWCTU. See Nishizawa, "Female Networks and Social Stratification," 265.

Given Orio's connections to the Church and the Okayama Temperance Society, it seems possible that she, too, helped to found San'yō gakuen in 1886 though sources credit only Kan'ichirō along with several other men and one single woman, Nakagawa's cousin Ōnishi Kinu.[48] We know Kan'ichirō was present in Okayama to give a speech on temperance in 1887, but he would go to jail the following year. Whatever the case, it would be a mistake to assume that Orio was passively following Kan'ichirō's lead, especially when he was away frequently. As historian of Great Britain Anna Clark points out, scholars have tended to overlook women's role in maintaining social life and networks, and this seems to have been the case with Orio.[49]

Even after 1890, Orio may have helped Kan'ichirō campaign for election to the Diet, similar to how educator Hatoyama Haruko (1861–1938) helped her husband.[50] In spite of the ban on women's political involvement, campaigning for one's husband was not understood as a political activity. Similarly, OWFS founder Tsuge Kume continued to "encourage" (*bentatsu*) many former Liberal Party members in the 1890 elections.[51]

The Overlap in Men's and Women's Political Lives

The case of the Ishiguros illuminates the gendering of political culture in Meiji Japan, suggesting remarkable overlap in men's and women's political lives. Men and women engaged in similar activities in public in the 1880s, but most often in gender-specific associations, such as the temperance societies and single-sex political and social reform associations. Kan'ichirō joined the Liberal Party and helped found its local branch. He delivered speeches; in March 1882, he joined several others at a lecture meeting with some 3,500 members in the audience.[52] Orio meanwhile became a member of the OWFS, an organization that was not officially

48.   For a list of the initial founders, San'yō gakuen, *Ai to hōshi*, 14.
49.   Clark, "Leonore Davidoff," 8.
50.   Hastings, "Hatoyama Haruko," 89.
51.   San'yō shinbunsha, *Okayama-ken rekishi jinbutsu jiten*, 641.
52.   Terasaki, *Meiji Jiyūtō no kenkyū*, 65.

a political party but nevertheless espoused a political purpose. She then joined the Okayama WCTU, which also sponsored speeches and stressed the importance of cultivating knowledge; dues were used to purchase magazines for members to expand their learning.[53] Unlike the OWFS, the Okayama WCTU also drafted petitions (*kenpaku*) or memorials (*ikensho, kengi*) declaring opinions and appealing to higher authorities in the manner of the all-male San'yō Liberal Party we saw in chapter 3.[54]

Orio's membership in multiple groups throws into relief the shifting political landscape for women over the 1880s. The 1882 OWFS was more overtly political and subsequent groups—the Okayama Temperance Society, which became the Okayama WCTU—less so. By the end of the decade, the political possibilities for women activists were more circumscribed. The 1889 Okayama WCTU group's pledge remained silent about politics and promised to "correct evil customs, work for morality, endeavor to prohibit drinking and smoking and thereby promote women's dignity," marking a narrowing of, but not an end to, women's political life.[55]

Imagining a Political Couple

Much about the relationship between Orio and Kan'ichirō is unknowable, but semiautobiographical fiction may offer insights into the lives of couples like them. Former activist and speaker Kishida Toshiko's 1889 novella *A Famous Flower in Mountain Seclusion* (*Sankan no meika*, hereafter *A Famous Flower*) illuminates the life of a couple in similar circumstances to the Ishiguros.[56] As noted, Kishida helped inspire the founding of the

53. Article 8. It is unknown whether the Okayama WCTU had a *meiyaku* (pledge) in addition to a *kiyaku* (which was common for men's groups). The Okayama joshi konshinkai documents reference a *meiyaku*, but it does not appear to be extant.

54. For an example, see *Okayama-ken shi*, 30:202.

55. Quoted in Yoshizaki, "Nakamura Shizu," 6–7. For more on the WCTU in Japan, see Lublin, *Reforming Japan*.

56. The novella was published in the journal *Miyako no hana*. Kishida's pen name was Shōen. I am indebted to Dawn Lawson's award-winning translation: Nakajima Shōen (Kishida Toshiko), "A Famous Flower in Mountain Seclusion." I follow Yokozawa Kiyoko in identifying Kishida's birth date as 1861, though many sources say 1863. Yokozawa, *Jiyū minken ka*, 452.

OWFS with her speeches in Okayama in 1882. By the time she wrote *A Famous Flower*, Kishida's career as an orator and activist on the national stage for the People's Rights Movement had ended though she continued to teach school as well as publish fiction and public-facing writing for the journal *Jogaku zasshi*.[57] In 1886, Kishida married the politician Nakajima Nobuyuki (1846–1899), who was fourteen years older than she. Kishida was a mother figure to three stepchildren. Nakajima was expelled from Tokyo in 1887—as was Ishiguro Kan'ichirō—but both men continued to work for the cause. (Unlike Kan'ichirō, Nakajima Nobuyuki stood for election in 1890 and won.)

A *Famous Flower* can be understood to reflect some of Kishida's experiences. Set in the late 1880s, *A Famous Flower* looks back on the heyday of People's Rights activism in the early 1880s and depicts the actions of a married couple after the main phase of the People's Rights Movement had ended and when the Unity Movement was in full swing. It invites us to consider what wives thought about and did in the absence of the men.

A *Famous Flower* illustrates the relationship between a politically-engaged husband and his supportive wife Yoshiko, modeled on Kishida's situation. What is most compelling for our purposes is how Kishida describes the role of each partner. In Kishida's view, women should play a supportive role within the home because this is no longer a moment for women to be engaged overtly in the public political sphere. That is the job of men. As Yoshiko readily admits to her former students when they come to visit, her views on women's activism have changed over the years. In her opinion, educating women outweighs working for a vague notion of women's rights or delivering speeches around the country, as she herself engaged in for a time.[58] Yoshiko elaborates:

> There are some extraordinary women in the wider world, but putting them aside, it's going to be extremely difficult unless ordinary women are exposed to education and become able to raise their status themselves. We will not get our way in ten or twenty years. I have given up on anything except gradual progress, but it's not that I've thrown away my old ambitions and

57.   Yokozawa, *Jiyū minken ka*, 466–67.
58.   Nakajima Shōen (Kishida Toshiko), "A Famous Flower," 29.

seek only to be comfortable. The only difference is that I have not been putting my beliefs into speeches and actions.[59]

Her commitments have not changed, she assures the students, but her methods and outlook have.

Kishida espouses the ideal of companionate marriage, where the husband and wife work together as "one unit."[60] In Yoshiko, Kishida depicts a model protagonist who is socially aware, educated, and concerned about national matters but who also knows how to be modest and feminine. Yoshiko serves as a helpmate to her husband; she takes over the maid's domestic labor in order to save money in the household budget and supports her husband while he travels the countryside working for the cause of liberty. A serious woman, she has no interest in spending money keeping up with the latest fashions. She cares a great deal about how women appear in public. In her view, women should eschew direct involvement in politics, but they can help men. Women may cultivate political knowledge and opinions, but "any involvement in national affairs should take place quietly, behind the scenes, not out in public."[61] Women should guard the home when their husbands are away working for the country. Above all, they must cultivate an "inner strength" that will support their husbands and, by extension, the nation. Importantly, this stance was no affirmation of the status quo because she still discerns an active role for women.[62] At the same time, the protagonist eagerly defends her students against the charge that they act in an "arrogant and unfeminine" manner when they are in public.[63] But she cautions them to consider how others perceive them, lest their actions backfire. In an extended reflection on the encounter with the students after they leave, she opines, "As far as accomplishing anything for the benefit of society is concerned, it would be best if they [women] were able to achieve modest results through mild actions that sow the seeds of happiness in out-of-the-way places."[64]

59. Nakajima Shōen (Kishida Toshiko), "A Famous Flower," 29.
60. Nakajima Shōen (Kishida Toshiko), "A Famous Flower," 20.
61. Nakajima Shōen (Kishida Toshiko), "A Famous Flower," 29.
62. Nakajima Shōen (Kishida Toshiko), "A Famous Flower," 29–30.
63. Nakajima Shōen (Kishida Toshiko), "A Famous Flower," 30.
64. Nakajima Shōen (Kishida Toshiko), "A Famous Flower," 30.

The vision Kishida lays out in her novel is a gradualist one, one more muted and circumscribed than her stirring statements as a public speaker in the early 1880s. I have suggested that her novella might be read more expansively to illuminate how women like her imagined a way forward, but one that shielded them from the harsh eyes of the public. Women have a role to play, but they must take care and not attract much attention. Kishida's call for "modest results through mild actions" would seem to apply to Orio and other activists as they sought to clarify their role amid changing circumstances.[65]

A Spectrum of Political Activities

The story of the Ishiguros, together with the material in Kishida's novella, suggests that some aspects of Meiji political life took place in the home, conversations that nurtured ideas and commitments to the People's Rights cause. Of course, shared interests were not confined to politics. The Ishiguros devoted themselves to a constellation of other concerns: the Okayama Church, San'yō gakuen school, and the cause of temperance. Attempting to separate the causes is an artificial endeavor. In all cases, we find no absolute separation between men's and women's spheres. Anna Clark has made this point in a different context, but it nonetheless applies: "all categories, especially the public and private, and masculinity and femininity, were shifting, interrelated, and constantly renegotiated. The division between public and private was always more rhetorical than real, however powerful it was in shaping the way people thought."[66] Of course, nineteenth-century Japan had its own particularities and the vocabulary people used had distinct valences. Still, Clark's comments offer a useful way of thinking about the dynamic interpenetration of peoples' lives. The case of the Ishiguros indicates there were ways for men and women to participate in political life *together* around the movement in the early 1880s.

Increasingly, the paths of activism available to women and men diverged more sharply across the 1880s. The overtly political tenor of the

---

65. Translations of Kishida's work into English can be found in Copeland and Ortabasi, *The Modern Murasaki*; Sievers, *Flowers in Salt*; Mamiko Suzuki, *Gendered Power*.
66. Clark, "Leonore Davidoff," 8.

OWFS went by the wayside, reflecting shifts in the ways women of education and social standing could participate in public. However, conversations in the home no doubt continued in the years following 1890.

This sketch of a couple in the decades following the Meiji Restoration expands our understanding of who exactly was involved in Meiji political life. I have argued that married women played a role. Another category we do not often consider is single women, a group that performed an important and overlooked role in reform networks, as we saw in the case of Sumiya Koume. We turn to an examination of other single women now.

Single Ladies

In the Higashiyama cemetery on the hills overlooking the city of Okayama, three single women, all born between the 1850s and 1870s, are buried near each other: they are Sumiya Koume, Ōnishi Kinu, and Kajiro Yoshi. Descendants continue to care for Ōnishi's and Kajiro's graves, but Sumiya's grave lies mostly untended as those friends who erected it have long since passed away.[67]

Since Sumiya has already received attention in chapter 2, I address Ōnishi and Kajiro here and evaluate their contributions to social and religious networks in late nineteenth and early twentieth-century Okayama. Both were of former samurai background, and they faced the challenges of the Meiji Restoration with their families. They became Protestant Christians who had careers, participating in the same overlapping networks. The rich environment of Okayama, especially the institutions of the Okayama Church and San'yō gakuen school, provided them with possibilities for careers at a moment in which scholars have imagined women were mostly restricted to the home.

As mentioned, Ōnishi Kinu worked with other Japanese Protestant converts to set up San'yō gakuen in 1886. She helped run the school, including the dormitory, and worked as a substitute teacher. The much younger Kajiro taught at San'yō gakuen, studied abroad at Mt. Holyoke

---

67. Hamada, *Kadota kaiwai*, 86. See also "Okayama kojiin no kage no chikara," *San'yō shinbun*, 20 October 2008. Sumiya's grave was "rediscovered" by researchers in 2008. Today there is a small plaque placed next to the grave explaining who she was.

College in South Hadley, Massachusetts, and graduated in 1897. She returned to Okayama to teach at San'yō gakuen before becoming the school's principal in 1908. The women participated in the dense web of connections linking the Okayama Church, Okayama Orphanage, and the school.[68] Neither woman resided in Okayama between 1882 and 1884 and therefore did not participate in the OWFS.

What exactly did single Meiji women like Ōnishi and Kajiro do? What kind of labor and activism did they engage in? As I have noted, much existing scholarship focuses either on the creation of the "good wife, wise mother" paradigm or frames Meiji women's lives in terms of the new public spaces made available after the Restoration.[69] Those explanatory frameworks have merit but do not help us understand single women's work outside of the household and how the extant sources represent it. Although social and educational work in the late nineteenth century opened up opportunities for women to live as single women, people at the time and since have framed their labor—both their work at the school and other activism outside the home—in highly gendered terms. Women are conceived as maternal figures or wives, even though they lived as childless single women. To be sure, Ōnishi and Kajiro adopted male heirs, but they did not raise the children.[70] Tenacious ideas and assumptions about women have impeded a fuller understanding of their roles.

ŌNISHI KINU

Ōnishi had deep ties to the famous local notable Nakagawa Yokotarō. Nakagawa, we will recall, was both Ōnishi's first cousin and brother-in-law because he married her older sister, Yuki. Ōnishi attended the sermons he sponsored at his home beginning in the mid-1870s. She became an avid supporter of Christianity along with her mother Hide and her sisters, Yuki and Kayo; all four women were founding members of the Okayama

68.   While Ōnishi and Sumiya did not write about each other, the much younger Kajiro wrote about both of them after they died. Kajiro's contributions can be found in Murata Tomi, *Ōnishi Kinuko*; Onoda, *Tsuikairoku*.

69.   To name a few examples: Nolte and Hastings, "The Meiji State's Policy"; Koyama, *Ryōsai kenbo to iu kihan*; Lublin, *Reforming Japan*; Marnie Anderson, *A Place in Public*.

70.   Sumiya's case was different because she had a child, Toyo. Sumiya's uncle's family adopted a son-in-law to marry Toyo.

Church. Services were held at their home for a time.[71] They donated money to help buy land and fund a new building a few years later. Meanwhile, Ōnishi began teaching at a Sunday school founded by missionary John C. Berry.[72] Although some scholarship states that Ōnishi was a widow, other sources—including one compiled by her friends after her death—reveal that she had been briefly married and divorced.[73] This experience of marriage was notably short-lived for Ōnishi, and yet it looms much larger in accounts of her life than for those of male counterparts. Soon after the breakup of her marriage, she either attended or worked at the newly-opened Kobe Women's Bible Training School, founded in 1880. Scholars do not agree on what Ōnishi did at the school—whether she was an employee or a student—nor do we know when the divorce occurred. What is clear is that Ōnishi was in Kobe in 1884 and spent time at the school.[74]

Upon her return to Okayama, Ōnishi collaborated with others to found San'yō gakuen school. She was the only woman directly involved in the first stages of planning. Later, minister Kanamori Michitomo's future wife Nishiyama Kohisa (1864?–1912) came to Okayama from Kobe College to teach at the school. Nishiyama composed the school's founding statement, which declares, "If there is a way to save Japanese women from being men's slaves and playthings, it is to offer an education that includes knowledge and virtue. Christian morals should be the basis along with the goal to reform society."[75] Another section elaborates, "At the root of the nation's prosperity is the household. A household is a small empire. Men and women are like two wheels of a cart or two wings of a bird and have the [joint] obligation to protect the organization." The notion of men and women as two wheels of a cart was prevalent among commoners in the Tokugawa period.[76] In this vision, men and women worked

71. Nihon kirutokyōdan Okayama kyōkai, *Okayama kyōkai hyakunenshi*, 47.

72. Okayama joseishi kenkyūkai, *Kindai Okayama no onnatachi*, 65.

73. Murata Tomi, *Ōnishi Kinuko*, 1, 48; Nakai, "Ōnishi," 49.

74. Murata Tomi, *Ōnishi Kinuko*, 1. On the divorce, see Nakai, "Ōnishi," 47, 51.

75. San'yō gakuen, *Ai to hōshi*, 15. The statement can be found on 356–59. Patessio summarizes the document in *Women and Public Life in Early Meiji Japan*, 92–93.

76. For another case of the metaphor "two wheels of a cart," see Walthall, "The Life Cycle of Farm Women," 58. On commoner ideals, see Miyazaki, "Networks of Believers

together for a greater cause. Here the notion reflected the heterosocial networks that created the school.

Three years later in 1889, Ōnishi took a job as the dorm supervisor and manager, a position that included living with the students and running the school's finances.[77] She worked in this role from 1889 to 1908, nearly twenty years.[78] It is worth emphasizing that Ōnishi, Nishiyama Kohisa, and the other founders made a conscious decision *not* to make the school a mission school, an approach that would have made it eligible for foreign financial support. Rather, the founders wished to shape the curriculum specifically to promote Japanese ideals of femininity rather than the Western models espoused by mission schools.[79] To the founders, women's education on their terms represented a most urgent concern, deeply tied to the national interest. Missionary John Hyde DeForest (1844–1911) later explained this desire to a Western audience in an article focusing on Kajiro. He noted that when Kajiro was abroad in Boston, Massachusetts, giving speeches on behalf of the school, a local woman had suggested that Kajiro put the school in the care of a mission board so that it could fundraise more effectively. DeForest knew the woman "meant well" but explained that "the glory of Miss Kajiro's work is that it is not Western work supported from Boston, but it is one of those glorious developments of large Christian work outside of missionary control, bearing the lamp of life where no missionary could ever go."[80] He did not mention Ōnishi here but was doubtless aware of her critical work at the school.

What kind of a person was Ōnishi? Depictions varied and tried to make sense of her using established templates. Abe Isoo regarded her as fiercely intelligent, one of many such women in Okayama. In a short piece commemorating her life, Abe wrote about how he lived with Ōnishi when

---

in a New Religion." There are similarities with Kishida's call for wives and husbands to act as "one unit."

77. Ōnishi held the job until 1908. See Nakai, "Ōnishi," 45. Okayama joseishi kenkyūkai, *Kindai Okayama no onnatachi*, 69.

78. Nakai, "Ōnishi," 45.

79. Okayama joseishi kenkyūkai, *Kindai Okayama no onnatachi*, 70. San'yō gakuen, *Ai to hōshi*, 12, 17–21.

80. John DeForest, "Well Done, Miss Kajiro," *The Christian Endeavor World*, 26 November 1908.

he first came to Okayama as a young pastor, and she looked after him. Abe notes that Ōnishi was not just "warm" (*onjū*) like "conventional Japanese women" (*zairai no Nihon fujin*) but also "resolute" (*kizen*), unbending (*kusshinai*), and in possession of a "man's attitude" (*danseiteki taido*). He continued: "Some said she lacked warmth because she did not have children but that was not correct . . . she had maternal love for her students and that is her immortal commemorative stone."[81] He thus attempts to redeem her as a maternal figure. School trustee Kōmoto Otogorō (1869–1944) observed that Ōnishi's "most beautiful virtues were her bravery and her strong will."[82] Other friends pushed her onto more familiar gendered territory, noting that she had "married" the school, terminology the much younger Kajiro would also apply to herself.[83] These approaches suggest the paucity of ways available to describe women's contributions, whether by women themselves or those around them.[84] Writer Lucy Worsley makes a similar point in her biography of author Jane Austen (1775–1817): "Jane's claim that her books were her children is cliché of clichés for the childless lady-writer, but it has also been pointed out that she had no choice other than to present her achievement in such terms. *There wasn't much else that women were congratulated for doing* [emphasis mine]." Even though the contexts and time periods remain distinct, we see a cross-cultural pattern of placing exceptional women in established frameworks even when they do not in fact apply.

The explanation of women as mothers and wives, even when the reality was different, may relate to a need to place single women in institutions since they were not based in typical households. Aya Takahashi makes a similar point about unmarried Japanese Red Cross nurses during these same years. She argues that they were able to adapt ideas about the household (*ie*) to their profession, creating a "virtual-'*ie*'" in order to maintain their status as unmarried working women.[85] This practice seems

81. Murata Tomi, *Ōnishi Kinuko*, 50.
82. Okayama joseishi kenkyūkai, *Kindai Okayama no onnatachi*, 71 (quoting Onoda Gen).
83. On Kajiro using the language of marrying the school: Okayama joseishi kenkyūkai, *Kindai Okayama no onnatachi*, 82.
84. Worsley, *Jane Austen at Home*, 89.
85. Takahashi, *The Development of the Japanese Nursing Profession*, 73–74. I thank Sally Hastings for this insight and reference.

to have been increasingly common in Meiji Japan, whereas in the Tokugawa period, long-term single women remained rare.[86]

Ōnishi's skills resulted from her education in a samurai household in the late Tokugawa and early Meiji periods. Her background was eclectic: she knew the tea ceremony, the art of flower arranging, how to play the koto (and later the organ), as well as how to cook, dance, and sew. Abe saw her as a product of the superior education available to women in Tokugawa-era Okayama.[87] As a substitute teacher, she taught ethics, sewing, food preparation, calligraphy, and music, all the while enjoining her students not to show the bottom of their socks (*tabi*) when they walked, like a good samurai woman.[88] Ōnishi bore many of the school's difficulties of the early to mid-1890s largely on her own, without Kajiro, who studied abroad at Mt. Holyoke from 1893 to 1897. One evening, Ōnishi bravely confronted a burglar in the dormitory. She intimidated him with her imposing posture, and he left the premises without taking a thing.[89]

Some accounts of Ōnishi and other women like her portray their actions in terms of jealousy. After several years in Okayama, Ōnishi moved in 1908 to Tokyo, where she worked for the Young Women's Christian Association (YWCA). Her seemingly abrupt move has led to scholarly debate. One source attributes her departure to a rivalry with Kajiro, who had just taken over as principal.[90] Another notes that Ōnishi suffered from an eye disease and went to Tokyo to recover.[91] This latter account does not explain, however, why she went to work for the YWCA if her health was so poor. Perhaps she needed an occupation. Whatever the case, we do not currently have the sources to piece together a full story. Further, I caution against the assumption of jealousy—a quality coded as feminine—in light of the lack of evidence (scholars, to my knowledge, never discuss whether or not the Meiji oligarchs were "jealous" of each other). Accounts of women's lives are necessarily fragmentary, and we

---

86. Cornell, "Why Are There No Spinsters in Japan?"

87. Murata Tomi, *Ōnishi Kinuko*, 49.

88. Okayama joseishi kenkyūkai, *Kindai Okayama no onnatachi*, 72, 74–75.

89. Okayama joseishi kenkyūkai, *Kindai Okayama no onnatachi*, 75. For a similar anecdote about Shibue Io who confronted a burglar with a knife (while naked), see McClellan, *Woman in the Crested Kimono*, 71–72.

90. Okayama joseishi kenkyūkai, *Kindai Okayama no onnatachi*, 73–74.

91. Nakai, "Ōnishi," 56. She had family in Tokyo.

must be careful about the assumptions we carry when interpreting the evidence. Kōmoto Otogorō suggested that the two women got along well and had "different bodies but were of one mind" (*itai dōshin*).[92] Whatever the case, Kajiro and Ōnishi worked together successfully for over a decade from 1897 to 1908.

This record shows Ōnishi's involvement in multiple networks—her work was not limited to the school but extended to other areas of her life. In addition to working at San'yō gakuen and teaching Sunday school, Ōnishi Kinu was part of the Okayama WCTU—along with Ishiguro Orio—and Ōnishi served as the secretary.[93] There was no clear line separating work and activism for single women like Ōnishi.

Today, Ōnishi remains largely forgotten, even by historians who write about local history. Kajiro outshone her in more "public" venues as did Ōnishi's nephew and heir, the philosopher Ōnishi Hajime, who was the third son of her sister Kayo. Even though Hajime died young, he has remained much better known than she.[94] Ōnishi provided key labor at the school, and yet her work falls between the cracks. Like other women who taught and mentored others, she never quite made it into the public eye. Ōnishi complicates our picture of what Meiji women did and the variety of circumstances they faced. She also raises the issue of how they were perceived and their actions explained.

KAJIRO YOSHI

Whereas Ōnishi converted to Christianity as an adult, Kajiro was born to a family that converted to Protestantism when she was still a child. In part, this difference can be attributed to timing—Kajiro was fourteen years younger than Ōnishi. Kajiro went on to occupy a far more influential position than any of the other single women taken up here, serving as the principal of San'yō gakuen for fifty-one years and teaching there for sixty-six years. She spoke English fluently and had studied abroad. Her

92. Nakai, "Ōnishi," 56. For original, see Murata Tomi, *Ōnishi Kinuko*, 15. We have few sources in Ōnishi's hand. All are letters held by Waseda University and come from the papers of her nephew and adopted son. Nakai, "Ōnishi," 45.

93. Yoshizaki, "Nakamura Shizu," 7.

94. On Ōnishi Hajime, see Marra, *Modern Japanese Aesthetics*, 79–83.

high local stature meant that when she died in 1959, over 1,500 people attended her funeral.[95]

Although Kajiro spent much of her adult life in Okayama, she was born in Ehime Prefecture and moved to Osaka shortly after. After her father Tomoyoshi (1852–1921) converted in the 1870s, he helped missionaries found Baika Girls' School (Baika jogakkō) in Osaka together with educator Naruse Jinzō (1858–1919). Kajiro studied with Naruse, who is best known for the school he later founded, Japan Women's University (Nihon joshi daigaku). After her mother died when Kajiro was twelve, she lived in the dorm at Baika and stayed with missionary John Hyde DeForest and his family on weekends.[96] Meanwhile, Tomoyoshi began missionary work in various churches throughout the region, and in 1889, he went on a mission to Hawai'i.[97]

At Baika, Kajiro read about nurse Florence Nightingale (1820–1910) and Mt. Holyoke founder Mary Lyon (1797–1849); both single women were heroines to the Baika students.[98] In 1889, Kajiro graduated and moved to Okayama to teach at San'yō gakuen. Through missionary connections, she was able to attend Mt. Holyoke in the 1890s without the usual obligation of serving as a teacher at a denominational school on her return. DeForest's friend, the minister Albert J. Lyman (1845–1915), agreed to pay for her education.[99] Kajiro's higher education thus occurred in New England in the late 1890s, leaving her with a different skill set than Ōnishi. Her college transcript has not survived, but Mt. Holyoke's robust requirements included the study of classics, rhetoric and English literature, philosophy, ancient history, science (physics, chemistry, botany), math, elocution, Latin and Greek, French or German, and the Bible.[100] In other

---

95.　Okayama joseishi kenkyūkai, *Kindai Okayama no onnatachi*, 77. See also Matsumoto, *Midori fukaku.*

96.　Hamada, *Kadota kaiwai*, 180. An instance of intertwined networks: DeForest's daughter Charlotte graduated from Smith College in 1901 and served as the president of Kobe College from 1915 to 1940.

97.　*Nihon kirisutokyō rekishi daijiten*, 292.

98.　Okayama joseishi kenkyūkai, *Kindai Okayama no onnatachi*, 78.

99.　Hastings, "Mt. Holyoke College," 22. Okayama joseishi kenkyūkai, *Kindai Okayama no onnatachi*, 79; Hamada, *Kadota kaiwai*, 182.

100.　The course of study can be found in the Mount Holyoke College Catalog, 1894–1895, 10–25, https://compass.fivecolleges.edu/object/mtholyoke:46322, accessed 1 June 2021. The catalog contains an exhaustive list of the college's courses. At the time,

words, she received an education on the same level as that offered by elite male institutions like Amherst and Yale.

After graduation, she returned to Okayama, resuming her role as a teacher at San'yō gakuen, though she had other job offers with higher salaries from schools across the country. She also worked for a missionary family who "rejoiced that Kajiro Yoshi had retained her faith" when she returned from abroad.[101] This moment was particularly difficult for San'yō gakuen. Not only was the institution struggling financially—which Ōnishi had to cope with as the financial manager—but there was a rising distrust of Western ideas, especially those related to Christianity. The school consequently shifted its curricular emphasis. Heretofore, the school had focused on inculcating Christian morals and English study. Going forward, the focus centered on raising women to be good wives and wise mothers.[102] In 1899, San'yō gakuen became a state-approved higher school following the passage of the 1899 Higher Education Law. These moves allowed the school to flourish for many years.[103]

The record indicates that Kajiro was an inspiring and influential teacher. When a government directive banned the teaching of religion in government-licensed schools in 1899, Kajiro worked around the restriction by living in the dormitory and moving her instruction there. Additionally, she rented space in three nearby Buddhist temples to house the students and teachers who could not be accommodated in the school's overflowing dormitories. DeForest explained Kajiro's strategy: "She couldn't have prayers and Bible-study in her regular school buildings, but in these Buddhist temples her Christian Endeavor society, her Bible-instruction, and her prayer meetings were regularly held, without the slightest objection."[104] Dormitory students referred to Kajiro as "mother" and Ōnishi as "father." Perhaps students used these terms because of the

---

Mt. Holyoke was in the midst of a transformation, from an institution dedicated to training teachers to a full-fledged liberal arts college. See Horowitz, *Alma Mater*, 225–32.

101. Hastings, "Mt. Holyoke College," 25.

102. Okayama joseishi kenkyūkai, *Kindai Okayama no onnatachi*, 69–71, 80; San'yō gakuen, *Ai to hōshi*, 35–36.

103. San'yō gakuen, *Ai to hōshi*, 36–37.

104. John DeForest, "Well Done, Miss Kajiro," *The Christian Endeavor World*, 26 November 1908.

age difference between the two women.[105] That we do not know more about this practice is unfortunate given the potential for analysis, but again, the examples point to the ways people struggled to explain women's leadership, resorting to a vocabulary of familial roles, especially wives and mothers—or fathers, in this case.[106] One source concludes that, together, Ōnishi and Kajiro provided complementary models of womanhood. Kajiro did not leave the dorm until she reached her fifties. Perhaps it was the lack of a private life that led her to comment that she had "married San'yō."[107] We are left to wonder about Kajiro's impact as a single woman on her students. To be sure, the school promoted "good wife and wise mother" ideals by the turn of the century. Yet the students' most immediate role models were Kajiro and Ōnishi, and neither was a wife or a mother.

After Kajiro took over as the school's first woman principal in 1908, she mentored the students and encouraged alumnae to gather and cultivate themselves by learning more about home economics, cooking, and sewing machines, indicating they were learning to make Western-style clothing.[108] Sources detail how she built connections among alumnae and students alike, ensuring the school's success. These ties—including those with Mt. Holyoke—helped her rebuild San'yō gakuen after it was completely destroyed in the Allied firebombing of World War II.[109] In the early postwar years, some individuals discussed the possibility of Kajiro standing for election to the Diet.[110] She ultimately did not run but continued to advocate actively and publicly for peace and a ban on nuclear testing. Meanwhile, members of the Allied Occupation tried to

---

105.　Okayama joseishi kenkyūkai, *Kindai Okayama no onnatachi*, 82. Similarly, students at the Okayama Orphanage regarded Sumiya as the mother and Ishii as the father. Kibi, *Kyōdo no joketsu 50-nen*, 45. I thank an anonymous reader for the suggestion that the women's ages played a role here.

106.　Okayama joseishi kenkyūkai, *Kindai Okayama no onnatachi*, 82.

107.　Okayama joseishi kenkyūkai, *Kindai Okayama no onnatachi*, 82. On the impact of women's education in the early United States, see Kelley, *Learning to Stand and Speak*.

108.　Okayama joseishi kenkyūkai, *Kindai Okayama no onnatachi*, 85. On the history of the sewing machine in Japan, see Gordon, *Fabricating Consumers*.

109.　Okayama joseishi kenkyūkai, *Kindai Okayama no onnatachi*, 86–89. This section also discusses Kajiro's use of jingoistic wartime language.

110.　Hastings, "Mt. Holyoke College," 24.

purge her—presumably for her support of the Japanese wartime state—though she talked them out of it.[111]

Kajiro's primary role was as an educator, but she also engaged in work beyond the school. She served as a "deaconess" at the Okayama Church and the principal of the Kyokutō Sunday School, later known as the Pettee Memorial Sunday School, the same place Sumiya taught.[112] The school, begun by James Pettee and several Japanese Christian men in 1881, operated separately from the Okayama Church, initially at the missionaries' residence. Kajiro eventually took it over. The organization was unusual because it was not under the direction of a male pastor, allowing Kajiro considerable autonomy.[113]

Kajiro cultivated a close relationship with Ishii and the Okayama Orphanage. She fundraised for the institution while traveling abroad in 1907.[114] When foreign visitors came to visit the Orphanage, Kajiro served as the translator since her time at Mt. Holyoke left her with excellent English. Her life demonstrates once again the deeply-intertwined nature of institutional and interpersonal networks in Okayama.[115]

All the Single Ladies[116]

How should Ōnishi and Kajiro—and all the single ladies—and their work be understood? One method is to bear in mind historian Irwin Scheiner's point that in the aftermath of the Restoration, male former

111.   Okayama joseishi kenkyūkai, *Kindai Okayama no onnatachi*, 89. On the attempt to purge her: Kajiro Yoshi Biographical File, Folder 1, Mt. Holyoke College Archives and Special Collections.

112.   Mt. Holyoke Alumnae address list, 22 April 1957, in Kajiro Yoshi Biographical File, Folder 1, Mt. Holyoke College Archives and Special Collections. Hamada, *Kadota kaiwai*, 230–55.

113.   Hamada, *Kadota kaiwai*, 254.

114.   Hamada, *Kadota kaiwai*, 94–95.

115.   Her son Kōzō (1897–1984), whom she adopted in 1917, became a professor at Tokyo Medical University; he served as the eighth principal of San'yō gakuen beginning in 1966. San'yō shinbunsha, *Okayama-ken rekishi jinbutsu jiten*, 290.

116.   See the book of the same title by Traister, *All the Single Ladies* which takes its name from the artist Beyoncé's song "Single Ladies."

samurai found in Christianity a "meaningful path to power."[117] We can make a similar argument here, not only with these women but also with those in the JWCTU and its local organization in Okayama, the Okayama WCTU. Certainly, the power acquired through social work was not limited to Christians. Nevertheless, Christian networks helped women forge dense ties across several institutions centering on education and social reform.[118] What may be most unusual about Ōnishi and Kajiro—along with Sumiya—is that they were self-supporting.

Their roles as educators, however, were not so extraordinary given the history of women working as teachers in the late Tokugawa period. Some women also led schools, as Sugano Noriko's work has illustrated.[119] The Meiji era brought changes as education came under the purview of the new state. Importantly, Kajiro and Ōnishi worked at the school as unmarried women rather than as someone's wife or daughter. The language they used suggests the school took the place of the household as the unit that defined and protected them; it was where they devoted their time and labor.[120] And there were others like them. As Yamakawa Kikue once noted, "Almost all the female teachers of early Meiji . . . were the daughters of poor provincial samurai."[121] To be sure, Kajiro and Ōnishi fit this description in terms of their status background, though the Ōnishi family seems to have been relatively prosperous.

The sources shed no light on the women's apparently conscious decision not to marry. I note their choice marks a major shift from the Tokugawa period, when all people were expected to eventually marry. A notable exception can be found in the life of Kusumoto Ine (1827–1903), the daughter of Dutch physician Philipp Franz von Siebold (1796–1866), who lived in Japan, and a Japanese mother named Taki. Taki was von Siebold's concubine and later common-law wife. Their daughter Kusumoto Ine lived as a lifelong single woman in spite of her care obligations

---

117. Scheiner, *Christian Converts*, 6.

118. See Lublin, *Reforming Japan*; Yoshizaki, "Nakamura Shizu," 1–10.

119. Sugano, "Terakoya to onnakyōshi," 144–46.

120. This work was not limited to single women. Miwada Masako (1843–1937) supported her family as an educator after her husband died. Walthall, "Women and Literacy from Edo to Meiji," 228.

121. Yamakawa, *Women of the Mito Domain*, 144. Less clear is how many of the women Yamakawa referenced were single.

for her mother and daughter, conceived after a teacher raped her. Because of her work as a medical practitioner, she was able to provide for her family and to "reject the conventional female path of marriage or concubinage in favor of an independent life" even before the Meiji period.[122] Like her Meiji counterparts, she adopted a male heir—in this case, her grandson.[123] Unlike them, Kusumoto hailed from a commoner background.

What Kusumoto and the trio of single ladies shared was an environment and circumstances that enabled them to live as single women; they were able to support themselves and enjoy respectability in local circles. Japanese women read about single missionary women's work abroad and encountered women like Eliza Talcott and Julia Gulick. We do not, however, find evidence of a conscious choice or rebellion against marriage. If anything, women took pains *not* to draw attention to their status; they tolerated—or even encouraged—people to think about them as married to local institutions. This pattern shares much in common with how scholars have described foreign female missionaries. They stretched the norms of gendered behavior in practice without drawing attention to their actions—their "independence and professionalism often belied their rhetoric."[124] Consequently, we should interpret this situation less in terms of Japanese women "following" Western women and more a case where Japanese and foreign women expanded their spheres at the same historical moment.

We have seen how writers across time and place have conceived of women's labor and authority in gendered terms. As with Kajiro and her talk of marrying the school, the women themselves sometimes contributed to this tendency—they portrayed themselves as maternal or wifely figures, even though these roles did not reflect their lives. Kajiro and Ōnishi were leaders at the school—yet most texts do not highlight this information.

To name but one example, a 1929 piece in English for a missionary audience conceives of Kajiro's work in maternal language:

122.   Nakamura, "Kusumoto Ine," 10.

123.   This practice of adoption extended to single foreign missionary women. See also Seat, *Providence Has Freed Our Hands*, chap. 1.

124.   Siegel, "Transcending Cross-Cultural Frontiers," 192. See also Seat, *Providence Has Freed Our Hands*, chap. 1.

For many years Okayama has had a practical demonstration of the power of consecrated mother-love in the life and work of Miss Yoshiko Kajiro. More than thirty years ago she graduated from Mt. Holyoke College and since then has been the Principal of the Sanyo Jogakko, a leading private Girls' School in this city. Although she has never married, her great mother-heart has been a powerful influence in the lives of thousands of girls.[125]

Similarly, accounts of Ōnishi highlight her work as a caretaker rather than an agent in her own right. A 2016 article in *San'yō shinbun* discusses an exhibit put together by junior high and high school students at San'yō gakuen. The exhibit featured information about Ōnishi: "Her husband died young, and she cared for her nephew whose father died in a war." This passage overlooks her leadership role, though it mentions her work at the school. One student, after learning about Ōnishi Kinu, concluded: "I want to be someone who works for others" as Ōnishi had.[126]

Other sympathetic interpretations also demand scrutiny, such as Hamada Hideo's assertion that the women "awakened to an independent way of life" (*jiritsushita ikikata ni mezame*).[127] The record contains no evidence that the women understood their lives this way. They were part of deeply-intertwined networks, endeavoring at the institutions they served to make the world better. Rather than awakening to independence, they commanded authority as they went about working for reform. Such distinctions matter because the very terms we use to talk about women's labor can limit our understanding of the extent of their actions. Undoubtedly in the process, the women found "independent roles," in the sense that they were not tethered to husbands and children, nor was their work rooted inside households. They supported themselves financially.[128] Like Kajiro's role models Mary Lyon and Florence Nightingale, the women wished to serve society and the nation, but they did not do so as married women based in households. Their work calls to

125.   Genevieve Olds, "Okayama: A Lover of Little Children," *News Bulletin from the Japan Mission of the American Board*, vol. 33, no. 5 (December 1929), 1.

126.   "Josei kyōikusha temani kabe shinbun 22 mai: San'yō joshi chu-kosei ga to-shokan de tenji," *San'yō shinbun*, 23 November 2016.

127.   Hamada, *Kadota kaiwai*, 86.

128.   Dunch describes a similar situation in the case of Chinese Protestant converts: Dunch, "Mothers to Our Country," 324–50.

mind the original San'yō gakuen "statement of intention," which described men and women as "two wheels of a cart" engaged in labor together for a greater cause. Of course, the difference is that for single women, the work was carried out in a heterosocial network outside of the conjugal relationship.

In retrospect, it seems fitting that the women were buried near each other. They made distinct contributions, but their lives intersected at multiple points—at the Okayama Church, at the Sunday school, and in women's groups like the Okayama WCTU.[129] They were bound together by San'yō gakuen's financial challenges. They donated to the school, whether in the form of time or money. Ōnishi gave her salary when times were tight, and Sumiya offered expensive hairpins and dolls.[130]

The school's most difficult moment—when these women made their donations—coincided with Nakagawa's "living funeral" whose proceeds he donated to the school. Ultimately, his donations rather than theirs are the ones remembered—even on the school's website and other informational materials.[131] Yet men like Nakagawa and institutions like San'yō gakuen relied on these women and others like them. Their lives speak to new possibilities opened by modernity for careers outside the home and also to the gendered ways people at the time and since have conceived of their labor.

Conclusion

This chapter has sought fresh perspectives on activism in Meiji networks while analyzing some of the biases that shape the historical record, especially relating to gender and marital status. Much of the scholarly literature

129.   Hamada, *Kadota kaiwai*, 238–39. This is not to say that all three women were present in each place at the same time. Ōnishi taught at a different Sunday school, and Kajiro does not appear to have been involved in the WCTU.

130.   Murata Tomi, *Ōnishi Kinuko*, 61; Onoda, *Tsuikairoku*, 71–72. Ōnishi refused a pension from the school as well. Okayama joseishi kenkyūkai, *Kindai Okayama no onnatachi*, 76.

131.   For example, see the chronology on San'yō gakuen's website: http://sanyogakuen .net/history/story (accessed 7 November 2019).

on Japanese history suggests that women emerged in public with full force in the 1920s. The material presented here pushes this statement back by several decades to the 1880s. The stories I have told compel us to reconsider received views about the activities of married couples and single women and their importance in driving historical change. I have also analyzed how sources present the lives of men and women in ways that limit scholarly understanding. In the case of the Ishiguros, men's lives are framed by high politics to the neglect of other dimensions—Kan'ichirō figures primarily as a politician rather than as an active member of multiple Christian institutions—and married women like Orio appear as appendages to men rather than agents in their own right, if they appear at all.

Single women like Kajiro Yoshi seem to have a better chance of making it into the historical record than married women, especially since Kajiro headed an institution. But this point does not hold true in the case of Ōnishi Kinu, who was overshadowed by a man, her nephew and heir Ōnishi Hajime. In the case of both women, it is impossible to clearly distinguish between the women's work at the school and their devotion to social reform as they moved between the two realms seamlessly.[132]

A more robust account of Meiji activism must consider the full range of people involved in social life and the variety of activities in which they engaged. It should illuminate how people took advantage of new institutions like schools and churches while attending to how individuals interacted with each other, including at home. We need to acknowledge cases of married couples working together as well as single women. At the same time, we must bear in mind the problems that swirl around the constitution of the archive. In all cases, the underlying networks comprised men *and* women. Still, the ways individuals occupied space differed by variables including gender, age, and marital status. Of course, chronology matters too—what happened in 1884 with men and women joining together in public for a political event could not have happened a decade later.

132. The question of widowed women's experiences also deserves analysis. Ishizaka Mina's life, for instance, has many parallels with the single women I address here. Mina, like Sumiya, became a Bible Woman. Steele, "The Ishizaka of Notsuda," 71.

A major takeaway from this chapter, then, is that understandings of late nineteenth and early twentieth-century activism can no longer be centered only on men and high politics. The material introduced here demands that our narratives include the contributions of women. Both married women and single ladies provided critical labor—by supervising households, connecting people, bridging divides, and at times, heading up institutions.

EPILOGUE

After Meiji: The Legacy of the Okayama Networks

T he networks I have discussed in these pages lasted through the first two decades of the twentieth century, although underlying networks stretched and shifted over time in ways we cannot always trace. Changes in individual lives become noticeable after the turn of the twentieth century. Ōnishi Kinu went to live in Tokyo in 1908, while Sumiya and Kajiro remained in Okayama. Yet far from sedentary, Sumiya traveled the country to raise money for the Okayama Orphanage and to evangelize. Meanwhile, Kajiro, who had spent part of the 1890s at Mt. Holyoke, took an overseas trip to the United States and Europe to fundraise for San'yō gakuen school and the Orphanage.[1]

By the mid-1910s, early in the Taishō era (1912–1926), most of the central actors in this story had died or were nearing the end of their lives. Born in the late Tokugawa period, they had faced the challenges of the Meiji era, forging new roles even as their lives were shaped by the Tokugawa world in which they had grown up. We have seen examples of these new lives in Nakagawa as an eccentric reformer, Ishiguro Kan'ichirō as a modern politician, lawyer, and temperance advocate, and Ishiguro Orio and the other married and single women activists who formed the OWFS and the Okayama WCTU. In particular, I have drawn attention to single women—Sumiya Koume, Ōnishi Kinu, and Kajiro Yoshi, who managed

---

1. Kajiro's English-language diary for the United States section of the trip can be found in Kitajima, "Kajiro Yoshi eibun nikki."

careers at the Orphanage and San'yō gakuen school while acting as reformers in local networks. All three taught at local Sunday schools connected to the Protestant community (Kajiro and Sumiya taught at the same one, while Ōnishi taught at one founded by Berry).[2]

Ishiguro Orio and Kan'ichirō both died in 1917. By that time, Nakagawa had been gone for fourteen years, and Nishi had died shortly after his friend in 1904 in an apparent suicide.[3] Sumiya remained active until her death in 1920, and Ōnishi Kinu passed away over a decade later in 1933. Abe Isoo died in 1949 before the Occupation ended. Of all the central figures, only Kajiro Yoshi would live to see the post–World War II world. She presided for decades over San'yō gakuen school, ensuring her prominent local profile until her death in 1959. Visitors to the school today will find she continues to be regarded with great reverence; her personal effects, including books from her time at Mt. Holyoke, are kept in a special locked room, as I discovered when I visited the school in the summer of 2018.

Over the course of researching this history, I have been struck by the rich human stories that emerge, often in the context of cross-cultural encounters. For instance, Kume notes how a linguistically-challenged Dr. Berry advised a Japanese patient to eat more cat (*neko*) instead of meat (*niku*), much to the amusement of locals.[4] Similarly, Berry's daughter recounts the story of the first Western-style banquet in Okayama, held by the governor in the early 1880s. One Japanese guest showed up sporting a kimono with a necktie, and several Japanese attendees became ill after consuming large quantities of Worcestershire sauce, which they had assumed was like soy sauce.[5] Also striking are the accounts of the individual Japanese actors—the charismatic Nakagawa and his living funeral, Sumiya admonishing her daughter not to brag about her good works, and the single women Kajiro and Ōnishi heading up dormitory life at San'yō gakuen, where they served as parental figures. These human interactions are woven throughout my account of the Okayama networks and offer

2. On the formation of Sunday schools, see Hamada, *Kadota kaiwai*, 232; Okayama joseishi kenkyūkai, *Kindai Okayama no onnatachi*, 65.

3. San'yō shinbunsha, *Okayama-ken rekishi jinbutsu jiten*, 741.

4. Kume, *Kenbōsai itsuwashū*, 25.

5. Berry, *A Pioneer Doctor*, 124.

evidence of the bonds that hold networks together. The three single ladies were hardly radical—they acted quite conventionally, which is precisely what enabled them to do what they did. Unlike their male counterparts, women activists could *not* be both eccentric and effective.[6]

This book has analyzed how networks of local elites—almost all former samurai—shaped Okayama's modernization. By looking at their efforts and accomplishments, I have demonstrated how local people built modern Japan from the middle out. In their quest to remake local society, they created and maintained institutions, exchanged ideas, and forged an environment where reform efforts thrived. Individuals were not merely receiving "top-down" instructions from the central government in Tokyo. Nor, as local elites, does "bottom up" accurately describe who they were and what they did.

At the same time, this study reminds us of the centrality of the local level in defining peoples' lives. Louise Young has demonstrated how modern regional identities in Okayama and elsewhere were remade during the interwar period amid migration and social upheaval. But identities were not created whole cloth; earlier manifestations of these identities can be glimpsed in the late nineteenth century. Nakagawa and other local elites were eager to promote Okayama's development so that its infrastructure surpassed that of neighboring cities. Okayama Prefecture sent trained nurses to Hiroshima to tend wounded soldiers during the Sino-Japanese War in 1894 and 1895, a matter of local pride. The OWFS women at the boating party on the Asahi River in 1884 proclaimed their identities as local Okayama women, including eleven-year-old Kawaguchi Ume. At times, peoples' expressions of identity were framed not in terms of Okayama Prefecture but rather the larger region of "San'yō," referring to the area of southern Honshū facing the Inland Sea, stretching from southern Hyōgo Prefecture to Yamaguchi Prefecture. The way individuals constructed their identities slid back and forth depending on the situation, from city to prefecture, to region and nation, and back again to the local level.[7]

---

6. I thank an anonymous reader for making this point.

7. On local identity, see Shimoda, *Lost and Found*; Dusinberre, *Hard Times in the Hometown*.

Networks also had a transnational dimension. Through the Okayama Church, missionaries, and the local branch of the Freedom and People's Rights Movement, Okayama citizens had ties to people in Kobe, Kyoto, Tokyo, and the United States. Okayama residents Kajiro Yoshi and Abe Isoo studied abroad in the 1890s, with Kajiro at Mt. Holyoke and Abe enrolled at the Hartford Theological Seminary in Hartford, Connecticut. The cause of social reform, embraced by both the Okayama activists and the American Board missionaries, was also part of a global story.

Today's Okayama bears the imprint—however faint—of the Meiji past discussed here. The city is much larger than it was in the late nineteenth century, with a population of 719,000. The Okayama Church and San'yō gakuen are still around and operational, although the original Meiji-era buildings were destroyed in the June 1945 firebombing of the city; the Orphanage closed in 1926, and the People's Rights Movement waned in the 1880s. Other traces of the Meiji networks include Okayama hakuaikai (Benevolent society), a hospital that traces its roots to a settlement community of the same name founded by American Board missionary Alice Pettee Adams (1866–1937) in the early twentieth century. I have not covered Adams in this book in part because she arrived in Japan in 1891, over a decade later than the first group of missionaries, and my focus has been primarily on Japanese actors. But she deserves a brief mention here.

A lifelong single woman, Adams engaged in charitable work centered on poor relief, especially for impoverished children, in Okayama for forty-five years.[8] Her Hakuaikai was located next to the Okayama slums, a place where children routinely went hungry.[9] Adams was a cousin of James Pettee and a close friend of Kajiro Yoshi. She is the Western counterpart to Ōnishi and Kajiro, a woman who played a pivotal role in reform and an example of how women's work often flies under the radar, especially in retrospect. At the time, local people heralded her efforts to create a settlement house, with facilities that included childcare, a medical dispensary,

8. Hamada, *Kadota kaiwai*, 44–54.
9. "Hakuai" can be translated as charity, benevolence, or philanthropy. "Children's Lunches," *News Bulletin from the Japan Mission of the American Board*, 33, no. 5 (December 1929), 2.

a kindergarten, and a Sunday school. They gave her a "wild ovation" upon her retirement and departure from Japan in 1936.[10] On that occasion, Adams received the Sixth Order of the Sacred Treasure from the emperor, the first foreign missionary to receive such an award. This honor was unusual, not only because she was a woman but also because it was normally granted posthumously. On Adams's part, so great was her love for Japan that she was buried with the Japanese flag, at a cemetery in Newton, Massachusetts.[11]

In the hospital, school, and church, we see evidence of the rich social environment that was from the Meiji era so conducive to reform. One cannot but be struck by the key role of women, both single and married, in creating and sustaining these institutions: Adams in the case of the hospital, Ōnishi Kinu and Kajiro Yoshi with San'yō gakuen, and Nakagawa Yuki and her sisters, along with Ishiguro Orio and Sumiya Koume, at the Okayama Church. Western women also played a role. Sumiya was supported by Talcott and Gulick. And the students at San'yō gakuen had their imaginations sparked by stories of Florence Nightingale and Mary Lyon.

Although the underlying networks included women and men into the 1910s, the situation changed by the 1930s, when the networks themselves became largely single-sex. Part of the reason for this shift was that men increasingly did not have the time to maintain networks. As men began to work in greater numbers outside of the household as salaried workers and urban professionals, women were left to cultivate the bonds of community and family.[12] Then, in the 1930s, the government co-opted women's groups.[13] The large women's organizations of the era were

10. "Our Japanese Connection: Alice Pettee Adams," *Bridgewater Magazine* 1, no. 4 (1991): 6.

11. "Miss Alice Adams, Welfare Worker; American Woman Noted for 46 Years' Service in Slums of Japan Dies in Newton," *New York Times*, 10 May 1937.

12. Walthall, "Closing Remarks," 28. It goes without saying that poor women often had to work outside the home.

13. The male-dominated socialist world straddled both older and newer forms; it was heterosocial and had a separate women's organization. Faison, "Women's Rights as Proletarian Rights," 17, 20. Some scholars suggest the notion of "co-optation" is not accurate because the state and women's groups had a good deal in common. For example, Faison, "Women's Rights as Proletarian Rights," 25–26.

coordinated by government ministries; far from autonomous, they were local branches of national organizations.[14] By 1942, all organizations were amalgamated into a single group, the Greater Japan Women's Federation (Dai Nihon fujinkai), in a wartime effort to consolidate associational life. After the war, the tight connection between women and motherhood continued, part of an overall pattern of heightened gender differentiation across society. The earlier Meiji moment when local men and women worked together in close association was largely forgotten.

There are three main takeaways from this analysis of Okayama networks. First, the environment conducive to social activism during the early Meiji period persisted in later eras. A 1904 American Board annual report boasted, "There is no other city in Japan where so many varied forms of Christian work are sustained in connection with a single church organization with equal harmony, economy, and efficiency." The authors understandably portray activism as "emanating from the Christian church" and highlight the existence of several Sunday schools, Young Men's Christian Association (YMCA) chapters, Bible classes, a temperance union, a night school, poverty relief efforts, and the Okayama Orphanage.[15] Without denying the Church's role, activism in Okayama thrived in other quarters throughout the city and prefecture. By the 1910s, Okayama's high levels of activism made it a center of the Taishō democracy movement, beginning with the 1918 Rice Riots.[16] After World War II, activism bubbled up to the surface again in the 1960s, when Okayama civic groups and unions successfully opposed the governor's plan to build a "vast heavy-industrial zone that would cover the southern half of the prefecture" and merge thirty-three administrative units into a single unit, a "million city."[17] Here, too, local actors decisively shaped Okayama's path on their terms.

14. The first national women's group, the Women's Patriotic Association (Aikoku fujinkai) was founded by Okumura Ioko (1845–1907) in 1901 but became state-sponsored by the 1930s. Government ministries formed the national groups of the 1930s, including the Greater Japan Federated Women's Association (Dai Nihon rengō fujinkai) in 1931 and Greater Japan National Defense Women's Association (Dai Nihon kokubo fujinkai) in 1932.

15. *The Ninety-Fourth Annual Report of the American Board of Commissioners for Foreign Missions* (1904), 121.

16. Young, *Beyond the Metropolis*, 9.

17. Young, *Beyond the Metropolis*, 248.

The second takeaway is a reminder of the contingency at work in the forging of the modern political sphere in relation to modern gender roles. In other words, sex-segregated associational activity was not always the norm but was rather a product of Japan's modern transformation. We have seen women's political participation across the 1880s, even though the associations dedicated to politics and reform were women-only. It would be a mistake to assume that the pattern of sex segregation visible in networks by the 1930s reflects a timeless Japanese "tradition." But to uncover the many ways that men did *not* act alone, we must push back on the sources to arrive at these conclusions, bringing in other records and expanding our archives whenever possible to mitigate androcentric bias.[18]

A third point involves a more general consideration of women and networks in the Meiji period. Networks were not necessarily present in the same form across society. For example, historian Nishizawa Naoko has discussed how Meiji women in educator and journalist Fukuzawa Yukichi's circle, especially his wife and daughters, faced barriers in building social networks. Following the Restoration, Fukuzawa founded an alumnae group at his Keio University called the Kōjunsha to promote the "social cohesion" so necessary in the topsy-turvy world of the early Meiji period. However, the group was not open to women.[19] Based on this case, Nishizawa concludes that women's opportunities to network in modern Japan were severely circumscribed. Nishizawa's trenchant analysis of the women in Fukuzawa's orbit does not apply, however, to the people at the center of this book. To be sure, Sumiya, Ōnishi, Kajiro, Ishiguro Orio, and others were local rather than national elites like Fukuzawa—though he, too, began life as a lower-level samurai. We have seen that places like the Okayama Church, San'yō gakuen, and the Orphanage facilitated networking among women *and* men. Undoubtedly, women accessed space differently than men when it came to politics. And marital status mattered. Single women and widowed women were more active—or at least generally left more traces in the record. One clear change visible in the late nineteenth century is that modern associations were increasingly single-sex. But the nature of networks—and the degree of heterosociality

18.   On the different kinds of Meiji women's groups: Yoshizaki, "Nakamura Shizu."
19.   Nishizawa, "Female Networks and Social Stratification," 253–55.

within them—varied based on location, social status, and the presence of religious and educational institutions.[20] The question of how to assess these networks continues to divide scholars. What exactly was possible and when? Nishizawa Naoko sees groups like Fukuzawa's Kōjunsha as "transcend[ing] the boundaries of early modern human relationships," whereas Eiko Ikegami proposes that Tokugawa aesthetic associations had already achieved this.[21] The conclusions one draws seem to depend on the group under discussion rather than solely on chronology. One plausible interpretation is that historical change proceeds unevenly. Another is that scholars are likely to see possibilities in their own period of study that they do not discern for other periods.

This study has also confronted a problem one encounters when writing about networks. Networks clearly facilitated activism in Okayama, but the tendency of observers, including historians, to focus on the labor of a few figureheads often renders invisible the work of the larger group—particularly the work of women. In other words, Nakagawa, Nishi, and Ishii receive much more credit in the historical record than Sumiya and Ōnishi. The one exception in which a woman clearly played a leading role is Kajiro as head of San'yō gakuen.[22] Even scholars, like Hamada, who do not appear interested in women and gender have to address Kajiro because of her position. Meanwhile, informal networks, which are even more likely than formal networks to involve women, are usually under-documented. For instance, what about the women at the Okayama Church, especially the Ōnishi sisters and their mother? We know they were important, but the written evidence remains scant. Considering the full range of actors in a network—rather than a few of its more prominent members—allows a nuanced appreciation of the many hands necessary to bring about social change. In my attempt to provide a

20. Miyazaki Fumiko addresses the opportunities provided by religious networks in the late Tokugawa period: Miyazaki, "Networks of Believers in a New Religion." On the exceptional opportunities offered by some religious institutions, see Gramlich-Oka and Walthall, "Introduction," 12–13.

21. Nishizawa, "Female Networks and Social Stratification," 269; Ikegami, *The Bonds of Civility.*

22. While she is not a major figure in this book, I would include Alice Pettee Adams here given her role at the Hakuaikai. Hamada discusses Adams as well.

more holistic view, I have found useful Norton's notion of "history on the diagonal," which gives ample attention to the labor of women like Sumiya Koume and Ōnishi Kinu.[23]

Anne Walthall has pointed out that in the Tokugawa period, women and men worked together in households and "shared the same emotional universe and worked together to further family goals."[24] This dynamic continued into the Meiji period even as the circumstances shifted: families worked together to navigate challenges, including the difficulties surrounding the breakdown of the status system, the hardships incurred by the new tax structure, and the burdens of military conscription and mandatory universal primary education. Within and outside of households, networks of men and women, married and single, strove to operate within this new world, a world they were simultaneously in the process of creating.

A major takeaway from this study of Okayama networks, then, is an appreciation of the interdependence of men and women in households and social networks—of men and women working in close association. To grant credit to this larger constellation of actors remains a most challenging task for the historian.

23. Norton, "History on the Diagonal."
24. Walthall, review of *The Problem of Women in Early Modern Japan*, 91.

List of Characters

Abe Isoo 安部磯雄
Aikō fujinkai 愛甲婦人会
Aikoku fujinkai 愛国婦人会
Aoki Aiko 青木愛子
Aoki Toyo 青木豊; given name also rendered as 登与
Aoki (Sakasai) Yōkichi 青木(坂斎)要吉

Baika jogakkō 梅花女学校
bakufu 幕府
bengoshi 弁護士
bentatsu 弁達
Biryokusha 微力社
Bodhidharma 達磨
bunmei kaika 文明開化
Bunmei saidai genso zaiyokuron 文明最大元素・在欲論
burakumin 部落民

Daidō danketsu 大同団結
daigennin 代言人
Dai Nihon fujinkai 大日本婦人会
Dai Nihon kokubo fujinkai 大日本国母婦人会
Dai Nihon rengō fujinkai 大日本連合婦人会
Dajōkan 太政官

danseiteki taido 男性的態度
danson johi 男尊女卑

eiwa 英和
Enomoto Takeaki 榎本武揚
eta 穢多

Fujidō 富士道
Fujin eigakusha 婦人英学舎
Fuju fuse 不受不施
Fukuda (Kageyama) Hideko 福田(影山)英子
Fukuzawa Yukichi 福沢諭吉
fūzoku taihai 風俗頽廃

Gakumon no susume 学問のすすめ
Gakusei 学制
"Geisha to tekake to ni susumezu" 芸者と手掛とに勧めず
Gensen gakkai 源泉学会
Gensenkai 源泉会
gidayū 義太夫
gobō 牛蒡
Gokajō no seimon 五箇条の誓文
gondaizoku 権大属
gonshōzoku 権少属
Gotō Shinpei 後藤新平

haikai 俳諧
Han Feizi 韓非子
happi 半被
Hara Kei 原敬
harenchi waisetsu 破廉恥猥褻
hatamoto 旗本
Hatoyama Haruko 鳩山春子
Higemaru 鬚丸
hinin 非人
Hoan jōrei 保安条例
hokkisha 発起者
Hoshi Tōru 星亨

Ichi Nihonjin 一日本人
ie 家
*Igakushi Kiyono-kun sōkokubetsu enzetsu
　narabini jo* 医学士清野君送告別演説并序
Ikeda 池田
ikensho 意見書
iki 粋
Inoue Kaoru 井上馨
Ishiguro Kan'ichirō 石黒涵一郎
Ishiguro Orio 石黒織尾
Ishii Jūji 石井十次
Ishii Shina 石井品
Ishizaka Kensō 石坂堅壮
Ishizaka Kōreki 石坂公歴
Ishizaka Mina 石坂美那
Ishizaka Shōkō 石坂昌孝
Ishizeki-machi 石関町
Itagaki Taisuke 板垣退助
itai dōshin 異体同心
Itō Hirobumi 伊藤博文
Iwamoto Yoshiharu 巌本善治

Jikkōsha 実行社
Jingū Kōgō 神功皇后
jiritsukei 自立形
jiritsushita ikikata ni mezame 自立した生き
　方に目覚め
jiyū 自由
Jiyū minken undō 自由民権運動
Jiyū no tomoshibi 自由燈
Jiyūtō 自由党

Jogaku zasshi 女学雑誌
Jōkō gakusha 蒸紅学舎
Jūjika ni tsuite no meisō 十字架に就いての
　瞑想

kachō 花鳥 flower and bird
kachō 蚊帳 mosquito net
Kadota kaiwai no michi 門田界隈の道
Kagawa Toyohiko 賀川豊彦
Kageyama Ume 景山楳
Kajiro Kōzō 上代浩三
Kajiro Tomoyoshi 上代知新
Kajiro Yoshi 上代淑
Kanamori Michitomo 金森通倫
kanbun 漢文
Kaneji 金次
Kanzei gakkō 関西学校
Katsu Kaishū 勝海舟
Katsurada Fujirō 桂田富士郎
Kawaguchi Ume 河口梅
kazoedoshi 数え年
keishū kunsai no mi 閨秀裙釵の身
kengi 建議
kenpaku 建白
kesa 袈裟
kijin 奇人
Kimata Kayo 木全嘉代
Kishida (Nakajima) Toshiko 岸田 (中島)
　俊子, pen name Shōen 湘煙
kiyaku 規約
kizen 毅然
kō 講
Kobayashi Kusuo 小林樟雄
Kobayashi Tei 小林貞
Kōbe eiwa jogakkō 神戸英和女学校
Kōbe jogakuin 女学院
Kōbe joshi shingakkō 神戸女子神学校
Kōjunsha 交詢社
koku 石
Kokuseiji 国清時
Kōmoto Otogorō 河本乙五郎
Konishi Masutarō 小西増太郎
Konkōkyō 金光教
koshōgumi umayaku 小姓組馬役

koto 琴
Kōtō jogakkō rei 高等女学校令
Kume Ryūsen 久米龍川
Kumiai 組合
Kunitomi Shōrinji 国富少林寺
Kurosawa Tokiko 黒澤止幾子
Kurozumikyō 黒住教
kusshinai 屈しない
Kusumoto Ine 楠本イネ
Kusunose Kita 楠瀬喜多
Kyōiku chokugo 教育勅語
Kyokutō nichiyōbi gakkō 極東日曜
　日学校
kyūmin 旧民

Laozi 老子

Matsumura Midori 松村緑
Matsu-no-e 松の江
Matsuo Taseko 松尾多勢子
Matsushita Chiyo 松下千代
meibōka 名望家
Meiji seika 明治製菓
Meiji seitō 明治製糖
meiyaku 盟約
Miwada Masako 三輪田真佐子
Miyako no hana 都之花
Morishita Tachitarō 森下立太郎, later
　Kagenao 影端
mugaku monmō 無学文盲
Murasaki Shikibu 紫式部
Murasame Nobu 村雨のぶ
muyō no yō 無用の用

nagauta 長唄
naijokei 内助形
naishoku 内職
Nakagawa Kamenoshin 中川亀之進
Nakagawa Naname 中川斜
Nakagawa Shigeru 中川蕃
Nakagawa Tateichi 中川竪一
Nakagawa Yokotarō 中川横太郎,
　pen name Kenbōsai 健忘斎
Nakagawa Yuki 中川雪

Nakajima Nobuyuki 中島信行
Nakamura Masanao 中村正直
Nakamura Shizu 中村静
Nakayama Miki 中山みき
Narita Ume 成田梅
Naruse Jinzō 成瀬仁蔵
neko 猫
Nichiren 日蓮
Nihon joshi daigaku 日本女子大学
Nihon kirisutokyō fujin kyōfūkai 日本キ
　リスト教婦人矯風会
Niijima Jō 新島襄
Niijima Yae 新島八重
niku 肉
niōdachi 仁王立ち
Nishi Kiichi 西毅一, pen name Bizan 薇山
Nishi Tsuyako 西つや子 also 艶子
Nishiyama (Kanamori) Kohisa 西山
　(金森)こひさ
nisshi 日誌
nōryōkai 納涼会
Nozaki Bukichirō 野崎武吉郎

Ōhara Magosaburō 大原孫三郎
Okayama fujin kinshukai 岡山婦人禁酒会
Okayama fujin kyōfūkai 岡山婦人矯風会
Okayama hakuaikai 岡山博愛會
Okayama joshi konshinkai 岡山女子
　懇親会
Okayama kojiin 岡山孤児院
Okayama kyōkai 岡山教会
Ōkuma Shigenobu 大隈重信
Okumura Ioko 奥村五百子
Ōnishi Hajime 大西祝, pen name
　Sōzan 操山
Ōnishi Hide 大西秀
Ōnishi Kinu 大西絹
Ōnishi Sadamichi 大西定道
onjū 温柔
Ono no Komachi 小野小町
Ozaki Yukio 尾崎行雄

rakugo 落語
Risshisha 立志社

rōkotsu 老骨
Ryōbisaka sangoku 両備作三国
ryōsai kenbo 良妻賢母

Saigō Takamori 西郷隆盛
Sakurada Momoe 櫻田百衛
Sankan no meika 山間の名花
San'yō gakuen 山陽学園
San'yō jiyūtō 山陽自由党
San'yō shinbun 山陽新聞
San'yō shinpō 山陽新報
Sei Shōnagon 清少納言
Shibusawa Eiichi 渋沢栄一
Shichiichi zappō 七一雑報
shinheimin 新平民
"Shinkō no hitsuyō" 信仰の必要
shinmin 新民
shiri metsuretsu 支離滅裂
shizoku 士族
shizoku jusan 士族授産
Shizutani gakkō 閑谷学校
shōteikoku 小帝国
shuisho 趣意書
Shūkai jōrei 集会条例
Shūkai oyobi seisha hō 集会及政社法
shukutoku o migaku 淑徳を磨く
Shūshin yōryō 修身要領
Soejima Taneomi 副島種臣
sōrōbun 候文
Sumiya Koume 炭谷小梅
Sumiya Koume-shi tsuikairoku 炭谷小梅
　姉追懐録
Sugiyama Heisuke 杉山平助
Sugiyama Iwasaburō 杉山岩三郎

tabi 足袋
tachi 立

Takasaki Itsumu 高崎五六
Takeuchi Hisa 竹内寿
Takeuchi Masashi 竹内正志
Tanima no sakura 谷間の桜
tenchi no kōdō 天地の公道
tenka no kōdō 天下の公道
Tenrikyō 天理教
tensei no dendōsha 天成の伝道者
terakoya 寺子屋
Tomeoka Kōsuke 留岡幸助
Tomoe Gozen 巴御前
tondenhei 屯田兵
Toyohashi fujo kyōkai 豊橋婦女協会
Tōyō no fujo 東洋の婦女
Toyotake Roshō 豊竹呂昇
Tsuge Kume 津下久米
Tsuge Masagorō 津下正五郎

Ueki Emori 植木枝盛
Uemori Misao 上森操
ura 裏

waga Nihon 我日本

Yamamoto Baigai 山本梅崖
Yamamoto Tadasaburō 山本唯三郎
Yamamoto (Ishiguro) Taki 山本（石黒）多喜
Yamamoto Ushi 山本宇志
Yamamuro Gunpei 山室軍平
Yamazaki Hokka 山崎北華
yoko 横
Yomiuri shinbun 読売新聞
yuigon 遺言
yūshisha 有志者

zairai no Nihon fujin 在来の日本婦人
zange 懺悔

Bibliography

Place of publication for Japanese-language texts is Tokyo, unless indicated otherwise.

All citations of archival materials and of newspapers and periodicals are given in full in the notes upon first citation.

Archival Materials

American Board of Commissioners for Foreign Missions, ABC 1-91, Houghton Library, Harvard University
Mt. Holyoke College Archives and Special Collections, South Hadley, Massachusetts
Okayama Prefectural Archives, Okayama

Newspapers and Periodicals

Annual Report (American Board of Commissioners for Foreign Missions)
Asahi shinbun
Bridgewater Magazine
The Christian Endeavor World
Jiyū no tomoshibi
Jiyū shinbun
Jogaku zasshi
Life and Light for Woman
Megumi
Missionary Herald
Mission News
News Bulletin from the Japan Mission of the American Board
New York Times
Nihon rikken seitō shinbun

San'yō shinbun, previously *San'yō shinpō*
Sekai fujin
Yomiuri shinbun

Other Sources

Abe Isoo. *Shakai shugisha to naru made.* Kaizōsha, 1932. Reprint, Meizensha, 1947.

Adelman, Jeremy. "What Is Global History Now?" *Aeon.* 2 March 2017. https://aeon.co/essays/is-global-history-still-possible-or-has-it-had-its-moment.

Ambaras, David R. *Bad Youth: Juvenile Delinquency and the Politics of Everyday Life in Modern Japan.* Berkeley: University of California Press, 2005.

Ambros, Barbara. "Nakayama Miki's Views of Women and Their Bodies in the Context of Nineteenth Century Japanese Religions." *Tenri Journal of Religion,* no. 41 (2013): 85–115.

Amos, Timothy D. *Embodying Difference: The Making of the Burakumin in Modern Japan.* Honolulu: University of Hawai'i Press, 2011.

Anderson, Emily. *Christianity and Imperialism in Modern Japan: Empire for God.* London: Bloomsbury Academic, 2014.

Anderson, Marnie S. "Critiquing Concubinage: Sumiya Koume and Changing Gender Roles in Modern Japan." *Japanese Studies,* 37, no. 3 (2017): 311–29.

———. "From Status to Gender in Meiji Japan." In *The Cambridge History of Japan,* vol. 3, edited by Laura Hein. Cambridge: Cambridge University Press, forthcoming.

———. *A Place in Public: Women's Rights in Meiji Japan.* Cambridge, MA: Harvard University Asia Center, 2010.

———. "Women's Agency and the Historical Record: Reflections on Female Activists in Nineteenth-Century Japan." *Journal of Women's History* 23, no. 1 (March 2011): 38–55.

Baxter, James C. *The Meiji Unification through the Lens of Ishikawa Prefecture.* Cambridge, MA: Harvard University Asia Center, 1995.

Beardsley, Richard K., John W. Hall, and Robert E. Ward. *Village Japan.* Chicago: University of Chicago Press, 1959.

Berry, Katherine Fiske. *A Pioneer Doctor in Old Japan: The Story of John C. Berry, MD.* New York: Fleming Revell, 1940.

Botsman, Daniel V. "Freedom without Slavery: 'Coolies,' Prostitutes, and Outcastes in Meiji Japan's Emancipation Moment." *American Historical Review* 116, no. 5 (2011): 1323–47.

Bowen, Roger W. *Rebellion and Democracy in Meiji Japan: A Study of Commoners in the Popular Rights Movement.* Berkeley: University of California Press, 1984.

Boylan, Anne M. *The Origins of Women's Activism: New York and Boston, 1797–1840.* Chapel Hill: University of North Carolina Press, 2002.

Brecher, W. Puck. *The Aesthetics of Strangeness: Eccentricity and Madness in Early Modern Japan.* Honolulu: University of Hawai'i Press, 2013.

Burks, Ardath W. "Administrative Transition from Han to Ken: The Example of Okayama." *Far Eastern Quarterly* 15, no. 3 (1956): 371–82.

Burton, Antoinette. *Dwelling in the Archive: Women Writing House, Home, and History in Late Colonial India.* Oxford: Oxford University Press, 2003.

Campbell, Gavin James. "'To Make the World One in Christ Jesus': Transpacific Protestantism in the Age of Empire." *Pacific Historical Review* 87, no. 4 (2018): 575–92.

Canning, Kathleen. *Gender History in Practice: Historical Perspectives on Body, Class, and Citizenship*. Ithaca, NY: Cornell University Press, 2006.

Cary, Otis. *A History of Christianity in Japan*, vol. 2. New York: Fleming Revell, 1909. Reprint, London: Routledge Curzon, 1994.

Clark, Anna. "Leonore Davidoff: A Tribute to Her Work." *Gender and History* 27, no. 1 (2015): 6–9.

Copeland, Rebecca L. *Lost Leaves: Women Writers of Meiji Japan*. Honolulu: University of Hawai'i Press, 2000.

Copeland, Rebecca, and Melek Ortabasi, eds. *The Modern Murasaki: Writing by Women of Meiji Japan*. New York: Columbia University Press, 2006.

Cornell, Laurel L. "Why Are There No Spinsters in Japan?" *Journal of Family History* 9, no. 4 (1984): 326–39.

Craig, Christopher R. J. "The Middlemen of Modernity: Local Elites and Agricultural Development in Meiji Japan." Ph.D. diss., Columbia University, 2015.

Dalby, Liza. *Geisha*. Berkeley: University of California Press, 1998.

Davidoff, Leonore. "Regarding Some 'Old Husbands' Tales': Public and Private in Feminist History." In *Worlds Between: Historical Perspectives on Gender and Class*, 227–76. New York: Routledge, 1995.

Davison, Kate. "Early Modern Social Networks: Antecedents, Opportunities, and Challenges." *American Historical Review* 124, no. 2 (2019): 456–82.

di Leonardo, Micaela. "The Female World of Cards and Holidays: Women, Families, and the Work of Kinship." *Signs* 12, no. 3 (1987): 440–53.

Downs, Laura Lee. "Gender History." In *Debating New Approaches to History*, edited by Marek Tamm and Peter Burke, 101–15. London: Bloomsbury Academic, 2019.

Dunch, Ryan. "Mothers to Our Country: Conversion, Education, and Ideology Among Chinese Protestant Women, 1870–1930." In *Pioneer Chinese Christian Women: Gender, Christianity, and Social Mobility*, edited by Jessie Lutz, 324–50. Bethlehem, PA: Lehigh University Press, 2010.

Dusinberre, Martin. *Hard Times in the Hometown: A History of Community Survival in Modern Japan*. Honolulu: University of Hawai'i Press, 2012.

Edelstein, Dan, Paula Findlen, Giovanna Ceserani, Caroline Winterer, and Nicole Coleman. "Historical Research in a Digital Age: Reflections from the Mapping the Republic of Letters Project." *American Historical Review* 122, no. 2 (2017): 400–424.

Edwards, Louise. *Gender, Politics, and Democracy: Women's Suffrage in China*. Stanford, CA: Stanford University Press, 2008.

Eide, Brock, and Fernett Eide. *The Dyslexic Advantage: Unlocking the Hidden Potential of the Dyslexic Brain*. New York: Plume, 2012.

Faison, Elyssa. "Women's Rights as Proletarian Rights: Yamakawa Kikue, Suffrage, and the 'Dawn of Liberation.'" In *Rethinking Japanese Feminisms*, edited by Julia C. Bullock, Ayako Kano, and James Welker, 15–33. Honolulu: University of Hawai'i Press, 2017.

Flaherty, Darryl E. *Public Law, Private Practice: Politics, Profit, and the Legal Profession in Nineteenth-Century Japan.* Cambridge, MA: Harvard University Asia Center, 2013.

Fujime Yuki. "The Licensed Prostitution System and the Prostitution Abolition Movement in Modern Japan." Translated by Kerry Ross. *positions* 5, no. 1 (1997): 135–70.

Fujimoto, Hiro. "Women, Missionaries, and Medical Professions: The History of Overseas Female Students in Meiji Japan." *Japan Forum* 32, no. 2 (2020): 185–208.

Fukuda Hideko. *Fukuda Hideko shū.* Edited by Murata Shizuko and Ōki Motoko. Fuji shuppan, 1998.

———. "Jōkō gakusha setsuritsu no shuisho." In *Fukuda Hideko shū,* 405–6.

———. *Warawa no hanseigai.* In *Fukuda Hideko shū,* 13–76.

Fukuzawa Yukichi. *An Encouragement of Learning.* Translated by David A. Dilworth. New York: Columbia University Press, 2012.

Ginzberg, Lori D. *Untidy Origins: A Story of Woman's Rights in Antebellum New York.* Chapel Hill: University of North Carolina Press, 2005.

Glasnovich, Ryan. "Return to the Sword: Martial Identity and the Modern Transformation of the Japanese Police." Ph.D. diss., Harvard University, 2019.

Gluck, Carol. "The End of Elsewhere: Writing Modernity Now." *American Historical Review* 116, no. 3 (2011): 676–87.

———. *Japan's Modern Myths: Ideology in the Late Meiji Period.* Princeton, NJ: Princeton University Press, 1986.

Gordon, Andrew. *Fabricating Consumers: The Sewing Machine in Modern Japan.* Berkeley: University of California Press, 2011.

Gramlich-Oka Bettina, and Anne Walthall. "Introduction." In Gramlich-Oka et al., *Women and Networks,* 1–18.

Gramlich-Oka, Bettina, Anne Walthall, Miyazaki Fumiko, and Sugano Noriko, eds. *Women and Networks in Nineteenth-Century Japan.* Ann Arbor, MI: University of Michigan Press, 2020.

Hall, John Whitney. *Government and Local Power in Japan, 500–1700: A Study Based on Bizen Province.* Princeton, NJ: Princeton University Press, 1966.

Hamada Hideo. *Kadota kaiwai no michi: Mō hitotsu no Okayama bunka.* Okayama: Kibito shuppan, 2012.

Hane, Mikiso. *Reflections on the Way to the Gallows: Rebel Woman in Prewar Japan.* Berkeley: University of California Press, 1988.

Hardacre, Helen. *Kurozumikyō and the New Religions of Japan.* Princeton, NJ: Princeton University Press, 1988.

Harootunian, Harry. "The Economic Rehabilitation of the Samurai in the Early Meiji Period." *Journal of Asian Studies* 19, no. 4 (1960): 433–44.

Hastings, Sally A. "A Christian Institution in Nineteenth-Century Japan: Ishii Jūji and the Okayama Orphanage." In *Orphans and Foster Children: A Historical and Cross-Cultural Perspective,* edited by Lars-Goran Tedebrand, 35–49. Sweden: Umea University, 1996.

———. "Hatoyama Haruko." In Walthall, *The Human Tradition in Modern Japan,* 45–60.

———. "Mt. Holyoke College: Teachers to Japan, Students from Japan." *Asian Cultural Studies* 38 (March 2012): 17–29.

Hein, Laura. *Post-Fascist Japan: Political Culture in Kamakura after the Second World War.* London: Bloomsbury Academic, 2018.

Hōgō Iwao. *Okayama no kijin henjin.* Okayama: Nihon bunkyō shuppan, 1977.

Hollinger, David A. *Protestants Abroad: How Missionaries Tried to Change the World but Changed America.* Princeton, NJ: Princeton University Press, 2017.

Horowitz, Helen Lefkowitz. *Alma Mater: Design and Experience in the Women's Colleges from Their Nineteenth-Century Beginnings to the 1930s.* New York: Alfred A. Knopf, 1985.

Hosoi Isamu. *Ishii Jūji to Okayama kojiin: Kindai Nihon to jizen jigyō.* Mineruba shobō, 1999.

Howell, David L. *Geographies of Identity in Nineteenth-Century Japan.* Berkeley: University of California Press, 2005.

Howland, Douglas. *Translating the West: Language and Political Reason in Nineteenth-Century Japan.* Honolulu: University of Hawai'i Press, 2001.

Huffman, James L. *Creating a Public: People and Press in Meiji Japan.* Honolulu: University of Hawai'i Press, 1997.

———. *Down and Out in Late Meiji Japan.* Honolulu: University of Hawai'i Press, 2018.

Ikegami, Eiko. *The Bonds of Civility: Aesthetic Networks and the Political Origins of Japanese Culture.* Cambridge: Cambridge University Press, 2005.

Inada Masahiro. *Jiyū minken no bunkashi: Atarashii seiji bunka no tanjō.* Chikuma shobō, 2000.

———. *Jiyū minken no keifu: Kindai Nihon no genron no chikara.* Yoshikawa kōbunkan, 2009.

Ion, Hamish. *American Missionaries, Christian Oyatoi, and Japan, 1859–73.* Vancouver: University of British Columbia Press, 2009.

Irokawa, Daikichi. *The Culture of the Meiji Period.* Translation edited by Marius B. Jansen. Princeton, NJ: Princeton University Press, 1988.

Ishii, Noriko Kawamura. *American Women Missionaries at Kobe College, 1873–1909: New Dimensions in Gender.* New York: Routledge, 2004.

Ishii Jūji. *Nisshi.* 32 volumes. Miyazaki: Ishii kinen yūaisha, 1956–1983.

Isshiki Aki. "Kirisutokyō to jiyū minken undō no rentai shiron." *Kirisutokyō shakai mondai kenkyū* 43 (1994): 134–65.

Jansen, Marius B. *The Making of Modern Japan.* Cambridge, MA: Harvard University Press, 2002.

Jaundrill, D. Colin. *Samurai to Soldier: Remaking Military Service in Nineteenth-Century Japan.* Ithaca, NY: Cornell University Press, 2016.

Johnston, William D. "Buddhism Contra Cholera: How the Meiji State Recruited Religion against Epidemic Disease." In *Science, Technology, and Medicine in the Modern Japanese Empire*, edited by David G. Wittner and Philip C. Brown, 62–78. New York: Routledge, 2016.

Judge, Joan. "Talent, Virtue, and the Nation: Chinese Nationalisms and Female Subjectivities in the Early Twentieth Century." *American Historical Review* 103, no. 3 (2001): 765–803.

Kagawa Toyohiko. *Jūjika ni tsuite no meisō*. Kyōbunkan, 1931.

———. *Meditations on the Cross*. Willet, Clark, and Company, 1935.

Karlin, Jason G. *Gender and Nation in Meiji Japan: Modernity, Loss, and the Doing of History*. Honolulu: University of Hawai'i Press, 2014.

Katō Shōzō. "Kenbōsai Nakagawa Yokotarō." In *Kyōdo ni kagayaku hitobito*, 1–27. Okayama denki bunko, vol. 5. Nihon bunkyō shuppan, 1958.

Kelley, Mary. *Learning to Stand and Speak: Women, Education, and Public Life in America's Republic*. Chapel Hill: University of North Carolina Press, 2006.

Kibi Gaishi (Watanabe Chisui). *Kyōdo no joketsu gojūnen. Chisui sōki*, vol. 27. Okayama: Self-published, 1959.

Kido Terayasu, ed. *Nihon teikoku kokkai giin seiden*. Tanaka sōeidō, 1890.

Kim, Kyu Hyun. *The Age of Visions and Arguments: Parliamentarianism and the National Public Sphere in Early Meiji Japan*. Cambridge, MA: Harvard University Asia Center, 2008.

Kitajima Eriko. "Kajiro Yoshi eibun nikki." *Kajiro Yoshi kenkyū* 1 (1996): 83–132.

Kōchi shiritsu jiyū minken kinenkan. *Meiji no joseishi ten zuroku*. Kōchi: Kōchi shiritsu jiyū minken kinenkan, 1996.

Kohiyama, Rui. "'No Nation Can Rise Higher Than Its Women': The Women's Ecumenical Missionary Movement and Tokyo Women's Christian College." In *Competing Kingdoms: Women, Mission, Nation, and the American Protestant Empire, 1812–1960*, edited by Barbara Reeves-Ellington, Katherine Kish Sklar, and Connie Shemo, 218–39. Durham, NC: Duke University Press, 2010.

Kornicki, Peter. "Women, Education, and Literacy." In *The Female as Subject: Reading and Writing in Early Modern Japan*, edited by P. F. Kornicki, Mara Patessio, and G. G. Rowley, 7–37. Ann Arbor: University of Michigan Center for Japanese Studies, 2010.

Kovner, Sarah. *Occupying Power: Sex Workers and Servicemen in Postwar Japan*. Stanford, CA: Stanford University Press, 2012.

Koyama Shizuko. *Ryōsai kenbo to iu kihan*. Keisō shobō, 1991.

Kume Ryūsen. *Kenbōsai itsuwashū*. Okayama: Okayama kenjinsha, 1937.

Lewis, Michael. *Becoming Apart: National Power and Local Politics in Toyama, 1868–1945*. Cambridge, MA: Harvard University Asia Center, 2000.

Lotus Sutra. Translated by Burton Watson. New York: Columbia University Press, 1993.

Lublin, Elizabeth Dorn. *Reforming Japan: The Woman's Christian Temperance Union in the Meiji Period*. Honolulu: University of Hawai'i Press, 2010.

Mackie, Vera. *Feminism in Modern Japan: Citizenship, Embodiment, and Sexuality*. Cambridge: Cambridge University Press, 2003.

Maier, Charles S. *Leviathan 2.0: Inventing Modern Statehood*. Cambridge, MA: Harvard University Press, 2012.

Mann, Susan. *Gender and Sexuality in Modern Chinese History*. New York: Cambridge University Press, 2011.

Marra, Michele. *Modern Japanese Aesthetics: A Reader*. Honolulu: University of Hawai'i Press, 1999.

Marran, Christine L. *Poison Woman: Figuring Female Transgression in Modern Japanese Culture.* Minneapolis: University of Minnesota Press, 2007.

Mason, Michele. *Dominant Narratives of Colonial Hokkaido and Imperial Japan: Envisioning the Periphery and the Modern Nation-State.* New York: Palgrave Macmillan, 2012.

Matsumoto Sachiko. *Midori fukaku: Kajiro Yoshi shiden.* Okayama: San'yō gakuen, 1986.

Matsumura Midori. "Ōnishi Sōzan zakki: Enkosha toshite no kenbun." *Nihon bungaku* 14 (April 1960): 65–80.

Matsuzaki Rumi. "Meiji ishinki no jendā kenkyū no kadai." *Rekishi hyōron* 812 (2017): 49–59.

Matsuzawa Yūsaku. *Jiyū minken undō: "Demokurashī" no yume to zasetsu.* Iwanami shoten, 2016.

Maus, Tanya. "Ishii Jūji, the Okayama Orphanage, and the Chausubaru Settlement: A Vision of Child Relief Through Communal Labor and a Sustainable Local Economy, 1887–1926." Ph.D. diss., University of Chicago, 2007.

Maza, Sarah C. *Thinking about History.* Chicago: University of Chicago, 2017.

McClellan, Edwin. *Woman in the Crested Kimono: The Life of Shibue Io and Her Family Drawn from Mori Ōgai's "Shibue Chusai."* New Haven: Yale University Press, 1985.

Mitsunaga Ippachi, ed. *Ishiguro Kan'ichirō-kun no enzetsu hikki.* Okayama: Shiomi Teruyoshi, 1890.

Miyachi Masato, ed. *Meiji jidaikan bijuaru waido.* Shōgakukan, 2005.

Miyagi-ken shi. Vol. 4. Edited by Miyagi-ken shi hensan iinkai kankōkai. Sendai: Miyagi-ken shi kankōkai, 1982.

Miyazaki Fumiko. "Networks of Believers in a New Religion: Female Devotees of Fujidō." In Gramlich-Oka et al., *Women and Networks,* 145–75.

Mizuuchi Masayasu. "Hyakunen mae ni rentai yūgō o yume mita otoko." *Buraku* 43, no. 535 (1991): 44–45.

Moriya Tomoe. "Auto sutēshon kara sutēshon e: Okayama sutēshon no keisei to chiiki shakai." In *Amerikan bōdo senkyōshi: Kōbe Ōsaka Kyōto sutēshon o chūshin ni, 1869–1890,* edited by Dōshisha daigaku jinbun kagaku kenkyūjo, 99–127. Kyōbunkan, 2004.

Mullins, Mark R. "Christianity as a Transnational Social Movement: Kagawa Toyohiko and the Friends of Jesus." *Japanese Religions* 32, nos. 1–2 (2007): 69–87.

Murata Shizuko. "Hyōden." In Fukuda Hideko, *Fukuda Hideko shū,* 627–42.

Murata Tomi, ed. *Ōnishi Kinuko sensei yohō: Denki Ōnishi Kinuko.* Self-published, 1934. Reprint, Ōzorasha, 1992.

Najita, Tetsuo. *Hara Kei in the Politics of Compromise, 1905–1915.* Cambridge, MA: Harvard University Press, 1967.

———. *Ordinary Economies in Japan: A Historical Perspective, 1750–1950.* Berkeley: University of California Press, 2009.

Nakagawa Yokotarō, ed. *Igakushi Kiyono-kun sōkokubetsu enzetsu narabini jo.* Okayama: Self-published, 1889.

Nakagawa Yokotarō and Yoshimoto Tetsusaburō. *Bunmei saidai genso zaiyokuron.* Okayama: Self-published, 1882.

Nakai Mariko. "Ōnishi Kinu to sono ichizoku." *Kajiro Yoshi kenkyū* 2 (1997): 45–59.

Nakajima Shōen (Kishida Toshiko). "A Famous Flower in Mountain Seclusion." Translated with an introduction by Dawn Lawson. *The Asia-Pacific Journal—Japan Focus* 17, no. 1 (January 2019): 1–35.

Nakamura, Ellen. "Kusumoto Ine (1827–1903): A Feminist Reappraisal." *Japanese Studies* 40, no. 3 (2020): 1–18.

————. "Working the Siebold Network: Kusumoto Ine and Western Learning in Nineteenth-Century Japan." *Japanese Studies* 28, no. 2 (2008): 197–211.

Nenzi, Laura. *The Chaos and Cosmos of Kurosawa Tokiko: One Woman's Transit from Tokugawa to Meiji Japan.* Honolulu: University of Hawai'i Press, 2015.

Nihon josei undō shiryō shūsei. Vol. 1. Edited by Suzuki Yūko. Fuji shuppan, 1996.

Nihon kirisutokyōdan Okayama kyōkai, ed. *Okayama kyōkai hyakunenshi.* Volume 1. Okayama: Nihon kirutokyōdan Okayama kyōkai, 1985.

Nihon kirisutokyō rekishi daijiten. Edited by Nihon kirisutokyō rekishi daijiten henshū iinkai. Kyōbunkan, 1988.

Nihon kokugo daijiten (second edition). 13 volumes. Shōgakukan, 2001.

Niijima Jō. *Niijima Jō zenshū,* vol. 3. Edited by Niijima Jō zenshū hensan iinkai. Kyoto: Dōhōsha, 1987.

Nishi Kiichi (Bizan). *Nakagawa Yokotarō-kun ryakureki.* Okayama kenjinsha, 1935.

Nishizawa Naoko. "Female Networks and Social Stratification in Meiji Japan: From the Perspective of Fukuzawa Yukichi." In Gramlich-Oka et al., *Women and Networks,* 246–74.

Nolte, Sharon, and Sally Ann Hastings. "The Meiji State's Policy Toward Women, 1890–1910." In *Recreating Japanese Women, 1600–1945,* edited by Gail Lee Bernstein, 151–74. Berkeley: University of California Press, 1991.

Norton, Mary Beth. "History on the Diagonal." *American Historical Review* 124, no. 1 (2019): 1–19.

O'Brien, Suzanne G. "Splitting Hairs: History and the Politics of Daily Life in Nineteenth-Century Japan." *Journal of Asian Studies* 67, no. 4 (2008): 1309–39.

Okayama danjo kyōdō sankaku suishin sentā, ed. *Jidai o hiraita Okayama no joseitachi.* Okayama: Okayama danjo kyōdō sankaku suishin sentā, 2005.

Okayama joseishi kenkyūkai, ed. *Kindai Okayama no onnatachi.* Sanseidō, 1987.

————. "Okayama joshi konshinkai ni tsuite." *Rekishi hyōron* 204, no. 10 (1983): 2–18.

Okayama-ken shi. Vol. 10. Edited by Okayama-ken shi hensan iinkai. San'yō shinbunsha, 1986.

Okayama-ken shi. Vol. 30. Edited by Okayama-ken shi hensan iinkai. San'yō shinbunsha, 1987.

Okayama minken undōshi kankei shiryōshū. Vol. 4. Edited by Aoki Mitsuko and Mitsuda Kyōko. Okayama: Okayama minken undō hyakunenshi kinen gyōji jikkō iinkai, 1982.

Ōki Motoko. *Jiyū minken undō to josei.* Domesu shuppan, 2003.

Old, Hughes Oliphant. *The Reading and Preaching of the Scriptures in the Worship of the Christian Church.* Grand Rapids, MI: Eerdmans, 2007.

Onoda Tetsuya. *Sumiya Koume-shi tsuikairoku.* Kurashiki: Hayashi Genjūrō, 1941. Reprint, Okayama: Okayama sōgō bunka sentā, 1984.

Ōta Ken'ichi. "Nakagawa Yokotarō no enzetsu 'Shiri metsuretsu' no shōkai; Meiji 32-nen 'nama sōrei' no haikei." *Kajiro Yoshi kenkyū* 1 (1996): 73–81.

———. "Nakagawa Yokotarō to Sumiya Koume." In *Nihon no kyōiku, Okayama no joshi kyōiku,* edited by San'yō gakuen tanki daigaku shakai sābisu sentā, 272–98. Okayama: San'yō gakuen daigaku, 2006.

Ōta Ken'ichi, ed. *Zusetsu Okayama, Bizen, Tamano no rekishi.* Kibito shuppan, 2010.

Ōta Ken'ichi and Takeuchi Ryōko, eds. *Aru Meiji jogakusei nikki: Okayama, San'yō Jogakkō sei "Ishihara Tomeko" no kiroku.* Okayama: Kibito shuppan, 2007.

Ozaki Yukio. *Autobiography of Ozaki Yukio: The Struggle for Constitutional Government in Japan.* Translated by Fujiko Hara. Princeton, NJ: Princeton University Press, 2001.

Partner, Simon. *The Merchant's Tale: Yokohama and the Transformation of Japan.* New York: Columbia University Press, 2018.

Patessio, Mara. *Women and Public Life in Early Meiji Japan: The Development of the Feminist Movement.* Ann Arbor: University of Michigan Center for Japanese Studies, 2011.

Perry, Adele. *Colonial Relations: The Douglas-Connolly Family and the Nineteenth-Century Imperial World.* Cambridge: Cambridge University Press, 2015.

Pettee, James Horace. *The Japan Mission: 1869–1895.* Boston, MA: American Board, 1895.

———. *Mr. Ishii and His Orphanage: A Japanese Apostle of Faith and His Asylum at Okayama.* Okayama: Asylum Press, 1894.

Platt, Brian. *Burning and Building: Schooling and State Formation in Japan, 1750–1890.* Cambridge: MA, Harvard University Asia Center, 2004.

———. Review of *Isami's House: Three Centuries of a Japanese Family,* by Gail Lee Bernstein. *Monumenta Nipponica* 61, no. 3 (2006): 418–22.

Putnam, Lara. "The Transnational and the Text-Searchable: Digitized Sources and the Shadows They Cast." *American Historical Review* 121, no. 2 (2016): 377–402.

Putney, Clifford. *Missionaries in Hawai'i: The Lives of Peter and Fanny Gulick, 1797–1883.* Amherst, MA: University of Massachusetts Press, 2010.

Pyle, Kenneth. "Meiji Conservatism." In *Cambridge History of Japan,* vol. 5, edited by Marius Jansen, 674–720. Cambridge: Cambridge University Press, 1989.

Ravina, Mark. *The Last Samurai: The Life and Battles of Saigo Takamori.* Hoboken, NJ: John Wiley, 2005.

———. *To Stand with the Nations of the World: Japan's Meiji Restoration in World History.* Oxford: Oxford University Press, 2017.

Roberts, Luke. *Performing the Great Peace: Political Space and Open Secrets in Tokugawa Japan.* Honolulu: University of Hawai'i Press, 2012.

———. "Women's Roles in Men's Narratives of Samurai Life." In Gramlich-Oka et al., *Women and Networks,* 21–41.

Saitō Yoshiko. "Meiji-ki Okayama-ken ni okeru kirisuto kyōkai jogakkō ni kansuru ichi-kōsatsu." *Kagawa tanki daigaku kiyō* 36 (2008): 1–10.

Sakamoto Kiyone. "Ūmanzu bōdo to Nihon dendō." In *Rainichi Amerika senkyōshi: Amerikan bōdo senkyōshi shokan no kenkyū 1869–1890*, edited by Dōshisha daigaku jinbun kagaku kenkyūjo, 119–50. Gendai shiryō shuppan, 1999.

Sale, Joseph. "The Moral Code of Fukuzawa Yukichi." *Open Court*, no. 613 (June 1907): 321–29.

San'yō gakuen, ed. *Ai to hōshi: San'yō gakuen sōritsu hyakusanjūshūnen kinenshi*. Okayama: Kibito shuppan, 2016.

———. *San'yō gakuen hyakunenshi*. Okayama: San'yō gakuen, 1986.

San'yō shinbunsha, ed. *Okayama-ken rekishi jinbutsu jiten*. Okayama: San'yō shinbunsha, 1994.

Scheiner, Irwin. *Christian Converts and Social Protest in Meiji Japan*. Berkeley: University of California Press, 1970.

Seat, Karen K. *"Providence Has Freed Our Hands": Women's Missions and the American Encounter with Japan*. Syracuse, NY: Syracuse University Press, 2008.

Sekiguchi Sumiko. "Confucian Morals and the Making of a 'Good Wife and Wise Mother': From 'Between Husband and Wife There Is Distinction' to 'As Husbands and Wives Be Harmonious.'" *Social Science Japan Journal* 13, no. 1 (2010): 95–113.

Seki Tamiko. *Edo kōki no joseitachi*. Aki shobō, 1987.

Shiba Keiko. "Building Networks on the Fly: The Travails of Travel for Domain Lords' Women." In Gramlich-Oka et al., *Women and Networks*, 113–42.

Shibata Hajime. *Kinsei gōnō no gakumon to shisō*. Shinseisha, 1966.

Shimizu Takichi. *Kageyama Hide-jo no den: Jiyū no gisei, joken no kakuchō*. Kinrindō, 1887.

Shimoda Hiraku. *Lost and Found: Recovering Regional Identity in Imperial Japan*. Cambridge, MA: Harvard University Asia Center, 2014.

Siegel, Mona. "Transcending Cross-Cultural Frontiers: Gender, Religion, Race, and Nation in Asia and the Near East." *Journal of Women's History* 27, no. 1 (2015): 187–96.

Sievers, Sharon L. *Flowers in Salt: The Beginnings of Feminist Consciousness in Modern Japan*. Stanford, CA: Stanford University Press, 1983.

Sims, Richard. *French Policy towards the Bakufu and Meiji Japan, 1854–95*. New York: Routledge, 1998.

Siniawer, Eiko Maruko. *Ruffians, Yakuza, and Nationalists: The Violent Politics of Modern Japan, 1860–1960*. Ithaca: Cornell University Press, 2008.

Smith, Bonnie G. *The Gender of History: Men, Women, and Historical Practice*. Cambridge, MA: Harvard University Press, 1998.

Sotozaki Mitsuhiro. *Kōchi-ken fujin undōshi*. Kōchi shiritsu shimin toshokan, 1971. Revised and reprinted by Domesu shuppan, 1975.

———. *Ueki Emori to onnatachi*. Domesu shuppan, 1976.

Steele, M. William. *Alternative Narratives in Modern Japanese History*. New York: Routledge, 2009.

———. "The Ishizaka of Notsuda." In Walthall, *The Human Tradition in Modern Japan*, 66–71.

Stoler, Ann Laura. *Along the Archival Grain: Epistemic Anxieties and Colonial Common Sense*. Princeton, NJ: Princeton University Press, 2008.

Sugano Noriko. "Kishida Toshiko and the Career of a Public-Speaking Woman in Meiji Japan." In *The Female as Subject*, edited by P. F. Kornicki, Mara Patessio, and G. G. Rowley, 171–89. Ann Arbor: University of Michigan Center for Japanese Studies, 2010.

————. "Terakoya to onnakyōshi." In *Nihon joseishi ronshū*, vol. 8, edited by Sōgō joseishi kenkyūkai, 140–58. Yoshikawa kōbunkan, 1998.

Sugiyama Heisuke. *Ichi Nihonjin.* Shōbundō, 1925.

Suzuki, Mamiko C. *Gendered Power: Educated Women from the Meiji Empress' Court.* Ann Arbor: University of Michigan Center for Japanese Studies, 2019.

Suzuki, Norihisa. "Nobuta Kishimoto and the Beginnings of the Scientific Study of Religion in Modern Japan." *Contemporary Religions in Japan* 11, no. 3/4 (1970): 155–80.

Suzuki Shizuko. *"Danjo dōkenron" no otoko: Fukamauchi Motoi to jiyū minken no jidai.* Nihon keizai hyōronsha, 2007.

Suzuki Yūko. "Kaisetsu." In *Nihon josei undō shiryō shūsei*, 18–48.

Takahashi, Aya. *The Development of the Japanese Nursing Profession: Adopting and Adapting Western Influences.* New York: Routledge, 2004.

Tanaka Tomoko. *Kindai Nihon kōtō kyōiku taisei no reimei: Kōsaku suru chiiki to kuni to kirisutokyōkai.* Kyoto: Shibunkaku shuppan, 2012.

Taylor, Sandra C. *Advocate of Understanding: Sidney Gulick and the Search for Peace with Japan.* Kent, OH: Kent State, 1984.

Terasaki Osamu. *Meiji Jiyūtō no kenkyū.* Vol. 1. Keiō tsūshin, 1987.

Tomasi, Massimiliano. *Rhetoric in Modern Japan: Western Influences on the Development of Narrative and Oratorical Style.* Honolulu: University of Hawai'i Press, 2004.

Tomoyose Kagemasa. "Okayama no hisabtesu buraku to kirisutokyō." *Buraku kaihō kenkyū* 156 (2004): 61–72.

Traister, Rebecca. *All the Single Ladies: Unmarried Women and the Rise of an Independent Nation.* New York: Simon and Schuster, 2016.

Tsurumi, E. Patricia. *Factory Girls: Women in the Thread Mills of Meiji Japan.* Princeton, NJ: Princeton University Press, 1990.

Ueki Emori. *Ueki Emori shū*, vol. 2. Edited by Ienaga Saburō. Iwanami shoten, 1990.

Van der Veer, Peter. *The Modern Spirit of Asia: The Spiritual and the Secular in China and India.* Princeton, NJ: Princeton University Press, 2014.

Walthall, Anne. "Closing Remarks." *Report of the International Symposium on Women and Networks in Nineteenth-Century Japan 2, Sophia International Review* 27 (2015): 27–29.

————. "The Creation of Female Networks in Exile: Hirata Atsutane and Orise's Banishment to Akita." In Gramlich-Oka et al., *Women and Networks*, 67–87.

————. "Devoted Wives/Unruly Women: Invisible Presence in the History of Japanese Social Protest." *Signs* 20, no. 1 (1994): 106–36.

————, ed. *The Human Tradition in Modern Japan.* Lanham, MD: Scholarly Resources, 2002.

————. "The Life Cycle of Farm Women in the Tokugawa Period." In *Recreating Japanese Women, 1600–1945*, edited by Gail Lee Bernstein, 42–70. Berkeley: University of California Press, 1991.

————. "Masturbation and Discourse on Female Sexual Practices in Japan." *Gender and History* 21, no. 1 (2009): 1–18.

———. "Nishimiya Hide." In Walthall, *The Human Tradition in Modern Japan*, 66–71.

———. Review of *The Problem of Women in Early Modern Japan*, by Marcia Yonemoto. *Monumenta Nipponica* 72, no. 1 (2017): 87–91.

———. *The Weak Body of a Useless Woman: Matsuo Taseko and the Meiji Restoration*. Chicago: University of Chicago Press, 1998.

———. "Women and Literacy From Edo to Meiji." In *The Female as Subject*, edited by P. F. Kornicki, Mara Patessio, and G. G. Rowley, 215–35. Ann Arbor: University of Michigan Center for Japanese Studies, 2010.

Walthall, Anne, and M. William Steele, eds. *Politics and Society in Japan's Meiji Restoration: A Brief History with Documents*. Boston: Bedford St. Martins, 2017.

Wang, Zheng. *Finding Women in the State: A Socialist Feminist Revolution in the People's Republic of China, 1949–1964*. Oakland: University of California Press, 2016.

Waters, Neil. *Japan's Local Pragmatists: The Transition from Bakumatsu to Meiji in the Kawasaki Region*. Cambridge, MA: Harvard University Asia Center, 1983.

Wert, Michael. "Tokugawa Loyalism during Bakumatsu-Boshin War." In *Japan at War: An Encyclopedia*, edited by Louis Perez, 438–39. Santa Barbara: ABC-Clio, 2013.

Wolf, Maryanne. *Proust and the Squid: The Story and Science of the Reading Brain*. New York: Harper, 2007.

Worsley, Lucy. *Jane Austen at Home*. New York: St. Martin's Press, 2017.

Wright, Diana. "Female Combatants and Japan's Meiji Restoration: The Case of Aizu." *War in History* 8, no. 4 (2001): 396–417.

Yamakawa Kikue. *Women of the Mito Domain: Recollections of Samurai Family Life*. Translated by Kate Wildman Nakai. Stanford, CA: Stanford University Press, 2002.

Yasutake, Rumi. *Transnational Women's Activism: The United States, Japan, and Japanese Immigrant Communities in California, 1859–1920*. New York: New York University Press, 2004.

Yokoyama Yuriko. *Meiji ishin to kinsei mibunsei no kaitai*. Yamakawa shuppansha, 2005.

Yokozawa Kiyoko. *Jiyū minken ka: Nakajima Nobuyuki to Kishida Toshiko*. Akashi shoten, 2006.

Yoneda Sayoko. "Jiyū minken to fujin mondai." In *Jiyū minken hyakunen no kiroku*, edited by Jiyū minken hyakunen zenkoku jikkō iinkai, 80–88. Sanseidō, 1982.

Yoshizaki Shihoko. "Hōshi suru onnatachi." In *Kindai Okayama no onnatachi*, edited by Okayama joseishi kenkyūkai, 105–17. Sanseidō, 1987.

———. "Meiji no shijuku fujin eigakusha ni tsuite." *Kyōiku jihō* 424 (1985): 27–28.

———. "Nakamura Shizu to fujin kyōfūkai no shūhen." *Okayama chihōshi kenkyū* 71 (1993): 1–10.

———. "Sumiya Koume nitsū no shokan ni tsuite." *Okayama chihōshi kenkyūkai kaihō* 41 (1984): 1–3.

———. "Sumiya Koume nitsū no shokan ni tsuite: Sono ni." *Okayama chihōshi kenkyūkai kaihō* 42 (1984): 3–5.

Young, Louise. *Beyond the Metropolis: Second Cities and Modern Life in Interwar Japan*. Berkeley: University of California Press, 2013.

Index

Page numbers for figures are in italics.

Harvard East Asian Monographs

(most recent titles)